H

NUFFIELD EUROPEAN STUDIES

Series Editors: Joachim Jens Hesse and Vincent Wright

Editorial Advisory Board: Sabino Cassese, John S. Fleming, Yves Mény,
Johan P. Olson, Robert Putnam, Fritz W. Scharpf

LOBBYING IN THE EUROPEAN COMMUNITY

NUFFIELD EUROPEAN STUDIES

The purpose of the Nuffield European Studies series is to provide, for students and teachers in the social sciences and related disciplines, works of an interdisciplinary and comparative nature dealing with significant political, economic, legal, and social problems confronting European nation-states and the European Community. It will comprise research monographs as well as the edited proceedings of conferences organized by the Centre for European Studies at Nuffield College, Oxford. The general editors of the series are Joachim Jens Hesse, Ford-Monnet Professor of European Politics and Comparative Government in the University of Oxford and Director of the Centre for European Studies, and Vincent Wright, Official Fellow of Nuffield College.

LOBBYING IN THE EUROPEAN COMMUNITY

EDITED BY

SONIA MAZEY

AND

JEREMY RICHARDSON

OXFORD UNIVERSITY PRESS
1993

Oxford University Press, Walton Street, Oxford OX2 6DP

Oxford New York Toronto
Delhi Bombay Calcutta Madras Karachi
Kuala Lumpur Singapore Hong Kong Tokyo
Nairobi Dar es Salaam Cape Town
Melbourne Auckland Madrid
and associated companies in
Berlin Ibadan

Oxford is a trade mark of Oxford University Press

Published in the United States
by Oxford University Press Inc., New York

British Library Cataloguing in Publication Data
Data available

Library of Congress Cataloging in Publication Data
Lobbying in the European Community / edited by Sonia Mazey and Jeremy Richardson.
p. cm. – (Nuffield European Studies)
Includes bibliographical references.
1. Pressure groups–European Economic Community countries.
2. Lobbying–European Economic Community countries. 3. European
Economic Community countries–Politics and government. 4. European
Economic Community countries–Economic conditions. I. Mazey,
Sonia . II. Richardson, J. J. (Jeremy John) III. Series.
JN94.A792P754 1993 324'.4'094–dc20 92–42268
ISBN 0–19–827789–X

Set by Hope Services (Abingdon) Ltd.
Printed in Great Britain
on acid-free paper by
Biddles Ltd, Guildford and King's Lynn

Preface

Irrespective of the arguments which may rage over precise terminological definitions of the European Community (EC), its development into some form of federal state is now an accepted aspect of politics in Western Europe. In particular, the nature of the EC decision-making process is of growing concern to students of comparative public policy. Indeed, if one is analysing the policy process in any one of the twelve Member States, it is impossible not to take account of the influence of the EC. Equally, the role of the EC as an international actor is of increasing relevance in the whole field of international political economy and in such areas as global environmental policies. In practice, as power shifts to Brussels and Strasbourg, few policy areas—whether domestic or international—are not subject to some degree of EC influence.

As always, shifts in power are noted and acted upon by interest groups, who act as a type of weather-vane for the locus of political power in society. They quickly re-target their influence, once they realize that the power to take decisions which affect them has moved to a new institution or to new actors. As the Americans say, it is best to shoot where the ducks are! Whilst there is differential recognition by groups of the significance of the EC (for example British trade unions began to set up offices in Brussels as late as 1991), and different policy sectors exhibit differing degrees of EC influence, it is now difficult to find a major interest in Western Europe which is not mobilized to influence policy-making at the European level. Although the Commission may be described as an 'adolescent' bureaucracy, its remit now runs wide and probably outstrips its technical capacity.

One of the main consequences of these developments has been the explosion of lobbying both directly at the EC level and also via national administrations. Moreover, the Commission itself is very open to the lobbying process and has yet to devise fully effective standard operating procedures for managing the process of intermediation with groups. Its preference for dealing with Euro-groups is in practice difficult to realize. These potential 'pillars' of a pluralistic, or indeed neo-corporatist, system are not yet sufficiently strong to support an effective system of intermediation. In reality the intermediation process is one of muddling through, with many different models of policy-making in use—ranging from internalized policy-making to the use of rather loose and extended policy and issue networks.

The purpose of this volume is to provide both empirical evidence regarding the ways in which the lobbying system is developing, and to raise some of the more general analytical issues which must be addressed before we can hope to develop reliable models of the EC policy process and the role of groups within it. We believe that it is especially important to see the process from the perspective of practitioners, in what is very much the development phase of the EC lobbying process—hence our volume is a collection of analyses of the process through the eyes of some individual participants, and of the more conventional academic analyses from observers like ourselves.

In preparing this volume we owe a considerable debt to a number of organizations and individuals. Our own research is supported by the ESRC, but we also wish to acknowledge support from the Nuffield Foundation, the British Academy, and the Joint University Council for Social and Public Administration for helping to finance a Workshop for the contributors to this volume at the Centre for European Studies, Nuffield College, Oxford, in March 1991. We are also grateful to the Centre for its very considerable support in hosting the Workshop and in providing an excellent environment where academics and practitioners could meet. David Spence, of the European Commission, was especially helpful in putting us in touch with Commission officials who participated in the workshop and who have contributed to this volume. Finally, we wish to record our thanks to Alison Bennett and Margaret Leckie, of the Department of Government at the University of Strathclyde, for typing most of the chapters, and to Linda Watson Brown, also of the University of Strathclyde, who assisted in the final preparation of this book.

S.M. and J.R.

Cambridge and Warwick
October 1992

Contents

I THE EUROPEAN LOBBYING PROCESS

II SECTORAL STUDIES

Figures

Tables

Abbreviations

ACAM	Assembly of Corporate Associate Members
ACEA	Association of European Automobile Constructors
AFNOR	Association française de normalisation
Amcham	American Chamber of Commerce
APME	Association of Plastics Manufacturers of Europe
APPE	Association of Petrochemicals Producers in Europe
ARE	European Assembly of Regions
ASSILEC	EC Dairy Trade Association
BAGFW	Bundesarbeitsgemeinschaft der Freien Wohlfahrtspflege
BEUC	European Bureau of Consumer's Unions
BSI	British Standards Institution
CAP	Common Agricultural Policy
CBI	Confederation of British Industry
CCC	Consumers Consultative Council
CCE	Council of European Communes
CCMC	Committee of European Community Automobile Makers
CCME	Churches' Committee on Migrants in Europe
CEED	Centre for Economics and Environmental Development
CEFIC	European Chemical Industry Council
CEMR	Council of European Municipalities and Regions
CEN	Comité Européen de Normalization
CFCs	Chlorofluorocarbons
CGT	Confédération Générale du Travail
CLCA	Liaison Committee of the Automobile Industry of the Countries of the European Communities
CLEAR	Campaign for Lead-Free Air
CNPF	Conseil National du Patronat Français
COFACE	Confédération des Organisations Familiales de la Communauté Européenne
COGECA	Comité Générale de la Coopération Agricole de la CEE
Comitextil	Co-ordination Committee for the Textile Industries of the European Community
COPA	Committee of Professional Agricultural Organisations
COREPER	Committee of Permanent Representatives

COSLA	Convention of Scottish Local Authorities
CSU	Christlich-Soziale Union
DTI	Department of Trade and Industry
DTp	Department of Transport
EAGGF	Agricultural Guidance and Guarantee Fund
EAPN	European Anti-Poverty Network
EATP	European Association for Textile Polyolefins
ECAS	European Citizen Action Service
ECD(E)	European Community Department (External)
ECD(I)	European Community Department (Internal)
EEB	European Environmental Bureau
EEG	European Enterprise Group
EFD	European Funds Division
EIB	European Investment Bank
EIPA	European Institute for Public Administration
ENDS	Environmental Data Services
EOC	Equal Opportunities Commission
EQ(O)	European Questions (Official) Committee
EQ(S)	European Questions (Steering)
ERDF	European Regional Development Fund
ESAN	European Social Action Network
ESC	Economic and Social Committee
ESF	European Social Fund
ESRC	Economic and Social Research Council
ETUC	European Trade Union Confederation
EUROCOOP	European Community of Consumer Cooperatives
FCO	Foreign and Commonwealth Office
FDP	Freie Demokratische Partei
FEANTSA	European Federation of National Organizations Working with the Homeless
FEOGA	European Agricultural Guidance and Guarantee Fund
HE	Highlands and Islands Enterprise
HIDB	Highlands and Islands Development Board
IBN	Institut belge de normalisation
IGCPK	Industriegerwerkschaft Chemice-papier-Keramic
Incapen	Industry Council for Packaging and the Environment
IOPs	Integrated Operation Programmes
ISO	International Organisation for Standardisation

IULA   International Union of Local Authorities
JAMA   Japanese Association of Automobile Manufacturers
LEIs   Local Employment Initiatives
MAFF   Ministry of Agriculture, Fisheries, and Food
MFA   Multifibre Arrangement
MITI   Ministry of International Trade and Industry
MSF   Manufacturing, Science, and Finance (Union)
NFU   National Farmers Union
NGO   Non-governmental organization
NPCIs   National Programmes of Community Interests
OECD   Organization for Economic Cooperation and Development
OICA   Organisation of International Automobile Constructors
OPD   Ministerial Committee on Defence and Overseas Policy
OPD(E)   Ministerial Committee on Defence and Overseas Policy–Sub-committee on European Affairs
PCN   Packaging Communication Network
PWMI   European Centre for Plastics in the Environment
SDA   Scottish Development Agency
SE   Scottish Enterprise
SEA   Single European Act
SEAQ   Stock Exchange Automated Quotations
SFA   Securities and Futures Association
SGCI   Secrétariate Général du Comité Interministériel pour les Questions de Coopération Economique Européene
SIB   Securities and Investments Board
SME   Smaller Manufacturing Enterprises
SMMT   Society of Motor Manufacturers and Traders
SOAFD   Scottish Office Agriculture and Fisheries Department
SOED   Scottish Office Education Department
SOHHD   Scottish Office Home and Health Department
SOID   Scottish Office Industry Department
SRO   Self Regulating Organisations
STUC   Scottish Trades Union Congress
TC   Technical Committee
TERN   Trans-European Rural Network
UACES   University Association for Contemporary European Studies
UASG   UNICE Advisory and Support Group

UKREP	UK's Permanent Representation to the European Communities
UN-ECE	United Nations Economic Commission for Europe
UNICE	The Union of Industrial and Employers' Confederations of Europe

Contributors

LYNN COLLIE is Assistant Head of the Brussels Office of the Confederation of British Industry.

MARTIN DONNELLY works in the Cabinet of Sir Leon Brittan in the Commission of the European Communities.

DICK EBERLIE is Director of the Brussels Office of the Confederation of British Industry.

WYN GRANT is Professor of Politics, University of Warwick.

BRIAN HARVEY is a research and public-relations consultant and was formerly a researcher with the Community Development Foundation.

ROBERT HULL is Adviser to the Director-General, Environment, Nuclear Safety and Civil Protection in the Commission of the European Communities.

GRANT JORDAN is Professor of Politics, University of Aberdeen.

JEFFREY KNIGHT is Special Adviser, Federation of Stock Exchanges in the European Community.

ANDREW MCLAUGHLIN is a Research Fellow in European Integration at the Robert Gordon University.

SONIA MAZEY is Lecturer in Politics and Fellow of Churchill College, University of Cambridge.

JAMES MITCHELL is a lecturer in the Department of Government, University of Strathclyde.

JEAN-PIERRE PECKSTADT is Director-General of the European Association of Textile Polyolefins.

JEREMY RICHARDSON is Professor of European Integration and Director of the European Public Policy Institute, University of Warwick.

JANE SARGENT runs her own governmental-relations consultancy.

PART I

THE EUROPEAN
LOBBYING PROCESS

1

Introduction: Transference of Power, Decision Rules, and Rules of the Game

SONIA MAZEY AND JEREMY RICHARDSON

1. THE TRANSFERENCE OF POWER TO BRUSSELS

The adoption of the Single European Act (SEA) by the twelve EC Member States in 1986 marked an important stage in the development of the Community. The SEA commits Member States not only to the completion of the internal market by the end of 1992, but also to monetary and financial integration. Other sections of the document strengthen the legal basis and widen the scope of Community policies relating to European political co-operation, economic and social cohesion, research and technological development, the environment, and social policy. In order to facilitate the attainment of these objectives, the Act strengthened the legislative powers of the European Parliament and removed the need for unanimity within the Council of Ministers from those decisions pertaining to the single market. The impact of the SEA on EC policy-making is thus twofold: the scope of Community policies has been extended to include policy areas which were previously the responsibility of national governments; and reform of the EC decision-making process has weakened the policy-making influence of national governments at the EC level. The decisions reached at the Maastricht Summit in December 1991 have added further impetus to the process of European integration, with a continuation of the process of erosion of the powers of individual national governments. In short, the locus of policy-making power in an increasing number of policy areas has shifted from the national level to the EC, as the EC becomes more statelike and federal in nature.

These changes in the distribution of power within the European Community have prompted a proliferation of interest-group lobbying at the EC level. Whilst the phenomenon of European lobbying is not at all new, there has, in recent years, been a sharp increase in the number of groups and levels of resources devoted to influencing both the formulation and, more recently, the implementation of EC policy. Although this development is now well recognized, it is more difficult to produce a coherent characterization of the nature of the relationship between interest groups and decision-makers both at the European level itself and at the national level where much 'Euro-lobbying' takes place. Our own findings suggest that there is, as yet, no dominant model or style of EC-group relations. Whilst some interests have managed to become part of a cohesive policy community at the EC level, most are involved in less integrated types of policy networks. These differences in styles of policy-making within the EC can be explained to some extent by the particular characteristics of different policy sectors, as they can at the national level, of course. However, as highlighted below, the structural characteristics which underpin the EC policy-making process also inhibit the establishment of stable policy communities.

The peculiar features of EC policy-making also have important implications for the European Community itself, not least for those European Commission officials whose task is to manage the increasingly time-consuming business of group consultation. Despite popular mythology, the EC bureaucracy comprises fewer than three and a half thousand senior administrators who are collectively responsible for the drafting of EC policies. The extension of the Community's sphere of competence and the resultant explosion in European lobbying has—inevitably—imposed considerable strains upon an increasingly overloaded administration. For EC officials charged with the task of reconciling the interests of numerous groups from twelve Member States, as well as having to take account of the pressures exerted by the governments and interests of non-Member and aspirant Member States, the Single European Act has underlined the need for the Community to seek to develop a manageable and stable set of interactions with interest groups. The nature of interest intermediation at the EC level is thus in a state of flux; whilst groups seek to develop new strategies for effective EC lobbying, EC policy-makers face the increasingly difficult task of managing the consultation, information exchange, and implementation problems associated with the accelerating pace of European integration.

2. THE EXPANSION OF EC LOBBYING

European-wide interest group federations have existed since the early days of the EC in industrial sectors such as agriculture and coal and steel, where responsibility for policy-making had been given to the European Commission under the Treaty of Rome. By 1970 more than 300 Euro-groups existed (Butt Philip 1987: 75) and in 1980 the number of Euro-groups formally recognized by the Commission had risen to 439 (Economic and Social Committee 1980). Some industries—whose interests in EC matters were partic-ularly intense—have been relatively effective EC lobbyists for many years. In April 1974, for example, M. Alexander Mallat, President of ATO-Chemie (a branch of the Elf Aquitaine and Total group) ʌʌ called for an EC organization of the chemicals industry in order to combat intra-EC problems of over-production and the growing challenge from Comecon and the USA (*Le Monde*, 27 Apr. 1978). Similarly, in June 1978, the Association of Plastics Manufacturers of Europe (APME) asked the EC Commissioner for Industry Étienne Davignon, to defend import levies on Third World plastics in the next round of GATT negotiations and to cut Eastern Euro-pean imports (*Les Echoes*, 19 June 1978). A typical example of pol-icy benefits derived from lobbying arose in 1979 when the industry escaped all EC regulations concerning the free movement of goods and VAT harmonization. A year earlier the Commission had announced its intention of facilitating the circulation of pharma-ceutical goods. This had provoked an outcry from the industry, followed by a meeting of 150 delegates from pharmaceutical indus-tries in fourteen countries (including non-EC countries such as Switzerland, Austria, Sweden, and Norway) in Brussels (*Le Figaro*, 15 Mar. 1979).

Prior to the 1986 Single European Act, however, much EC lob-bying by national organizations or firms was conducted through national political and administrative structures (see Chapter 2 for a discussion of the continued importance of national channels). This tendency for groups to work through national ministries reflected the concentration of decision-making power within the Council of Ministers at the EC level. Since the 1966 'Luxembourg Compro-mise' effectively gave each national government a veto over pro-posals put to the Council by the European Commission, many groups relied almost exclusively upon national officials to defend them at the European level. Moreover, until the adoption of the SEA, many groups had no more than a passing interest in the EC policy process: though the principle of supremacy of EC law over national legislation was established early on, the scope of the Community's jurisdiction was in practice, limited. In short, most interest groups were far more interested in the content of national legislation, as this was still the main source of the regulatory frameworks under which they operated and national governments were still the main source of state intervention.

The Single European Act has prompted a number of changes to this pattern. It has formalized and strengthened the European Commission's powers to initiate Community policies in a number of areas as suggested above. Signatories to the Single European Act have also agreed to the phased introduction of full economic and monetary union, a commitment reiterated in the 1991 Maastricht agreements. Of more immediate importance, the Act commits Member States to implementation of the internal market (i.e. the free movement of goods, services, capital, and labour within the EC) by the end of 1992. This will require the introduction of 282 measures proposed in the Commission's original White Paper on the single market (EC Commission, *Completing the Internal Market,* COM(85) 530 Final). By the end of November 1991, 168 of the 282 measures were in force, 204 had been adopted by the Council of Ministers, and a further 78 measures proposed to the Council by the Commission were still to be considered. Thus, almost at a stroke the number and range of interests directly affected by EC policy-making has increased dramatically.

In consequence, there has been a sharp increase in recent years in the volume and diversity of interests represented in Brussels. Recent figures indicate that there are now 525 Euro-groups (i.e. those federations which are officially recognized by the Commission) represented in Brussels, although the membership, status, resources, and policy-making influence of these associations varies enormously. Whilst some groups such as COPA (Committee of Professional Agricultural Organisations), UNICE (The Union of Industrial & Employers' Confederations of Europe—see Ch. 12), the ETUC (trade unions), and BEUC (European Bureau of Consumers' Unions) have a broad membership base, most—such as the European Association of Hearing Aid Dispensers and the European

Herbal Infusions Association—are more narrowly focused with fewer members, fewer resources, and a more selective and intermittent interest in EC legislation. Many companies—particularly multi-product or multi-purpose firms, will be members of more than one Euro-group, as part of their strategy of using multiple channels of access (see Ch. 13). The nature of the Euro-groups reflects the corporatist nature of the origins of the EC. Industrial and commercial employers' interests account for almost 50 per cent of the Euro-groups, a further 25 per cent are connected with agriculture and food, around 20 per cent are related to the service industries (including the legal and banking professions), with just 5 per cent of the Euro-groups representing trade union, consumer, and environmental interests (European Commission 1990).

National associations also lobby independently at the European level—particularly on issues where they are at odds or competing with their European counterparts, or when they face particular policy difficulties with their national governments. Below this level, multinational companies and/or economically powerful firms and organizations such as British Petroleum and Shell, Imperial Chemicals Industries, British Aerospace, Ford Motor Company, the London Stock Exchange, and Unilever are as a matter of course represented in Brussels, either by their own public relations staff or by a professional consultant. Regional and local authorities throughout the EC have also become more active lobbyists in recent years (see Ch. 6).

Finally, non-EC groups and governments have also become more active in Brussels. For example, Japanese and American groups are among the most effective EC lobbyists. Especially influential, is the EC Committee of the American Chamber of Commerce (Amcham) which represents eighty US organizations including multinational such as ITT, IBM, Allied Signal Inc., Colgate Palmolive, General Electric, General Motors, etc., all of which have subsidiaries in EC countries (*Fortune*, June 1990: 78). Indeed Amcham is possibly the most effective lobbying organization in Brussels and has developed a complex and expert structure of specialist committees which represent an unrivalled network of advance intelligence within the EC. Individual American firms such as IBM are very conscious of the relevance of the EC to their business environment. For example, it mounted what is widely regarded as one of the most effective lobbying campaigns in the EC to persuade the Community to accelerate the deregulation of telecommunications (*Europe*, July/Aug. 1988: 25).

So, whilst several producer groups have been active EC lobbyists for many years, the amount of resources devoted to monitoring developments in Brussels has in virtually all cases increased since the mid-1980s. For example, the number of people employed in the Brussels office of the French employers' association, the Conseil National du Patronat Français (CNPF), has quadrupled since 1988 from seven to thirty-one (*Fortune*, June 1990: 78). Similarly, some Danish organizations report increased contacts with EC institutions. Bregnsbo and Sidenius report that between 1988 and 1991, 29 per cent of Danish trade associations and eight out of the eleven peak associations have increased their degree of contact with the Commission (Bregnsbo and Sidenius 1992: 19). Most Euro-associations are also increasing their level of staffing. The Association of European Food Processing Industries has increased its representation in Brussels, as has UNICE (see Ch. 12) and Leaseurope (the Euro-group of the national leasing company associations in the EC). However, the weakness of Euro-groups can itself be the cause of increased lobbying in Brussels by national associations (see Ch. 7). For example, the German Federation of Private Dairy Producers (Bundesverband der deutschen Milchwirtschaft) has found that the relevant Euro-group (ASSILEC—the EC Dairy Trade Association) has not been effective in representing the interests of the German industry and it has begun to contact EC officials directly (Private correspondence, 20 Aug. 1990). Most groups, however, cannot afford to employ their own 'EC watcher' in Brussels. Hence one of the most striking developments since the mid-1980s has been the rapid increase in the number of professional lobbyists, financial consultants, and law firms locating in Brussels. Thus, a single consultancy firm, Hill and Knowlton, employs no fewer than twenty-one consultants in Brussels (*Fortune*, June 1990: 81). In the absence of any official register of EC lobbyists, it is impossible to calculate exactly how many lobbyists actually operate at the EC level. One estimate put the figure for 1990 at 3,000—three times that of two or three years ago (*Fortune*, June 1990). It seems probable that the system has now reached saturation point, with the possibility that there will be some 'shake-out' of the professional lobbying firms as clients themselves become more sophisticated in their understanding of the EC and demand more than mere information-gathering.

Also the market expansion opportunities for new entrants are now limited by the fact that few significant commercial interests have yet to develop some form of European representation.

Despite Britain's reputation as a reluctant European, British groups have in several sectors been among the most enthusiastic supporters of European-wide organization. That the British should be reasonably advanced in at least this aspect of European integration is possibly not surprising, bearing in mind the very long tradition of an often symbiotic relationship between groups and government at the national level. Many producer interests, especially, have been well organized into national policy-making processes in Britain for at least a century (Richardson 1990). It comes naturally to them to seek a similar relationship with bureaucrats in Brussels, once the shift in the locus of power has been recognized. Significantly, the majority of professional lobbyists, consultants, and legal experts based in Brussels are also UK (and US) firms. This fact was frequently cited by non-UK groups and officials as giving Anglo-Saxon groups a considerable advantage over lobbyists from other EC countries—not least because of the considerable use made by the Commission itself of professional consultants for contract research. The 'procedural ambition' of many Commission officials to seek a stable and regularized relationship with the affected interests might be seen as presenting particular advantages to those lobbyists used to that type of policy style at the national level.

3. DECISION RULES AND RULES OF THE GAME

Whatever cultural attitudes govern the interaction between groups and policy-makers—whether these attitudes influence the behaviour of groups or bureaucrats (see Dogan 1975) or the propensity of organized interests to emerge from the various cleavages in society—there is no doubt that institutional and structural factors are also of very considerable importance in determining the role of groups in the policy process (Richardson 1993). This is as true for the EC as it is for national systems. The relative weakness of the European Parliament, for example, has similar implications for group lobbying in the EC as does the weakness of the UK Parliament or of the French National Assembly for lobbying in Britain or France (Jordan and Richardson 1987; Mény 1990).

Interest groups seeking to influence the content of EC legislation naturally focus their energies upon those Commission officials (often from more than one Directorate-General) responsible for preparing draft proposals. In fact, Commission officials are generally acknowledged by groups to be rather accessible and open to influence. Thus, the German Solicitors & Lawyers Association (Bundesrechtsanwaltskammer Körperschaft des Öffentlichen Rechts der Hauptgeschäftsführer) reported that 'relations with Brussels are certainly good and requests for talks have never been refused' (Private communication, 16 Aug. 1990). However, one reason for this greater openness is that the Commission is what might be called an 'adolescent bureaucracy'. It is still very dependent upon national experts and groups for detailed information about diverse technical standards, legislation, and organizational structures throughout the EC. The practical task of knowing what policies will actually work in twelve very different states is exceedingly difficult. Moreover, the political problems are also considerable. Thus the Commission, in early 1992, decided to set up a special unit to avoid insensitive action which could provoke more general hostility to the EC which could disrupt ratification of the Maastricht Treaty. A senior Commission official is reported as saying that the unit would offer advice on the timing of EC measures without trying to alter the substance (*Financial Times*, 20 Jan. 1992). In practice, it is virtually impossible for any single interest or national association to secure exclusive access to the relevant officials, let alone secure exclusive influence. As yet, there seem to be relatively few cases of 'agency capture' if only because of the enormous increase in the range of interests seeking representation in each policy area. The German Chemical & General Workers' Union (IGCPK—Industriegerwerkschaft Chemie-Papier-Keramic) reported to us that it found the Commission receptive, but was fearful that the increasing numbers of organizations seeking to influence the Commission would mean that the Commission would be incapable of dealing with all of them and would lose interest in talking to organizations as 'partners' (Private correspondence, 28 Aug. 1990). Indeed, draft proposals are invariably revised several times, sometimes quite radically, following diverse representations from Member States. This aspect of the EC policy process contrasts sharply with that of Britain and other Northern European states where groups can generally rely upon the fact that major or radical changes to published White Papers and their equivalents are relatively rare.

A related problem for groups is the unpredictability of the European policy agenda. Although the Commission announces its own legislative programme at the beginning of each year, other more pressing items may be added as a result of European Summit decisions. In addition, all national governments use their six-month presidency of the Council of Ministers to promote favoured projects (e.g. the UK Government and the internal market, the French Government and social policy) whilst MEPs, ambitious ministers, and interest groups all seek to push the Commission in certain directions. Keeping track of EC policy initiatives is therefore a major undertaking, further complicated by the highly compartmentalized structure of the Commission (despite its collegiate nature). The development of transnational co-ordination of EC lobbying strategies is consistent with the neo-functionalist theories of integration which accord organized interests a leading role in the integration process (see Chs. 8 and 14).

Since 1986 the European Parliament (EP) has become a somewhat more influential actor in the EC policy process and is likely to become more influential in future years. Previously, the EP had no legislative powers; although MEPs were consulted over legislative proposals, the Council of Ministers was under no obligation to take their views into account. In an attempt to redress the so-called 'democratic deficit' within the EC, the SEA introduced a new 'co-operation procedure' which grants the EP the right to a second reading of all Community legislation relating to the establishment and functioning of the internal market, social and economic cohesion, technological research and development, and certain aspects of EC social and regional policies. This provides MEPs with a further opportunity to propose amendments to the 'common position' adopted by the Council of Ministers which can then be overridden by the Council of Ministers only by a unanimous vote.

The co-operation procedure has undoubtedly provided MEPs with additional leverage over the details of much Community legislation. In the period between the introduction of the Single European Act in 1987 and November 1990, the Commission accepted 1,052 of the Parliament's 1,724 amendments to single-market laws, and of those the Council agreed to 719 (*The Economist*, 10 Nov. 1990). As Bogdanor (1989) has pointed out, the primary effect of the co-operation procedure has been to draw the Parliament into the early stages of the policy process in order that a policy compromise can be negotiated by the first-reading stage—before proposals are 'firmed up' in complex package deals worked out by Commission and COREPER (Committee of Permanent Representatives) officials. For groups, the EP has thus become a useful means of achieving amendments to EC legislation. In consequence, groups now pay more attention to the European Parliament. For example, 12 per cent of Danish trade associations are reported to have increased their contacts with the European Parliament between 1988 and 1991 (Bregnsbo and Sidenius 1992). Our own evidence suggests that virtually all groups interested in influencing EC policy pay some attention to the European Parliament but that the degree of attention is influenced by two factors. First, groups which are weak at the national level or which lack the resources to sustain continuous contact with Commission officials on very technical matters often see the Parliament as an alternative policy-making arena—particularly in terms of agenda-setting. Thus, environmental groups, unions, and various voluntary organizations view the Parliament as a very useful forum. Secondly, certain issues are more influenced by parliamentary activity than others. This is especially true in the environmental and social policy field. However, even well-resourced and strong groups, normally relying on contacts with national governments and the Commission, now acknowledge the need to maintain some contact with the EP, and occasionally they too may gain direct benefits from lobbying in that arena. One particular example of this is the way in which the tobacco industry, together with advertisers and publishing groups dependent upon advertising, successfully lobbied the EP in January 1992 in order to delay voting on proposed legislation banning the advertising of cigarettes. Although only a temporary delay, it was the result of the spending of much time and money by the industries in lobbying MEPs and journalists (*Independent*, 17 Jan. 1992). The more normal pattern for producer groups, however, is that they see the EP as very much a secondary arena for lobbying purposes. The German Dairy Producers, for instance, reported that 'very occasionally, we use the European Parliament as a place of lobbying. Although we have contacts with German MPs in the European Parliament, through whom we do lobbying from time to time, we do not think of the EP as an influential place' (Private communication, 20 Aug. 1991). In contrast, the German Chemical & General Workers' Union reported that

without doubt, the European Parliament has become more self-confident during the past years, especially in helping to create a new social structure for Europe. There has been a positive change in the moods of most MEPs towards progressive decisions. Therefore, the European Parliament is quite important to protect the rights of the workers, although the Parliament is not that powerful because of its difficulty in finding majorities and its lack of authority to prevent unanimous decisions by the Council of Ministers. (Private communication, 28 Aug. 1990)

The legislative powers of the EP remain—for the moment at least—limited. It has no right to initiate legislation, no legislative powers with regard to policies outside the policy areas listed above and until recently no powers to override decisions taken by the Council of Ministers. Moreover, parliamentary amendments to the common position require the support of an absolute majority of MEPs. Obtaining such support is far from simple given the lack of party discipline within the EP. Though MEPs sit in recognized transnational party groupings within the assembly these are without exception internally divided along national and doctrinal lines. However, the Maastricht agreement provides for an increase in the powers of the EP, giving it the power of veto in certain areas. The new Treaty introduces a procedure of co-decision-making between Parliament and Council which involves two readings and provides for Parliament to table amendments to proposed legislation, as can happen at present under the co-operation procedure. Whereas under the existing co-operation procedure Parliament's amendments at second reading can only stand if Council is divided, the new procedure provides for the convening of a conciliation committee comprising equal representation from both institutions, should both sides fail to agree and, as a last resort, allowing Parliament the right to reject the legislation if it is still not satisfied. Co-decision will apply to those areas where the Council takes a decision through qualified majority voting, namely, internal market rules, free circulation of workers, right of establishment including the treatment of foreign nationals, the recognition of qualifications, and general environment programmes. In addition, it will also apply to the new areas of competence—education and training, trans-European networks, health action, and consumer protection.

Also included are the research framework programme and culture, where Council decisions are taken by unanimity (*EP News*, 9–13 Dec. 1991).

The most powerful EC decision-making body remains the Council of Ministers. In contrast to the Commission and the Parliament, both of which are in a sense 'European' bodies, the Council is an intergovernmental body where national officials and ministers seek to secure the best possible deal for 'their' government. The fact that there is a considerable concentration of power within the Council, that its meetings are secret and closed, and that groups have no direct access to it, has significant implications for EC lobbying styles. Groups have little option at this stage but to rely upon the negotiating skills of national ministers, their civil servants, and COREPER officials. However, as the Commission is a major participant in all Councils of Ministers, continued lobbying of Commission officials gives an important element of continuity, at least for those arguments or lobby points which have a European validity.

In the past, each Member State could effectively block proposals which, in theory, might have been adopted by a qualified majority by invoking (or more usually by threatening to revoke) the right of national veto granted by the Luxembourg Compromise. The SEA has—as Mrs Thatcher made clear at the time of its adoption—left intact the Luxembourg Compromise. In practice, however, the extension of majority voting to new policy sectors (further extended at Maastricht to such areas as some aspects of environmental policy, development aid, public health, consumer protection, trans-European networks, individual research programmes, some aspects of transport and competition policy, some social policy, and the implementation of the social fund) has been accompanied by a diminution in the use of the Luxembourg Compromise. There appears to be agreement among the Member States that it should not be invoked with respect to those policy areas brought under the Community's jurisdiction for the first time in the SEA (e.g. the environment, research, and development). In addition, Member States have been generally reluctant to appear to be holding up legislation relating to the internal market. Thus, the extension of majority voting (54 out of 76 votes) to those sectors covered by the co-operation procedure has major implications for interest groups. By reducing the extent to which national govern-

ments within the Council are either willing or able to obstruct proposals, the greater use of majority voting has increased the incentive for groups to seek allies in other Member States in order to
achieve either a blocking minority or qualified majority.

Often overlooked, the European Court of Justice, which is
responsible for interpreting and enforcing EC law, is also of crucial
importance for EC lobbyists. In recent years, environmental organizations and women's groups, especially, have used the Court
(whose appellate powers resemble those of the US Supreme Court)
as a means of forcing recalcitrant national governments to implement EC legislation concerning the quality of drinking water and
equality between working women and men (for the latter, see
Mazey 1988). Indeed, the European Court's decision in May 1990
in the case of *Barber* v. *Guardian Royal Exchange*, that pensions
were part of pay and therefore that men and women had to be
treated equally, had enormous potential consequences for industry.
For example, it has been estimated that British industry alone
could have faced a bill of £40 billion. In fact the *Barber* case provoked what is probably the most costly and intense lobbying campaign yet seen in Brussels. In the event, the Maastricht Treaty
redefined Article 119 of the Treaty of Rome so that pensions
should not be treated as pay prior to the date of the *Barber* decision. Increasingly, therefore, individual cases are being brought to
the Court with the backing of organized interests. This relationship
between individual cases and group lobbying can be seen in an
October 1991 case in which a British speech therapist succeeded in
having her pay parity case referred to the Court. She believed that
her salary as a speech therapist was less than that of clinical psy-
chologists and principal pharmacists on a comparable grade within
the same hospital. As 99 per cent of speech therapists are women
and the majority of those in the other jobs are men, she argued
that the pay difference amounted to unintentional, indirect sex dis-
crimination (*Financial Times*, 27 Oct. 1991). Her case was supported by the union MSF (the general technical union) and by the
Equal Opportunities Commission (EOC). Indeed, the EOC, as an
official agency in the UK, was not afraid to enter into conflict with
the UK Government in the field of equal opportunities. The Chair-
woman of the EOC was a pioneer in the radical use of European
law to fight British women's battles. She is pledged to continue to
use the Court in a 'creative and strategic way' (*Guardian*, 21 Jan.

1992). The UK branch of Friends of the Earth also continued the campaign by environmental groups against Britain's non-implementation of EC water laws by taking the UK to the Court, in early 1992, over the UK Government's failure to implement directives relating to the level of nitrates in drinking water. It would be wrong, however, to exaggerate the policy influence of the Court at this stage in its development. Nevertheless, as O'Brien notes in relation to the US Supreme Court, 'the fact that the court decides an issue is more important than what it decides' (1986: 320).

Even without resort to the Court, the supremacy of EC law over national legislation means that no group can afford to ignore EC legislative developments which might undermine policy compromises being negotiated nationally. This is especially important in such areas as industrial policy and regional policy, where intervention by national governments can be overruled and reversed by the EC as being contrary to the principles of the single market. Equally, for those groups given a frosty welcome by national policy-makers, EC lobbying may also prove a more successful means of influencing national legislation, and we can expect an increase in the propensity of groups to shift their lobbying to Brussels in the early stages of national policy disputes. A good example of this tendency can be seen in the way in which senior telecommunications managers in Britain very quickly went to Brussels when British Telecom announced that it was proposing to introduce a one-digit addition to Britain's telephone codes. The Deputy Chairman of the Telecommunication Managers Association, pointed out that the change could cost industry between £10 billion and £100 billion to adjust to the change. He therefore took the issue to Brussels at a meeting of senior industrial users of telecommunications systems, representatives of Europe's telecommunications operators, and equipment suppliers (*Independent*, 16 Jan. 1992).

The distinctive nature of EC policy-making thus has important implications for interest-group strategies. First, EC lobbying is a multi-lateral operation which requires interest groups to co-ordinate national and EC-level strategies, since national politicians remain important allies within the Council of Ministers and are usually influential in determining the manner in which EC legislation is to be implemented. As a rule, no group can afford to alienate national government ministers during the course of EC lobbying, both because on a whole range of other issues these ministers will still be influential policy actors at the national level, and because of the role of national governments in the Council of Ministers. Secondly, when it comes to EC policy-making, sectoral interest groups are often competing not only with their traditional adversaries (e.g. the CBI versus the TUC), but also with their counterparts from other Member States. Moreover, one should not underestimate the enduring strength of national sentiments and their capacity to undermine the formulation of stable transnational policy communities. Witness, for instance (even with the relatively stable agricultural community), the recurrent violent clashes between British and French farmers prompted by the impact of UK lamb imports on French lamb prices. Thirdly, both the compartmentalized nature of the Commission and the problem of competitive agenda-setting make it very difficult for groups to monitor EC policy developments. More generally, the EC decision-making and implementing process is not a stable one in the sense that national policy-making systems have very long histories and traditions. Changes in voting rules within the Council of Ministers and the strengthening of the European Parliament are in effect changes in the decision rules of the EC and have implications both for the organization of EC lobbying and for its effectiveness. The further institutional reforms agreed at Maastricht and future enlargement of the Community will undoubtedly further affect the way in which groups lobby the EC in the future and indeed may lead to significant 'overcrowding' of policy sectors (see Gustafsson and Richardson 1980).

4. CHANGING AGENDAS AND THE POLITICS OF UNCERTAINTY

Whilst there are significant cross-sectoral differences in terms of the policy impact of the EC, it is not difficult to find a range of illustrative examples to show that more national groups must either develop their own EC lobbying strategies (combining attempts to influence their own government and the EC) and/or they must join (or form) European-wide groups. As with lobbying at the national level, much group activity is of course concerned with technical issues which are of low political salience to other than the affected interests. As always, therefore, it is necessary to distinguish between what Hoffmann (1966) described as 'high' politics and 'low' politics. Just as national groups may find it difficult (or impossible) to influence issues such as nuclear deterrence or the broader aspects of energy policy, so groups operating at the European level experience difficulties in influencing such 'high' politics issues as monetary union, German reunification, relations between the EC and the USA or Japan, or Community enlargement. Thus, in emphasising the increased scope and importance of lobbying at the European level—directly and indirectly via national governments—we also need to recognize that some of the really big issues like political and monetary union are processed in quite a different way to those technical issues such as the long-standing dispute over standards in the field of high-definition cinema-quality television (HDTV) or the kind of issues concerning the polyolefins industry (see Ch. 9). Although the background influence of groups (such as those involved in the field of social policy) was evident at Maastricht in December 1991 for example, it would be misleading to argue that groups played a really important role. Essentially, the decisions were matters of high politics and groups found it difficult to exert any direct influence on outcomes.

Nevertheless, even issues which are properly characterized as high politics can be 'unpacked' into more manageable—and therefore bargainable—issues more susceptible to group influence. In particular there is evidence that EC officials wish to develop something akin to national 'policy communities' at the European level, as a means of managing the increasingly burdensome consultation process. EC environmental policy is a good example of this development. Though the political debate surrounding the general principles of this policy attracted widespread public interest, the Commission has sought to achieve its objectives by breaking down issues of high political salience into more technical issues around which it is possible to construct a more cohesive policy community. Thus, within DG XI (Environment) an *ad hoc* consultative group on chlorofluorocarbons (CFCs) has been established comprising groups which have a direct interest in CFCs—i.e. representatives from the chemicals industry and refrigerator, foam-rubber, plastics, and aerosol manufacturers and users. The Commission's aim is to negotiate with these groups a means of meeting targets set by the Council of Ministers for reducing the use of CFCs. Significantly, environmental and consumer interests are not directly represented in this policy network which resembles the more restricted 'policy community' model of policy-making than the 'issue network' model which allows a more loosely regulated and less structured form of group participation in the policy process. Other policy issues—e.g. many problems in the field of social policy—appear to be processed in a manner closer to the 'issue network' model (see Ch. 10). The question of finding appropriate policy-making models to capture the essence of the EC policy process is discussed more fully in Chapter 14. However, it is important to note at this stage that there is certainly not *one* model appropriate for describing the EC's policy process. Even at the national level, different styles of policy-making are evident (Hayward 1982; Dyson 1982; Richardson, Maloney and Rüdig 1991), but with the EC it is extremely difficult to predict in advance the precise nature of the way in which a particular problem will arrive on the agenda and how it will be processed.

Groups are also increasingly interested in the implementation of EC policies. The British seem to be particularly anxious to raise the question of the EC's 'implementation gap', as they have one of the best records in the EC for the actual implementation of EC laws and have come to recognize that cross-national differences in implementation may present significant modifications to the concept of a level playing field. This concern with implementation may be of specific importance in terms of cross-national differences in lobbying styles. The Engineering Employers' Federation's Director-General wrote to the Employment Secretary welcoming the commitment which Britain had secured from the EC Social Affairs Commissioner, Vasso Papandreou, to make regular reports to the Council of Ministers 'on the records of member states in implementing European legislation'. The UK minister is reported as saying: 'the UK takes its legal responsibility very seriously and we are concerned that others do likewise. There is sometimes a difference between what people say about employment and social matters and what they do in practice' (*EFF News*, Apr. 1990: 5). British groups are by tradition used to a high degree of compliance with laws in the context of a highly centralized state and will therefore go to great lengths to ensure that the original decision is acceptable to them, on the assumption that whatever is decided will be implemented by a strong central government. This may be less true in other EC states where there is a tradition of non-compliance built into their political cultures. Evidence for this view is provided by the Commission's reports on the application of EC legislation which show that whilst Denmark and the UK have incorporated 80 per cent of the single market directives into national law, in Italy 70 per cent of the directives were still outstanding at the beginning of the year—despite the introduction of new national legislative procedures designed to facilitate implementation of EC legislation (European Commission 1989: 10).

Whatever cross-national differences in lobbying styles exist at present, as the Community becomes far more assertive and state-like, so more and more interests will be sucked into the European policy process, with ever-increasing emphasis on Euro-level groups. The Federal Association of German Meat Processors commented that in the long term they expect more issues to be handled by their Euro-association in Brussels, 'whereas the national associations will deal with questions of information and interpretation' (Private communication, 9 Aug. 1990). Part and parcel of this development has been increased public acceptance of the legitimacy and desirability of European legislation in a number of policy areas. For example, by the end of 1990, very high levels of citizen support were being recorded for joint decision-making among the Member States in such areas as science and technology research (75 per cent), environmental protection (71 per cent), and even rates of value added tax (50 per cent) (see *Eurobarometer 34*, Dec. 1990: 23). We might also expect to see a continuation of the process of competitive agenda-setting within the EC. While many policy issues will be common across national boundaries, others may be country-specific or there may be cross-national variations in the position of common items on the agenda. Industrialists whom we interviewed commonly suggested to us that agenda-setting is their main weakness. This produces a reactive style of lobbying on their part. More often than not, firms and industries are conducting rearguard or fire-brigade campaigns in response to agendas set by others—often by the environmentalists for example. Indeed, environmental policy is a classic example of the differing emphases found in EC states and of the EC's own agenda being pushed along by certain enthusiastic actors. EC action on lead in petrol owed much to the campaign in Britain conducted by CLEAR (Campaign for Lead-Free Air) which goaded the UK Government to press for the issue to be resolved at a European level. Similarly, domestic 'green' pressure in West Germany led its government to take the initiative in pressing for limits on car exhaust emissions, although the issue soon became more complicated than a single conflict between environmentalists and polluters (see Ch. 7). The 1991/2 controversy over possible EC controls on packaging is another case of a national agenda impinging on the EC's policy agenda. The German 'Packaging Decree', implemented in January 1992, placed responsibility upon manufacturers and distributors to the German market for the collection and disposal of all packaging materials, with further restrictions coming into force in April 1992 and January 1993. German interest in the issue has had a knock-on effect at the EC level, where a draft directive on packaging is currently being prepared. Fear that something like the German legislation will be introduced at the EC level has caused consternation in the European packaging industry. A representative of the Euro-federation, the Industry Council for Packaging and the Environment (Incapen), commented on the German proposals as follows: 'Never mind the Nimby factor (Not In My Back Yard), they seem to be suffering from the Banana syndrome—Build Absolutely Nothing Anywhere Near Anyone' (*Independent*, 10 Sept. 1991).

An added problem—leading to further agenda uncertainty—is that the Commission, despite being 'technocratic', is, as suggested earlier, relatively small and inexpert (in the sense of lacking detailed, technical knowledge, especially across twelve nations) and is therefore often reliant on external evidence either from groups or national 'experts'. Brussels bureaucrats may, therefore, be susceptible to the phenomenon identified in Britain by C. D. Foster, who argued that lack of professional expertise in bureaucrats leads to a lack of confidence in formulating policies and to a greater reliance upon interests (1971: 63). Butt Philip has also noted a special dependency relationship between officials and groups (though he does not use the term 'dependency'). He comments that

The Commission, for its part both wants and needs contact with the many interest groups in Europe. It too needs information about the variety of positions and aspirations of Euro-groups and national pressure groups, as well as factual information which may be slow in arriving from national governments. Such information will often be essential material upon which to construct proposals and policies which will have a community application. (Butt Philip 1985: 42)

Commission officials face an apparent dilemma with regard to group consultation which has yet to be resolved. On the one hand, those officials interviewed by us stressed their commitment to (as well as need for) the widest possible consultation with groups. On the other hand, they also acknowledged the increasing difficulties of achieving this given the speed with which the growing amount of legislation must be prepared and the badly organized nature of many interests. Almost against their will it seems, Commission officials are in danger of being drawn into quasi-clientelist relationships with the limited number of groups which are really able to keep pace with and respond to Commission proposals. These groups are in practice often national-level organizations and firms, or multinational companies rather than Euro-associations. This is because the most common feature of Euro-groups is that they find difficulty either in reacting quickly to EC draft proposals, or that their internal divisions are such that they find it difficult to say anything which would be really useful to Commission officials. This has two consequences. Not only do the officials find themselves regularly ignoring the official injunctions to rely on Euro-groups, but also the nature of the interests themselves undermine the possible development of effective Euro-groups by lobbying directly. One British-owned multinational told us that although it joined every relevant national and Euro-association (and there were many, as it was a multi-product company), it still did much of its lobbying directly as this was the only way to ensure effective representation of its own interests.

Both the size and nature of the Commission, together with the fact that twelve national governments and twelve different sets of interest groups have an input into the policy process, means that the market for policy ideas within the EC policy process is much broader and is more dynamic than in any one national policy system. This is no doubt beneficial in terms of policy innovation, but the ensuing process is more difficult for everyone—including groups—to manage. Thus one characteristic of Brussels decision-making (compared to the relative predictability of, say, UK decision-making) is that new ideas and proposals can emerge from nowhere with little or no warning, simply because the Commission has seen fit to consult a particular group or a particular expert.

One of the primary advantages (to organized interests) of making policy via well-defined policy communities—namely, the prospect of a 'negotiated order' (Strauss 1987; Richardson and Jordan 1979) is usually lacking at the EC level, or at least is much more difficult to achieve. As J. P. Olsen (1977) suggests, organizations try to avoid uncertainty by arranging 'negotiated environments'. Uncertainty and risk, as well as conflict and competition, are avoided at the national level through the formation of stable relationships between actors. In very many policy areas at the EC level, there is not the intimate knowledge that often exists between policy actors at the national level, and neither is there sufficient common interest between them to underpin the development of stable agendas and processes. As suggested in the case of the stock exchanges (see Ch. 8) the structure of national sectors is often so different that it is almost impossible to develop an effective common position. Likewise, the German Solicitors' and Lawyers' Association has found that the Euro-group is 'less than optimal' in part because the range of interests of all twelve Member States is expressed in the different structures of law, economy, and social systems (Private communication, 16 Aug. 1991). These conflicting policy objectives and fluctuating participation in the policy process inhibit the formulation of stable policy agendas and the development of standard operating procedures for processing policy issues. Hence, lobbying may be especially about what one Washington lobbyist described as his basic task in the US system—namely not changing the world but minimizing his surprises!

Moreover, the Commission itself seems less of a 'bureaucratic village' than are many national bureaucracies. This is partly because the bureaucrats are not drawn from common cultures and do not pass through common selection systems or common training. It is also due to the high degree of sectorization/segmentation of policy-formulation even within Directorates. Of course, such problems also exist at the national level. The difference is one of degree; at the EC level, the absence of stable policy communities, the increasing assertiveness of certain Commission DGs since 1986, and the extremely compartmentalized nature of the Brussels bureaucracy undoubtedly render such conflict more difficult to avoid than at the national level. As Butt Philip suggests, 'Incoherent and inconsistent policy stances can easily emerge from the Commission because the Directorates-General make policy decisions separately rather than jointly' (1985: 53).

Openness and a willingness to consult and a desire to unpack big issues into more manageable technical problems all assist group influence at the European level. Yet the picture is one of enormous complexity, with a vast and proliferating range of groups, conflicting national interests, a strongly sectorized but small bureaucracy, unpredictable agendas, and changing decision rules. The most successful groups will be those which exhibit the usual professional characteristics—namely, resources, advance intelligence, good contacts with bureaucrats (and with parliamentarians when the need arises), and especially an ability to put forward rational and technical arguments which will assist in the formulation of practical policies at the European level.

Streeck and Schmitter have argued that the European policy process is, even more than in the United States, characterized by 'a profound *absence of hierarchy and monopoly* among *a wide variety of players of different but uncertain status*' (1991: 159). Our purpose, in this volume is to contribute to the understanding of what they describe as an American-style pattern of 'disjointed pluralism' or 'competitive federalism' organized over three levels of government—regions, nation-states, and 'Brussels'.

We have divided the volume into two distinct, but related parts. In the rest of Part I, the chapters continue with the analysis of the broader institutional and structural factors which are at work. For example, Wyn Grant, in his overview of European lobbying, emphasizes the continuing importance of national channels of lobbying and David Spence describes the system of EC policy-making within one national administrative system—Britain. Martin Donnelly and Bob Hull, both EC officials, provide an insider's view of the EC policy process into which groups must be accommodated. In Part II, we address a number of sectoral issues. The accelerating trend for both public and private regional interests to mobilize as lobbyists in the European policy process is analysed by Mazey and Mitchell. The problems of forming and running Euro-associations are addressed by McLaughlin and Jordan; Knight, Mazey and Richardson; and Peckstadt, Mazey and Richardson. Subsequent chapters examine the behaviour of certain sectoral interest groups—the development of cross-national networks in the voluntary sector (Harvey); the Confederation of British Industry (Eberlie); the Union of Industrial & Employers' Confederations of Europe (Collie); and the multiple strategies employed by corporate lobbyists (Sargent). Finally, we conclude with an analysis of the general trends in European lobbying and ask whether it is possible that a European policy style is emerging.

Notes

This chapter is based on information obtained from interviews with a range of British interest groups engaged in EC lobbying and senior EC Commission officials. We wish to thank David Judge, Keith Dowding, David Bellamy, Martin Smith, Ella Ritchie, David Spence, and various Commission officials for their comments on an earlier draft of this chapter and Christian-Martin Czypull for assisting with the analysis of types of Euro-groups. We also wish to acknowledge the financial support of the ESRC.

References

Bogdanor, V. (1989) 'The June 1989 European Elections and the Institutions of the Community', *Government and Opposition*, 24: 199–214.

Bregnsbo, Henning, and Sidenius, Nils Chr (1992) 'Danish Lobbying in Brussels', paper presented to the conference 'The Impact of National Traditions on European Public Affairs', Leuven, Holland, 16–17 Jan. 1992.

Butt Philip, A. (1985), *Pressure Groups in the European Community*, UACES Occasional Paper 2 (London: University Association for Contemporary European Studies).

——(1987), 'Pressure Groups in the European Community and Informal Institutional Arrangements', in R. Beuter and P. Taskaloyannis (eds.), *Experiences in Regional Co-operation* (Maastricht: EIPA).

Commission of the European Communities (1985), *Completing the Internal Market* (COM(85) 530 Final).

——(1989), *Communications from the Commission on Implementation of the Legal Acts Required to Build the Single Market* (COM (89) 422, 7 Sept. 1989).

——(1990), *Directory of European Community Trade and Profession Associations* (Brussels: Delta).

Dogan, M. (ed.) (1975), *The Mandarins on Western Europe* (New York: Halsted).

Dyson, Kenneth (1982), 'West Germany: The Search for Rationalist Consensus', in J. J. Richardson (ed.) *Policy Styles in Western Europe* (London: Allen & Unwin), 17–46.

Economic and Social Committee (1980), *The Right of Initiative of the Economic & Social Committee of the European Communities* (Brussels: Delta).

European Commission, see Commission of the European Communities.

Foster, C. D. (1971), *Political Finance and the Role of Economics* (London: Allen & Unwin).

Gustafsson, Gunnel, and Richardson, J. J. (1980), 'Post-Industrial Changes in Policy Style', *Scandinavian Political Studies*, 3/1: 21–37.

Hayward, Jack (1982), 'Mobilising Private Interests of the Dual French Policy Style', in J. J. Richardson (ed.), *Policy Styles in Western Europe* (London: Allen & Unwin).

Hoffmann, S. (1966), 'Obstinate or Obsolete? The Fate of the Nation State and the Case of Western Europe', *Daedalus*, 95/3: 862–915.

Jordan, A. G., and Richardson, J. J. (1987), *British Politics and the Policy Process* (London, Unwin & Hyman).

Mazey, Sonia (1988), 'European Community Action on Behalf of Women: The Limits of Legislation', *Journal of Common Market Studies*, 27/1: 63–84.

Mény, Y. (1990), 'Les Groupes et L'État en France: Collaboration et contestation, arrangements et corruption', paper presented to VI International Colloquium of the Feltrinelli Foundations, 'Organised Interests and Democracy: Perspectives on West and East', Cortina, Italy, 29–31 May 1990.

O'Brien, David M. (1986), *Storm Center: The Supreme Court in American Politics* (New York: W. W. Norton and Co.).

Olsen, J. P. (1977), *Organised Participation in Government* (Bergen: University of Bergen).

Richardson, J. J. (1990), *Government & Groups in Britain: Changing Styles* (Strathclyde Papers on Government & Politics No. 69, Glasgow).

——and Jordan, A. G. (1979), *Governing Under Pressure: The Policy Process in a Post-Parliamentary Democracy* (Oxford: Martin Robertson).

——(1993), *Pressure Groups* (Oxford Readings in Politics and Government; Oxford: Oxford University Press).

——Maloney, W. and Rüdig, W. (1991), *Privatising Water* (Strathclyde Papers on Government and Politics No. 80; Glasgow).

Strauss, A. (1987), *Negotiations, Values, Contexts, Processes and Social Order* (London: Jossey Bass).

Streeck, Wolfgang, and Schmitter, Philippe C. (1991), 'From National Corporatism to Transnational Pluralism: Organized Interests in the Single European Market', *Politics & Society*, 10/2: 133–64.

2

Pressure Groups and the European Community: An Overview

WYN GRANT

1. INTRODUCTION

Before examining interest organization at the Community level, it is important to reflect on the nature of the Community itself. Much of the research and reflection on interest-group activity in Western countries over the last thirty years has emphasized not just government as a target of group activity, but also the way in which government influences, intentionally or not, the structure, scope, and character of activity by interest organizations. The state as a shaper of interest groups has been a central theme of the recent literature on pressure groups (Wilson 1990). Although the Community does not qualify as a state *per se*, it has some statelike characteristics and does have a capacity to influence the extent, form, and direction of pressure-group activity within its boundaries. This theme has a particular relevance in the case of the Community, as an earlier generation of theorists saw interest-group activity as a major integrating force (Haas 1958).

The development of the European Community in the run up to 1992 can be regarded as a process of state formation, an unusual opportunity for social scientists to observe an experiment taking place in front of them. Of course, what emerges is likely to vary in some respects from our conventional conceptions of a state. It is something more than yet another international organization, but something less than a fully fledged state. Perhaps the most useful way of looking at the Community is as a confederation, 'a union that falls short of a complete fusion or incorporation in which one or all of the members lose their identity as states' (Forsyth 1981: 1). Because the Community is not yet a fully fledged state, and because the central decision-making institution (the Council of Ministers) is a forum for interstate bargaining, this means that pressure-group behaviour is still heavily weighted in favour of working with national governments.

The Community's abiding weakness is that it is largely dependent on the Member States to implement its decisions, and even lacks the resources to monitor whether they are doing this properly. Indeed, this creates an additional role for interest organizations as the Community is dependent on 'whistle blowing' by environmental and other public-interest groups to let it know when Community decisions are not being implemented properly. For example, the case against Britain's 'dirty' drinking water was fuelled by information from environmental interest groups.

Some of the recent writing on interest organization at the Community level has emphasized the way in which the Single European Act, and the internal market project, have transformed the importance of the Community level to interest organizations (Greenwood and Ronit 1991). These are important developments, but we must be aware of the limits of their impact. For example, while approximately 70 per cent of the measures necessary for the creation of the internal market were in place by early 1991, the ones that had not then been achieved related to the most difficult issues.

2. THE CONTINUING USE OF NATIONAL CHANNELS

My cautious and sceptical approach leads me to emphasize the continuing importance to interest organizations of channels of access through national governments. If a national interest organization is worried about, say, a draft Community directive, then its best course of action may well be to use its established contacts with the national government. If the national government can be persuaded to adopt the association line as the national line, then the association has the assurance that its position will be defended in the place where final decisions are actually taken, the Council of Ministers.

The great advantage of this strategy is that there is no need to reach compromises with business interests in other Member States. It is, however, risky for two reasons. First, with the general use of qualified majority voting, no Member State has a veto on a particular measure. Secondly, decision-making in the Council of Ministers often takes place through a process of negotiation by exhaustion. All night meetings on a complex agenda finally lead to trade-offs of positions because of the necessity of reaching some conclusion. For example, in the autumn of 1989 the Council of Agricultural Ministers reached a complex three-way deal on New Zealand butter exports to the UK, New Zealand lamb exports to the UK, and the Community sheepmeat regime, including the abolition of the variable deficiency payment enjoyed by British sheep farmers. In trade-offs of this kind, a government may suddenly abandon its position on a particular issue, meaning that the associ-ation has lost everything.

Of course, interest organizations are not so naïve as to rely solely on one channel of access. The exact combination of channels that is used, and the relative emphasis that is placed upon them, will depend on the particular issue being addressed. As well as being in contact with their own national government, it is likely that they will be working through their European-wide federation and making direct approaches to the Commission on their own behalf. Certainly, as the Community has developed in importance as a decision-making body, representation in Brussels has become increasingly important. One indicator of this is the extent to which large multinational firms increasingly find it necessary to have permanent government affairs representatives in Brussels.

Although national channels of access remain important, the actual content of the work of business associations has been substantially affected by the development of the Community. When one looks at what national business associations actually do, European Community business often tops their agenda these days. There are, of course, variations from one sector to another: for example, the construction industry is less affected by the actions of the Community than the food-processing industry. If one looks beyond the business area, the professions are still essentially nationally based. For example, policies in areas such as health, education, and culture are still largely determined by national politics.

In the industrial area, the range and complexity of the matters being dealt with means that firms cannot hope to deal with all these issues on their own, so an important rationale for supporting business associations is their ability to handle EC matters. It should also be noted that once it comes to the implementation stage, contacts with national officials will be important in influencing the drafting of the regulations which give effect to Community decisions. It could be argued that an important characteristic of the EC policy process is implementation failure, and that this in part reflects the influence exerted by national-level pressure groups when Community directives are translated into domestic legislation.

3. COMMUNITY-LEVEL BUSINESS REPRESENTATION

The activities of pressure groups at the national level have been comprehensively documented (Jordan and Richardson 1987; Grant 1991). Rather less has been published about pressure-group activity at the Community level. Hence, the rest of this chapter will focus on such Community-level activity. This does not undermine the central argument that the national level remains important. However, as the Community develops as a political entity, pressure-group activity at that level is likely to become more important.

There are several hundred associations representing business interests operating at the Community level. If one takes just one sector, chemicals, excluding pharmaceuticals, the writer's own data base, which is certainly incomplete, identifies nine major European sectoral or subsectoral associations, and sixty-five product-level associations. Some of these product associations have very narrow, highly technical domains of concern. This is not surprising when one recalls that the Community is often dealing with highly product-specific, technical questions in areas such as environmental policy. The matters that product-specific associations deal with can be of vital importance to their member companies.

In dealing with the national-level impact of Community business, national associations are operating through well-established—and well-researched—channels. Rather more needs to be said about the roles of the European-level federations of business associations, that is the organizations which bring together the relevant national associations, sometimes also covering Western European states outside the Community. These associations exist at cross-sectoral, sectoral, subsectoral, and product levels. Three generalizations can be made about them which are, of course, subject to qualification in particular cases: they are inadequately resourced in relation to the range and complexity of tasks they attempt to undertake; they largely react to an agenda set by the Commission; and they often have great difficulty in reconciling the divergent national interests of the member organizations. In short, they are often rather ineffective, and leading multinationals have become increasingly exasperated with them, a point returned to later (see also Ch. 13).

Levels of resources vary considerably, but all the European federations are constrained by the fact that they have to raise funds from member associations who have to come up with the funds from their generally hard-pressed budgets (even if they are not actually hard-pressed, they often behave as if they were). Consequently, many European-level associations are run by a director-general and a secretary: if the director is lucky, he or she may have an executive assistant as well. There are, of course, better staffed organizations such as the European Chemical Industry Council (CEFIC) which represents the chemical industry.

The lack of resources means that federations cannot do very much more than react to an agenda set by the Commission in terms of proposals for directives, etc. They are helped by the fact that the Commission is a very open bureaucracy and is generally anxious to consult with relevant groups. The process of decision-making is usually a very long drawn out one, and very often the activities of groups will concentrate on slowing it down even further. However, it is also subject to sudden spurts of activity, when documents will suddenly reappear from drawers where they have been lingering for a long period, and quick responses will be required.

Reconciling the divergent interests of the member associations is a very time-consuming process. Often the only way in which agreement can be reached is through arriving at a 'lowest common denominator' policy which is so vague and general that it is unlikely to have any impact on the development of Community policy. Indeed, sometimes agreement is not possible. In April 1991 British and Irish electricity suppliers refused to sign a paper agreed by Continental members of Eurelectric on how to introduce more competition into European Community power networks. It is difficult to accept Eurelectric's argument that this open split in its ranks did not damage its lobbying power with the Commission. Even when a policy is arrived at, it often tends to be rather inflexible. Modifying it in any way may mean starting the bargaining process all over again, as once one part of it has been unstitched, the whole garment tends to unravel. This makes it very difficult for the Euro-groups to respond very effectively to new initiatives emerging from the Commission.

Even so, most of the lobbying activity is directed at officials in the various DGs of the Commission, some of which are more receptive to approaches from business interests than others. Another tactic may be to approach the cabinet of a commissioner, not necessarily the cabinet of the commissioner dealing with the matter, as the Commission does function as a collective decision-making body. The European Parliament is being given more attention as it becomes more significant, but the work of handling the Parliament is often subcontracted to specialists who work on behalf of a number of European associations.

4. CEFIC AS AN EFFECTIVE EUROPEAN-LEVEL ORGANIZATION

CEFIC is generally regarded as one of the best organized European-level pressure groups, and an analysis of its particular features may assist an understanding of how effective European-level pressure groups can emerge. An empirically based study of the politics of the chemical industry found that 'CEFIC was regarded by every person who was interviewed both in firms and the Commission as a relatively well organized sector body' (Grant, Paterson, and Whitston 1988: 187).

An analysis of why this should be the case needs to take account of both 'logic of membership' (characteristics of the category of interest) and 'logic of influence' (impact of government, in this case, EC) factors. On the logic of membership side, the European chemical industry has a highly international orientation and is predisposed to view the EC as a single market. The EC therefore represents a principal focus of attention for the industry. The industry is made up of a relatively small number of large companies, so that the large firm–small firm tensions which undermine so many business organizations are not generally present. The companies are usually highly profitable and can afford to fund a well-resourced association, and to lend their own experts for association work. The companies have a long tradition of associating with one another in cartels (which continue to the present day), thus predisposing them to co-operative activity.

On the logic of influence side, the chemical industry is a major focus of attention for the Community. The industry is particularly affected by the development of the Community's environmental policies. However, a number of other Community policies have a substantial impact on the industry. Many of its joint venture activities require clearance under Community competition policy. Community trade policy is a central concern of the industry, particularly in relation to the possible conclusion of a free-trade agreement with petrochemical-producing countries in the Middle East.

While CEFIC remained a federation of national chemical associations, there were recurrent tensions about the extent of direct participation by the major multinational firms in the organization's decision-making. Directors of the national business associations, sometimes regarded as middle ranking bureaucrats, were perceived as exercising a disproportionate influence. Companies saw themselves as paying for the organization, but having a limited input into its decisions. The first step to resolving these tensions was taken when Sir John Harvey-Jones of ICI was president in 1985. Individual companies were brought into a consultative, non-voting body, the Assembly of Corporate Associate Members (ACAM). Although seen as a useful change, this created a complex internal structure, and still left the companies in something of an outsider role. In 1991 CEFIC gave full membership to companies and developed a bicameral structure which created a shared balance of power between its historic national federation members and the individual chemical companies.

The major challenge now facing CEFIC (and other European-level associations) is coping with the consequences of change in Eastern Europe. The chemical industry federations in Poland and Hungary (as well as that in Turkey) have applied for membership. Enlargement beyond the existing base of fifteen member federations may make the organization more difficult to manage. Difficult issues to be resolved include the attitude of applicant federations to environmental and dumping issues. CEFIC has set up a working group under its director-general to study these problems and to assess what conditions new members ought to meet.

5. LARGE FIRMS AND THE WEAKNESSES OF THE EUROPEAN-LEVEL FEDERATIONS

Despite the relative success of the CEFIC reforms, the problem of reforming the associations from within is that many of the weaknesses of these bodies are apparently endemic. Any serious attempt at reform is likely to arouse opposition from those interests who stand to lose from the reform process. The weaknesses of many of the European-level federations have increasingly exasperated senior executives of major multinational companies as the European dimension has become increasingly important. They have therefore increasingly decided to appoint their own public affairs specialists in Brussels and have also formed individual direct membership associations at the European level.

Major firms have, however, increasingly relied on their own government relations representatives in Brussels (e.g. ICI, Exxon). It is particularly interesting that the German chemical firms, who traditionally relied on working entirely through their association, have appointed high-level European co-ordinators to oversee their relations with Brussels.

In understanding the work of these government affairs representatives, it is important to note that Brussels is more like Washington as a setting for lobbying than any European capital. Everything, of course, happens on a much smaller scale than in Washington, and there is no equivalent of the White House as a central focus. However, there is a proliferation of lobbyists working for firms, or offering their services to firms, working in an environment where the administration is very open. Much depends on informal social contacts, in which power is the currency of social exchange. Any contact will be exploited if it gives access to decision-makers. The presence of a considerable number of American law firms in Brussels may reinforce the American flavour of much of the lobbying there.

Something else which is also like Washington, but very different from London, is that the government relations representatives are closely involved in the work of the relevant Euro-associations. One of the tasks of ICI's representatives in Brussels was to act as a progress chaser on CEFIC matters. This also happens where the company chairman is not directly involved. In Britain, government relations and trade association activities are kept in separate compartments. It should be noted that, just as in Washington, government affairs representatives are usually located away from their corporate headquarters, giving them more autonomy of action.

Another type of response by multinational companies dissatisfied with existing arrangements for European-level representation has been to form direct membership associations at a Community level restricted to multinational or very large companies. So far this is happening on a small scale, but the fact that it is happening at all reflects the significance of the Community to large firms. The case of the petrochemical industry is discussed here, but another example is motor vehicle manufacture.

At the sectoral level, the Association of Petrochemicals Producers in Europe (APPE) was formed as part of the Harvey-Jones reforms of CEFIC. Membership is confined to multinational companies who have to be represented at meetings by very senior executives. It is no accident that one of the first direct membership associations at the EC level was formed in a globally oriented industry. APPE states, 'The rising costs of research mean that Europe's petrochemical . . . producers have to seek global markets. Even continental sized markets like the United States are no longer sufficiently large to repay the cost of developing a new speciality chemical.' APPE has been active and influential in the areas of the overcapacity problem, and EC trade relations with the Gulf Cooperation Council countries, a matter of vital importance to petrochemical companies.

At the cross-sectoral level, the European Business Round Table is made up of the chief executives of forty leading European business firms (including firms from countries outside the EC). It has met twice a year, focusing on cross-sectoral issues which are regarded as being of crucial importance to business. It enjoys access to European heads of government, as well as to the Commission. One of its claims is that it was one of the original driving forces behind the adoption of the internal market proposal.

One other cross-sectoral body representing major firms which deserves mention is the EC Committee of the American Chamber of Commerce which portrays itself in its publicity material as the 'eyes, ears and voice of American business in the European Community'. It meets regularly with commissioners and their top officials. A lunch is usually organized to discuss current issues with the delegation about to start its six-month presidency of the Council.

Nevertheless, the model of the direct membership association does not offer a means of overcoming fundamental differences of opinion between member firms, particularly where there have been decision rules that require unanimity. The difficulties that can arise are illustrated by the recent split among European car firms over the question of Japanese imports into the EC after 1992. The chairman of Peugeot has been a leading opponent of such imports. He was reluctant to see the Committee of European Community Automobile Makers (CCMC) adopt a system of qualified majority voting, even with a tough 80 per cent requirement. His view was that he should not be allowed to take part in a majority vote on matters which could jeopardize the life of his company. The other eleven firms therefore walked out of the CCMC and formed their own new organization.

The chairman of Peugeot was also opposed to opening up the new organization to Volvo which is, of course, now linked with Renault. The new auto industry organization will include non-EC car-makers including General Motors and Ford (see also Ch. 7). This raises another issue about direct membership associations: should they admit non-EC companies? When Fujitsu acquired an 80 per cent stake in ICL, the formerly British company was suspended from the European Information Technology Round Table. The Round Table's view was that because its purpose was to enhance the global position of the European information technology industry, the group should be confined to truly European-owned companies, but it was later admitted.

Direct membership associations at the European level seem most likely to be formed where three conditions are met. First, the industry should have an international orientation in terms of its structure and marketing strategies. The industry will be one in which 'global firms responding to changing international marketing conditions and engaged in a complex network of relationships with other firms are the crucial actors' (Martinelli and Grant 1991: 297). Secondly, the sector's activities should be substantially influenced by decisions taken by the European Community. Thirdly, it should have a relatively small number of large firms, reducing (although not eliminating) conflicts which inhibit co-operation, and enabling

the sector to provide the resources necessary to sustain a sophisticated European-level association.

6. THE AGRICULTURAL LOBBY

Two-thirds of the EC's budget continues to be devoted to a Common Agricultural Policy (CAP) which represents dubious value for
money by any criteria. Not surprisingly, the agricultural lobby,
represented by the Committee of Professional Agricultural Organisations in the European Community (COPA), is often regarded as
the most successful Community-level pressure group. 'COPA's relationship with DG VI is . . . very close' (Smith 1990: 161).

There is nothing 'surprising' about the influence of the farm
lobby in the EC; it is what happens in every OECD country.
OECD statistics show that the cost of supporting agriculture in its
member states nearly doubled between 1979–81 and 1986. Producer
subsidy equivalents, an attempt to provide a comprehensive measure
of farm subsidies, rose on average in OCED countries from 30 per
cent in 1979–81 to 47 per cent in 1986. In all Western countries,
agricultural policy decisions are taken in a distinct policy network;
highly insulated from the political process as a whole, and usually
involving agricultural ministries, farmers' organizations (and, particularly in the US) specialist legislative committees. The only differences in the EC are that the Council of Agricultural Ministers
gives a central decision-making focus to a network that is often
more diffuse in the Member States, and that agricultural expenditure is the dominant budget item. The frequency of meetings of the
Council of Agricultural Ministers, and the relative stability of its
membership, with particular long-serving ministers playing a pivotal role, tends to produce a collective outlook which is protective
of what are perceived as the interests of Community agriculture
(Swinbank 1989: 304–6).

The agricultural lobby has been more intensively studied than
any other aspect of interest organization in the Community, if only
because of the central role it has enjoyed in the decision-making
process over a long period of time. In many ways, COPA (and
its sister organization, COGECA, representing agricultural co-
operatives) act as one would expect to act at the Community level.
In other words, they have well-developed and regular contacts with

Commission officials, but also make representations to the European Parliament and the Economic and Social Committee. Although direct representations are made to the Council of Agri-. cultural Ministers, the more usual channel is indirect representation at the national level.

The one aspect of COPA's operations that distinguishes it from other European-level pressure groups is the importance it attaches to the advisory committees set up by the Commission in connection with the operation of the CAP. There is one of these committees for each of the products covered by the CAP regime, and COPA usually has 50 per cent of their membership. These committees provide a valuable opportunity for institutionalized participation in the development and implementation of policy. 'The farmers are in an institutionally privileged position within the EEC. They have access to, and involvement in, agricultural decision making' (Smith 1990: 162).

It has been argued that such changes as the introduction of milk quotas and budget stabilizers provides some evidence that the influence of the farm lobby has peaked. A more restricted budget provides more opportunities for national differences of opinion, arising from differences in farm structure and the range of products produced, to come to the surface. Moyer and Josling observe, 'the farm lobby appears increasingly divided as different farm interests compete for scarce funds, resulting in a loss of influence' (1990: 209). Smith notes, 'As the Common Agricultural Policy has continually failed to deal with increasing costs and production, controversy over food policy has increased and farmers have been unable to defend the position that the only important policy goal is increasing production' (1991: 249).

It may be, of course, that the influence of the farm lobby per se, as distinct from the existence of a separate decision-making network for agriculture, has been exaggerated in the past. It is too easy to take the existence of a sophisticated and well-resourced farm lobby on the one hand, and the maintenance of a CAP that provides considerable financial support on the other, and come to the conclusion that there is a monocausal relationship from one to the other. Smith (1990) has argued in the British context that agricultural policy outcomes in the post-war period can be explained in terms of the maintenance of a productionist agenda by a closed policy community. The politically privileged position of the NFU was a consequence of the dominant ideology rather than a source of it. More generally, Moyer and Josling have argued that to blame agricultural policy inertia 'on the power of farm lobbies does not seem particularly helpful . . . The major farm policies survive because of the particular sets of institutions involved in the setting of policy and the structure of the decision framework in which they operate, as well as the pressure from interest groups' (1990: 203).

Budgetary pressures have led the Community to take a rigorous attitude towards agricultural spending. As the CAP began to threaten the budgetary stability of the whole Community, the agricultural policy-making process became exposed to new, external influences, introducing political forces into the agricultural decision-making process with different priorities from those of the farm lobby. COPA member organizations are often rather slow in developing bargaining positions, and national positions can be relatively inflexible once they have been arrived at. A slow, rather rigid mechanism for arriving at bargaining positions may be able to cope with a decision-making process which is essentially incremental (as the CAP used to be), but not with one where fundamental changes are at least on the agenda and, in some cases, actually being implemented (the CAP in the late 1980s/early 1990s). A complicating factor is that southern enlargement has expanded and changed the overall mix of commodity regimes. Enlargement of the EC to include countries such as Sweden and Norway is of particular concern to southern Member States who feel that the political balance in agricultural issues might swing further against them.

Budgetary crises, however, provide only relatively short-term pressures for change. Once the budgetary crisis has been apparently 'solved', the focus of political attention shifts elsewhere. The complexity of the agricultural sector also means that it is possible to 'fudge' outcomes so that they are more generous to the agricultural sector than appears to be the case. One illustration is the adoption of the green ECU which is based on the Deutschmark rather than a basket of currencies. Hence, agricultural prices were favourably influenced by the appreciation of the Deutschmark relative to other currencies. 'Agricultural policy makers are skilled at introducing changes which appear to produce more fundamental reforms than they actually deliver' (Grant 1991: 110). The introduction of milk quotas did go some way towards redressing (although not eliminating) the imbalance of supply and demand for milk, but it also gave existing dairy farmers a new and valuable asset. The debate about the current crisis in the CAP shows how difficult it is to produce any fundamental reform package, as any solution suggested is likely to offend the interests of at least one Member State. All too often, the result is immobilization and another temporary solution.

The failure of the GATT talks in Brussels, largely over the agricultural issue, once again illustrates the weight attached to the priorities of the agricultural sector compared with more general interests. Admittedly, the talks later reached a conclusion, but then provoked considerable dissent in France. Once again, however, one should not see the breakdown of the GATT talks as an illustration of the power of the farm lobby, but rather of the insulation of agricultural policy issues from wider concerns. This reflects not just the way in which farmers are organized as interests, but also the complexity of agricultural issues which imposes a high political entry price, and the separate institutional organization of agriculture within government at both national and Community level.

The longer run prospects for policy change depend in part on the extent to which hitherto excluded groups are able to establish themselves as participants in the decision-making process. Environmental considerations are increasingly impinging on agricultural policy, with a debate on the merits of an 'extensive' as distinct from an 'intensive' agricultural policy. Issues such as water pollution resulting from fertilizer use provide a new opening for environmental groups into agricultural policy. In the long run, severe restrictions on the use of fertilizers in certain areas could substantially change the pattern of British agriculture.

The agricultural agenda has become more complex as new issues have been introduced by new groups. However, one must be aware of the limits of this process. Farmers remain a well-entrenched interest in the Community, not least because of their influence on political parties in government, notably the CSU and the FDP in Germany. Consumer groups remain relatively excluded, but the losses of the CAP to the individual consumer are relatively small compared to the potential loss for producers. Above all, 'The greatest problems in terms of subordinating narrow interests have come at the level of the Council of Agricultural Ministers' (Moyer and Josling 1990: 210). Once again, this reflects the continuing

importance of bargained compromises between Member States in
the Community's decision-making process.

7. WEAKER GROUPS: ORGANIZED LABOUR,
ENVIRONMENTALISTS, AND CONSUMERS

In terms of the language adopted by the 1972 Paris Summit, the
trade unions are one of the 'social partner' organizations enjoying a
special status in the eyes of the Community. However, it would be
difficult to argue that the influence of the European Trade Union
Confederation (ETUC) has approached that of COPA, even though
the latter organization is operating in a much more restricted policy
arena. ETUC itself makes the relatively modest claim that 'concrete
work on health and safety has been our biggest success story'
(Interview information, Brussels, 28 Apr. 1986).

There are a number of reasons for the limited impact of the
ETUC which largely pre-date the emergence of governments
unsympathetic to trade unions in Member States such as Britain.
First, the ETUC sees itself as a European-wide rather than an EC
organization with member organizations from Turkey to Iceland.
Other organizations operating within the EC (e.g. CEFIC) draw
members from Western European countries outside the Community, but their main focus of action tends to be the Community.
Secondly, the national member organizations of the ETUC tend to
be predominantly domestically oriented organizations with a strong
desire to preserve their own autonomy. One important factor here
is that collective bargaining, the ultimate focus of all labour organizations, is not conducted at a Community level. The ETUC thus
faces considerable difficulties in co-ordinating policies across countries. As an ETUC official put it in interview, 'There are different
nuances about co-ordination, what it means. Actions? Statements?
Representation to the European Commission?' (28 Apr. 1986).
Thirdly, there are ideological divisions between the member organizations (indeed, two major confederations, the CGT in France
and the Workers' Commissions in Spain are not ETUC members).

With its interest in creating a 'social space' in Europe, and its
focus on health and safety matters, the ETUC concentrates much
of its effort in Brussels on DG V, the directorate-general for social

affairs. It has been developing contacts with DG XI, the environment directorate. Like other European-level interest groups, an ETUC official explained in interview that 'we ask our members to intervene directly with their governments on the basis of ETUC policy. The ways that unions are involved in compromises with their national governments can be important at the international level' (28 Apr. 1986). Given the various weaknesses and problems that have been outlined, the ETUC is probably closer to the environmental and consumer groups discussed below than the other producer groups in terms of being dependent to a considerable extent on Commission goodwill and interest for its ability to influence policy.

Environmental groups in the Community are represented at the EC level by the European Environmental Bureau (EEB) which has 150 membership organizations throughout the Community and is financed by grants from the Commission, from private foundations and from member subscriptions. Despite this assistance from the Commission, the EEB has often been seen as something of an 'outsider' group.

The situation has changed since then in so far as the Single European Act gives the Community specific environmental responsibilities. Even so, the EEB continues to be a reactive rather than a proactive group. The EEB is very dependent on its good contacts with the environment directorate (DG XI), and on the ability of DG XI to win intra-bureaucratic battles with the Commission. In many ways, the 'whistle blowing' activities of national environmental groups in drawing attention to failures by Member States in the implementation of Community directives may be of greater significance than the work of the EEB, although this is a subject on which further research is required. The work of environmental 'think tanks' and policy research institutes (such as the Institute for Environmental Policy) may make an important contribution to the policy agenda on environmental issues at the EC level.

Environmental pressure groups form part of a wider environmental movement which also includes political parties and other forms of social action. The success of environmental pressure groups is likely to be influenced by the progress made by this wider environmental movement. The higher politicians perceive environmental questions to be up the political agenda of voters, the more likely they are to respond to environmental pressure groups.

The evidence of the current standing of environmentalism is rather mixed. It would appear that the onset of recession in countries such as Britain has led voters to give a higher priority to more pressing material concerns. There is also perhaps a greater awareness of the impact that some environmentalist demands could have on jobs. The antics of some followers of the green cause may also have undermined the credibility of the environmental movement.

Given the trend-setting role of Californian politics, some commentators saw the defeat of the 'Big Green' initiative in a referendum there as a significant development. However, it may be that this is simply because the proposal itself was complex, over-ambitious, and poorly presented. The Greens seems to have recovered somewhat from their electoral set-back in the Bundestag elections in Germany and have made progress through joining coalition governments at *Land* level. These electoral developments need to be taken into account to a greater extent in discussing environmental pressure groups because evidence of public support is a key political resource for them.

There are three consumer organizations at the EC level, of which the most important is the European Bureau of Consumers' Unions (BEUC). EUROCOOP represents the interests of consumer co-operatives, while COFACE represents family organizations in the Community. Consumer groups remain very much outsiders at the Community level. The commitment of the Community to a consumer policy could be seen as being as much symbolic as substantive. Consumers are particularly difficult to organize because they are (small groups of industrial consumers aside) a very diffuse interest, and their difficulties are clearly compounded when an attempt is made to operate at an international level. As Moyer and Josling observe,

consumers have little incentive to organize and contribute the resources necessary to influence the policy debate . . . Moreover, consumer interests appear so diverse that consumer organizations have difficulty in forming positions generally acceptable to their membership. All this means that consumer organizations cannot make credible threats and promises to policy-makers . . . As a result neither the Council nor the Commission has much incentive to pay much attention to their views. (1990: 49)

The general picture that emerges is of a decision-making process in which the most influential groups are those that defend existing sectional interests, notably business and farmers. The CAP is the most firmly established Community policy, while the support and advice of business interests is important to the successful completion of the internal market. These interests therefore have more to offer the Community than those organizations who cannot influence the achievement of key Community goals. Organized labour and environmental groups have their points of entry in particular DGs, but still remain relatively marginalized. The most successful route for environmental groups to exert influence may be at either end of the policy process: influencing the construction of the policy agenda, and highlighting implementation deficiencies.

8. CONCLUSIONS

Although business interests are likely to remain the most important category of interests organized at the Community level, this is not the same thing as saying that business generally gets what it wants at the Community level. The Member States remain highly influential, and they have political objectives of their own which are often not the same as those of business. The Commission also has its own agenda which often does not coincide with that of business. Business itself is, of course, divided. Some firms (e.g. firms in industries threatened by international competition such as consumer electronics and motor vehicles) may welcome a relatively interventionist, 'European champion' industrial strategy by the Community. Others (e.g. international chemical firms) would prefer the Community to concentrate on removing those remaining barriers which obstruct the free flow of capital between Member States, and those regulations which impair the operation of the market mechanism on a Community-wide basis.

National level pressure-group activity to influence Community policy outcomes has not been discussed at length in this chapter because it is relatively well covered in the existing literature. Such emergent phenomena as direct membership associations and individual activity by firms have been emphasized as harbingers of possible future trends. One should not overlook the work done by the European-level associations of associations. Much of it is highly technical, and very little of it is glamorous, but it is of considerable importance in ensuring that the Community does not adopt policies which ultimately undermine the competitiveness of firms.

However, enlargement of the Community is likely to further compound the difficulty of arriving at policies which rise above the lowest common denominator. An important agenda item for the future organization of interests at the Community level must be to ensure that such associations of associations have the resources and the internal structure which will allow them to do an effective job on behalf of their members.

As emphasized in the introduction, the pace at which this happens will be considerably influenced by the speed at which the Community develops statelike properties, particularly in terms of its ability to directly implement policies and decisions (at present confined to some limited but significant areas such as cartel busting). As the Community enhances its capacity to make and enforce authoritative decisions, firms will consider that it is worth devoting more resources and decision-making authority to European-level pressure groups. The integration process will tend to drive the pattern of pressure-group activity, rather than the other way round, as was predicted at an earlier stage of the debate about the Community's development.

References

Forsyth, M. (1981), *Unions of States: The Theory and Practice of Confederation* (Leicester: Leicester University Press).

Grant, W. (1991), *The Dairy Industry: An International Comparison* (Aldershot: Dartmouth).

——Paterson, W., and Whitston, C. (1988), *Government and the Chemical Industry* (Oxford: Clarendon Press).

Greenwood, J., and Ronit, K. (1991), 'Organised Interests and the Internal Market', paper prepared for the annual conference of the Political Studies Association, Lancaster.

Haas, Ernst B. (1958), *The Uniting of Europe: Political, Social, and Economic Forces 1950–57* (Stanford, Calif.: Stanford University Press).

Jordan, G., and Richardson, J. (1987), *Government and Pressure Groups in Britain* (Oxford: Clarendon Press).

Martinelli, A., and Grant, W. (1991), 'Conclusion', in A. Martinelli (ed.), *International Markets and Global Firms* (London: Sage), 272–88.

Moyer, H., and Josling, T. (1990), *Agricultural Policy Reform* (Hemel Hempstead: Harvester Wheatsheaf).

Smith, M. J. (1990), *The Politics of Agricultural Support in Britain* (Aldershot: Dartmouth).

—— (1991), 'From Policy Community to Issue Network: *Salmonella* in Eggs and the New Politics of Food', *Public Administration*, 69: 235–55.

Swinbank, A. (1989), 'The Common Agricultural Policy and the Politics of European Decision Making', *Journal of Common Market Studies*, 27: 303–22.

Wilson, G. K. (1990), *Interest Groups* (Oxford: Basil Blackwell).

3

The Role of the National Civil Service in European Lobbying: The British Case

DAVID SPENCE

1. INTRODUCTION

This chapter examines the role of the UK's national administration, focusing on British officials in Whitehall and Brussels.[1] These two levels of the government machine are not merely geographical distinctions; they also demonstrate important conceptual points of relevance to the Community decision-making process itself. There are four important points to make. First, the national Official is clearly a lobbyist of European institutions and other Member States' Officials. But the Official is also a target for the national lobby and the 'foreign' lobby—whether of Community countries or elsewhere. Secondly, European policy-making is far more complex and less accessible to the lobbyist than at the purely national level. Thirdly, the stakes in Brussels are often higher and the institutional game more fraught with risk. The 'right' policy for the UK may simply be overruled if the Treaty base allows for a majority vote. Fourthly, arising from this, law-making and policy-making in the European context underline the degree to which international diplomacy and negotiating skills are now part of the domestic policy-making process. Community decision-making is the arena, *par excellence*, for positive-sum games, and it is here that the borderline between domestic and international policies is most blurred. Indeed, the originality of European decision-making lies in the supranationality of its outcomes and the blurring of the distinction between foreign and domestic policy in the process of international compromise that characterizes its procedures. Domestically, there is 'direct effect' and 'direct applicability' of Community legislation. In Brussels there is dilution of national viewpoints in the attempt to

find acceptable compromises for legislation applicable throughout
the Community.

2. THE LOBBIED LOBBYIST: THE ROLE OF THE NATIONAL OFFICIAL

National officials have two mirror-image but complementary roles
in the process of negotiating European legislation: they are simultaneously subjected to influence and called upon to exercise it. Yet,
unlike in the purely national framework, officials and politicians in
the UK do not set the Community agenda. Apart from when the
UK holds the Council Presidency, the organization and timing of
Community business is largely outside the control of the UK.
Indeed, even during the UK Presidency, much of the agenda is
determined by the previous Presidency and invariably influenced by
the Commission's own work programme. So, whereas a lobbyist
knows that in the context of national legislation, Whitehall is the
prime focus of law-making, in the European context the British
civil servant is but one of many points of access to the decision-
making process. In theory, the role of UK officials is to defend
national interests. However, the sources of influence on the officials
need not only be their own country's government and national
interest groups. Influence is also exerted by other Member States'
officials, and their organized interests. Extra-Community interests
also seek allies among Member States' officials. Equally, the influence exercised by UK officials may not only be on the European
institutions and other Member States' officials. It can also be
brought to bear on their own colleagues and those very interests
they are called upon to 'represent'. Thus, while national officials
are the key target for national lobbyists, for the latter to concentrate on the national officials alone would be foolhardy. The lobbying net needs to be spread much wider, since the traditional
relationship between national interest groups and 'their' government is diluted at the European level.

This phenomenon was predicted in the Community's early days
by neo-functionalist analysts of the European integration process
such as Leon Lindberg and Stuart Scheingold (1970) in their semi-
nal *Europe's Would-Be Polity*. Jean Monnet, founding father of the
European Coal and Steel Community, also believed (and hoped)

this would be the outcome of post-war attempts to integrate the economies of Western Europe: 'I was certain that the lessons that we learned day after day . . . would spread well beyond the confines of the ECSC, and that gradually, more activities, more people would live under common rules and common institutions' (1976: 578). Just as the focus of interest groups has shifted from the purely national level, so has the working environment of the civil servant. As national officials and politicians come to see this wider context they often appear to take on European rather than British priorities—a process described as 'going native'. This was said, for example, of Lord Cockfield when Mrs Thatcher refused to nominate him for a second term as European Commissioner. Former Labour Minister Tony Benn went so far as to claim that 'I think the Foreign Office in a deep way has transferred its allegiance from Britain to Brussels' (Young and Sloman 1982: 79).

It is true that compromises resulting from the confrontation of Member States' views in Brussels sometimes lead the national official to defend a view at variance with an original departmental line or a position advocated by a key interest group. Positions are watered down during the domestic co-ordination process and in negotiation with the Commission and other Member States. Sometimes the 'foreign' view makes sense or may have to be taken on board as part of a package deal where the cost of compromise is outweighed by negotiated advantage. In consequence, British officials often have to persuade their colleagues in Whitehall that the limits of negotiability have been reached. This can sometimes be more difficult than persuading other delegations to accept the British viewpoint. As one Foreign Office official has commented: 'the diplomatic challenge of dealing with Whitehall is more difficult than dealing with foreigners'. Readers of the literature on international negotiations will not be surprised by this. Gilbert Winham (1977), for example, has pointed out that international negotiations are often characterized by the preponderance of negotiating within the team in order to reach an agreed line, rather than with the other side. So, while 'going native' remains a term of abuse, seeing other viewpoints, whether those of other Member States, the Community as a whole, or of 'the lobby' has become the *sine qua non* of the effective national negotiator in the EC context.

Moreover, since the Single European Act expanded the scope of decisions taken by qualified majority, the government may be outvoted on issues where its 'ideal position' as set out in the 'line to take' agreed in Whitehall is simply not acceptable. Sometimes, the more nuanced 'realistic position' is not acceptable either and in the worst case, even the British 'fallback position' may fall on deaf ears (H. Wallace 1985). Even if the private lobbyist has convinced national officials and the relevant minister of his or her case, the game may anyway be lost in a majority vote. When the UK is in a minority at the 'high-political' level of the European Council, national defeats and successes hit the headlines. It is common knowledge, for example, that the UK was in a minority of one at the European Council in Strasbourg in December 1989 which agreed to introduce a 'Social Charter' and to hold an intergovernmental conference on economic and monetary union. Likewise, British isolation at Maastricht was front-page news—though it needed to be promoted by government officials as 'good sense' rather than isolation. Yet, in issues of more direct concern to most private lobbyists, outcomes of the many Council working groups of national officials go unreported. Nevertheless, it is precisely at this level that most European legislation is made, where most lobbying takes place and where most of the 'national interest' is defined and decided.

Other contributors to this volume underline how diverse the methods and targets of Community lobbying can be. Lobbying can take place in the agenda-setting phase of the decision-making process through influence on Commission officials at 'services' level (see Ch. 5) and on commissioners' *cabinets* before policy proposals are finalized (see Ch. 4). It may also be effective throughout the negotiation period. It is not difficult for interest groups to lobby Commission officials by visits, letters, and informal meetings. At *cabinet* level, lobbying may also be undertaken by interest groups themselves. The growing number of European public affairs consultants is constantly involved in effecting the relevant contacts. Frequently, however, national governments are the lobbyists involved. In the British case, attempts to influence Commission policy in this way occur either as a direct approach from a Whitehall department or as a line co-ordinated by the European Secretariat in the Cabinet Office and expressed through the UK Permanent Representation in Brussels. So, whilst commissioners' *cabinets* and the Commission services need to be informed of private sector interests, the route is rarely direct. Indeed, lobbying a *cabinet* is really only possible for the most highly organized and senior levels of private-sector pressure. For others, the usual route is via national officials and it is here that power routinely lies. The lobbyist's task is to convince the national official that his or her interest is consistent with the 'national' interest.

Just as there are conflicts between different interests and between organized interests and the government, so there are conflicts between Whitehall departments, between a department and its clients in the private sector, and between the Brussels team and the home team. Hence, the common assumption that conflict is between the Commission and the Member States or between the Member States themselves needs to be put into a much larger perspective than traditional institutional analysis allows. For the purposes of this chapter, there are two relevant features of such a larger perspective. The first concerns bureaucratic politics expressed as disagreements within and between Whitehall departments. There are political and ideological priorities involved in deciding what is actually in the 'national' interest. The Department of Health and public opinion may support the view that a ban on tobacco advertising is in the national interest, while the Department of Trade and Industry, the Treasury, the advertising profession, and the tobacco producers can invoke a string of ethical and financial arguments to demonstrate that such a ban would not be in the national interest. At one level such disagreements are usually about the implications for the policy sectors involved. In many cases, however, they also involve conflicts of departmental responsibility and power. There is therefore a need for an independent arbitration mechanism. In the British case this is provided by the European Secretariat in the Cabinet Office.

The second relevant feature concerns the conflict between government, Parliament, and the private sector about where the borderline between national and European policy-making should be drawn. In Euro-jargon this is known as the question of 'competence'. A considerable amount of time is spent in national capitals throughout Europe debating whether competence should pass from national to Community level. As with the shift in the focus of interest-group activity mentioned above, this 'functional spill-over' of competence was precisely what the founding fathers hoped and the neo-functionalist theorists of integration predicted would happen (Etzioni 1963; Haas 1958). Whilst the European Commission welcomes this development, the UK Government's primary objective is to prevent any further extension of Community competence. The institutional focus of the government's strategy is the Cabinet Office and the Foreign Office. For the lobbyist, the crucial point here is that getting the UK Government to identify with a particular interest is potentially dependent on political considerations going beyond the specific issue concerned.

3. THE CONDUCT OF EUROPEAN COMMUNITY AFFAIRS BY THE UK GOVERNMENT

What, then, are the roles and functions of UK officials in this complex process? There are two broad categories into which officials fit. First, there are those who are closely involved in the lobbying process both on the receiving end from interest groups and as lobbyists/negotiators themselves in Brussels and Strasbourg. Secondly, there are those officials whose job it is to co-ordinate EC policy and ensure the efficiency of the UK Government's negotiations and lobbying once a policy line has been decided. References to both categories are scattered throughout the analysis, which focuses on the four parts of the machinery of government involved in European policy co-ordination: the little known European Secretariat of the Cabinet Office; the Foreign and Commonwealth Office; the UK's Permanent Representation to the European Communities (UKREP), and lead departments, which are the prime targets for private-sector lobbyists. The three main co-ordination institutions and their staff are all committed to representing the 'national' interest, whereas lead departments tend to defend sectoral interests. The primary objective of this analysis is to show how civil servants arrive at defining the national interest and the mechanisms involved in reconciling differing departmental views on what the national interest might be and how it might best be defended. For the lobbyist, access to official decision-makers is crucial. Channels are open and interaction encouraged between lobbyists, lead departments, and UKREP. However, they become less open as one moves from officials concerned with the defence of a sectoral policy to the governmental machinery dealing with the co-ordination and reconciliation of conflicting departmental views.

3.1 The European Secretariat: Origins and raison d'être

The European Secretariat of the Cabinet Office is different from the other major secretariats by virtue of the very openness with which it is discussed. Though its precise terms of reference are not widely known, it is the only secretariat whose existence is generally admitted (Seldon 1990). The European Secretariat is responsible for overall policy co-ordination on European issues. This role is shared with the Foreign and Commonwealth Office (FCO), which retains responsibility for day-to-day operational co-ordination. The European Secretariat is rarely the target of private-sector lobbying, since policy itself is primarily made and implemented by Whitehall departments. As one senior Cabinet Office official commented to the author, 'we are not in the business of implementing policy, but in making sure there *is* a policy.' It is, however, the focus *par excellence* of departmental pressure in Whitehall.

Having made the decision not to join the Community at the outset, the British have been obliged to tussle with an administrative system at the EC level with traditions and procedures unlike those in Whitehall. Nevertheless, British arrangements for the co-ordination of European policy are generally reckoned to be the most effective of any of the Member States. The former (French) Secretary-General of the European Commission Émile Noel, told the *Financial Times* in October 1988 that the national administration for which he had the greatest respect was the British. His view has recently been endorsed by the results of a study undertaken at the European Institute of Public Administration in Maastricht which confirmed that the UK and Denmark scored highest on an efficient policy-making and co-ordination scale (Metcalfe and Zapico Goni 1991). The British pride themselves on their regular high score on the European Commission's own table of punctual implementation of Community legislation. One of the Cabinet Office's roles is to ensure such a high score.

The positive features of co-ordination by the European Secretariat are twofold: the non-partisan (i.e. in departmental terms) nature of the co-ordination arrangements and the accumulation of an objective centre of knowledge about Community affairs accessible to all government departments. Since the Cabinet Office is under the direct responsibility of the Prime Minister, EC policy-making is above the interests and objectives of individual ministers·

and their departments. In practice, much of the practical day to day co-ordination is run by the FCO and one might argue that it could take over the policy co-ordination role as well. But the FCO is just one department in Whitehall with its own interests to defend in cases where an interdepartmental line is needed. Since EC proposals typically affect several departments, it has been argued that Community policy should not be determined by the interests of any single government department (Central Policy Review Staff 1977; Edwards 1985). Co-ordination is necessary when a particular departmental policy line on a domestic issue conflicts with wider political objectives. Whilst it might suit a department to have a new Community policy in a particular area, if it means more government spending or has spill-over implications elsewhere, the line in European negotiations might well be cautious. A case in point was the Commission's decision to make proposals under Article 90 (EEC) to liberalize the telecommunications industry. While the government was content with the *laissez-faire* principles underlying the Commission's proposals, government lawyers were uneasy about the legal base involved. While the DTI was happy with the proposal, the Department of Energy believed that the precedent thereby set would have considerable implications for the gas and oil industries (Bender 1991).

The European Secretariat which provides 'good offices' to resolve such differences, escapes the accusations of partisanship often levelled at the co-ordination arrangements of other Member States. In Belgium and Germany, for example, responsibility for policy co-ordination is shared between the foreign and economics ministries. In Denmark the foreign ministry is responsible for co-ordination and in Greece, there is outright vying for power between the Ministry of the National Economy and the Ministry of Foreign Affairs. The system closest to British co-ordination is the French Secrétariat Général du Comité Interministériel pour les Questions de Coopération Economique Européene (SGCI) (H. Wallace 1973; Carnelutti 1988). However, a form of partisanship nevertheless occurs in France. The SGCI reports to the Prime Minister, though foreign affairs remain the reserved domain of the President. This may not matter in times of harmony between the two offices, but periods of 'cohabitation' between a President and a Prime Minister with different political allegiances, though hitherto rare in the system, present their own problems for policy co-ordination

(Lequesne 1987, 1988). Moreover, a senior official of the French Permanent Representation in Brussels once told the author that even in normal times 'the SGCI is the principle—interministerial vying is the reality'. The Cabinet Office arrangements, described by one senior Cabinet Office official as 'a bureaucrat's mechanism as opposed to a politician's' tend to carry more authority in Whitehall. This authority rests to a considerable extent upon the development of centralized legal and administrative expertise within the European Secretariat, upon which departments are able to draw.

3.2 Functions of the European Secretariat

It has long been the rule that Cabinet committees are not discussed by officials in public. The European Secretariat is increasingly breaking with this tradition. Its Deputy Head, Brian Bender, has described the tradition of Cabinet collective responsibility begun by King George III and formalized by the setting up of the Cabinet Secretariat by Lloyd George's coalition government of 1916. The principal duties of the Cabinet Secretariat, as Bender underlines, were:

to record the proceedings of Cabinet; transmit decisions to the departments concerned; prepare agenda papers, arrange for the attendance of Ministers and circulate papers required for discussion and to attend to correspondence connected with the work of Cabinet. In brief, collective responsibility means coordinated decision-making and it is the job of the Cabinet Office to see that the coordination happens. (1991: 16)

In achieving these objectives, the European Secretariat's functions are fivefold. First, it is responsible for the European items on the Cabinet's agenda and on the agenda of Cabinet committees. It aims to present issues to ministers at the right time and in the right form. Europe is only one issue on the Cabinet agenda and ministers only need to know about the major high-political questions to be resolved in Councils or those (fairly rare) instances where it has not been possible to reach an agreed interdepartmental line.

Secondly, the Cabinet Office is responsible for interdepartmental co-ordination. This is not merely a routine administrative task; a key role of the European Secretariat is to anticipate problems and potential opportunities to promote UK interests. At higher levels this entails the elaboration of complex negotiating strategies where, for example, agreement to boost spending on structural funds might permit the UK, as a net contributor to the Community budget, to require a corresponding commitment on the part of other Member States to budget discipline. At lower levels, any number of trade-offs in the drafting of a particular piece of legislation may serve UK interests in other areas (Edwards 1985). Whilst individual departments cannot be expected to predict the wider ramifications of a text in their specific area they are required to signal likely problem areas. As one senior official has commented 'what we want is lots of false alarms from departments'. Only then can the Cabinet Office be sure that it will pick up issues.

Once a co-ordination meeting is called, the role of the European Secretariat is to provide 'a neutral but purposive Chair for official level discussions; recording conclusions authoritatively and bludgeoning only rarely; and where necessary, remitting individual issues for Ministerial correspondence/discussion but in doing so isolating the key issues and presenting them clearly' (Bender 1991: 16). After such meetings a Cabinet Office minute, circulated to contacts in each department, becomes the general line to be adopted. The extensive circulation list for such papers ensures that all departments are informed and that no department can subsequently claim not to have been consulted.

This leads to the third function of the European Secretariat: providing authoritative guidance on Community issues of concern for overall UK policy. The Secretaries (civil service principal grade) provide occasional briefing papers designed to ensure that no official should be uninformed on a question of principle arising in a Community negotiation. Examples of such guidance include complex briefings on Community competence (and how to avoid its expansion), and explanations of 'comitology', i.e. the criteria involved in selecting the appropriate committee of national officials to discuss Commission implementation of secondary legislation. They also include instructions on the use of the Luxembourg Compromise and the rules regarding parliamentary scrutiny of proposed EC legislation. The European Secretariat thus functions as the collective memory and source of practical guidance for Whitehall departments on Community issues. While those Whitehall departments traditionally concerned by Community legislation—DTI, MAFF, Customs and Excise—have their own in-house expertise, newer departments on the Community scene, such as the Home

Office, the Department of Education, and the Department of Health have relied heavily on the European Secretariat for guidance.

The fourth function of the European Secretariat is monitoring the parliamentary scrutiny process. While the lead department in Whitehall has prime responsibility for the respect of procedures agreed with the parliamentary scrutiny committees, the Cabinet Office ensures that responsibilities are correctly assumed.

The fifth function of the European Secretariat is the monitoring of all Community legislation, both in terms of implementation deadlines and with regard to any legal proceedings in which the UK might be involved. Here, the Cabinet Office relies on the European Division in the Treasury Solicitor's Office to provide the necessary legal expertise. Implementation and litigation are largely the responsibility of the legal division of the lead department, but the Cabinet Office ensures that legal ramifications of a horizontal nature are borne in mind. Lawyers in the European Division of the Treasury Solicitor's Office do this first by providing legal advice both to the European Secretariat and at interdepartmental policy co-ordination meetings. Their second task is the co-ordination of views on legal issues among the legal advisers to government departments. Views on Community competence, the validity of a Treaty Article chosen by the Commission for a particular proposal, or on horizontal implications of European Court judgements are typical matters falling under this heading. Thirdly, the Treasury Solicitor's European Division has responsibility for the conduct on behalf of the UK of proceedings in the European Court of Justice, whether these are actions by the Commission against the UK under the terms of Article 169 of the EEC Treaty, references for provisional rulings under Article 177, or cases brought by individuals against HMG. Governments are also empowered by Article 173 (EEC) to challenge the validity of acts of the institutions and intervene in direct actions before the European Court in support of one of the parties. In all such cases the Cabinet Office, through the Treasury Solicitor's European Division, becomes involved.

3.3 The European Secretariat's Committee System

In practice, there is a mix of all functions described above at the various levels of the European Secretariat's responsibility. The most senior level is the Cabinet itself. Chaired, of course, by the Prime Minister, meetings are co-ordinated and minuted by the Cabinet Secretary. There is a European item at each week's Cabinet meeting, but unless there is an issue of great contention, this is designed to inform ministers rather than lead to discussion and debate. The Deputy-Head of the European Secretariat writes the first draft and the Head the final version of the briefing to the Cabinet Secretary. The Cabinet Secretary uses this briefing for his own brief to the Prime Minister. The brief is prepared in close collaboration with the head of the FCO's European Community Department (Internal) and thus ensures that the Foreign Secretary is informed about matters likely to be seized upon by the Prime Minister for further discussion. The Deputy-Head of the European Secretariat also consults closely with the private offices of other ministers likely to raise issues arising from recent or forthcoming meetings of the Council of Ministers.

The most senior committee involved in European affairs is the Overseas and Defence Committee (OPD). This Cabinet committee discusses issues pertaining to the Community only in so far as they impinge on foreign policy and security issues. OPD is also chaired by the Prime Minister and administered by the Cabinet Secretary. The subcommittee Overseas and Defence (Europe) (OPD(E)) deals with important political implications of more strictly European Community business (Edwards 1985). The expansion of Community competence after the Maastricht decisions on Political Union and in the aftermath of the events of 1989–91 in the Soviet Union, Central and Eastern Europe, makes increased activity by OPD and OPD(E) highly likely. EC issues requiring co-ordination at the Cabinet level, e.g. Council of Ministers meetings, therefore become the subject of prior OPD(E) meetings. OPD(E) currently meets about twice a month under the chairmanship of the Foreign Secretary, with the Head of the European Secretariat providing the administrative co-ordination, guidance, and reporting functions. Ministers from most departments attend OPD(E), since no department in Whitehall is now isolated from the Community context. OPD(E) meetings are prepared by senior officials in the framework of a committee entitled European Questions (Steering) and referred to simply as EQ(S). EQ(S) also meets frequently to decide strategic issues of overall importance to UK policy, such as major trade policy initiatives, budget questions, or North Sea policy (Edwards 1985, 1992).

However, the 'workhorse' of the system is the European Questions (Official) Committee, referred to throughout Whitehall as EQ(O). EQ(O) meets formally once or twice a week, but there are also frequent informal, swift co-ordination meetings (Edwards 1985). The EQ(O) network in Whitehall is extensive, but departments usually attend meetings only when a matter is of direct concern to them. Minutes of EQ(O) meetings are circulated to EQ(O) contacts throughout Whitehall. EQ(O) appears in the co-ordination process as a response to two kinds of demand. The first is line-clearing. Individual departments may know exactly what they require in terms of the negotiation of a specific piece of legislation, but must ensure that other departments are informed and have sorted out any contentious points. Or, they may lack the requisite expertise in a given area and wish to get 'cover' by ensuring there are no unforeseen legal implications. The Department of Health for instance, may have decided its own view on the Community's cancer action programme. Nevertheless, it needs to ensure that potential spill-over into neighbouring areas has been foreseen by the lawyers and that lines have been cleared with relevant departments. In fact, the cancer action programme led to a later Commission proposal for a total ban on tobacco advertising which had important implications for the DTI, the Treasury, and the Inland Revenue. Without the intervention of EQ(O), departments could remain oblivious to such Community developments.

The second role of EQ(O) is advisory. Individual departments may need guidance on three kinds of situation: procedural, tactical, and strategic. Departments may wish for procedural advice on the legal base of a Commission proposal, the scope of the Commission's powers, and whether or not to contest an issue in the European Court. Often, individual departments need guidance on Commission procedures. Tactical advice on negotiating techniques and procedures is also provided in the co-ordination meetings of the European Secretariat, where departments consult each other on negotiating tactics. Judging when to lobby a commissioner's *cabinet*, how far to involve Members of the European Parliament or whether a government minister should phone a commissioner are decisions often taken after consultation in EQ(O). Advice from the FCO on the conduct of bilateral 'pre-negotiations' to ensure sympathetic coalition-building may also be gained in this way. EQ(O) also considers the European policy implications of proposed domestic legislation. However, as highlighted by the recent decision of the European Court of Justice in the *Factor Tame* case, the system is not infallible (*Daily Telegraph*, 26 July 1991).[2] Increasingly, the European Secretariat, is becoming proactive, taking initiatives and offering advice. This requires Secretaries to keep their ears to the ground, read all the telegrammed minutes on negotiations, copies of interdepartmental correspondence, and negotiating briefs. They must also keep abreast of emerging Commission priorities and proposals. As Donoughue has stressed, 'The machine can actually influence and limit policies while nominally going through the merely administrative function of processing' (1987: 5).

4. BILATERAL AND MULTILATERAL NEGOTIATIONS: THE ROLE OF THE FCO AND WHITEHALL DEPARTMENTS

The Foreign Office has been transformed by UK membership of the EEC. It now intervenes in and is concerned with subjects which were not its proper province ten years ago. Foreign Office civil servants are interfering in agricultural prices; they are interfering in economic policy; they're interfering in energy policy. Naturally enough, the Foreign Office has an enthusiasm for continuing an institution that gives them this very substantial increased power. (Roy Hattersley, cited in Young and Sloman 1982: 81)

The FCO provides the institutional framework for the day to day co-ordination of EC policy through the Permanent Representation in Brussels and monitors departmental activity through its two European Community Departments in Whitehall. The main focus of private lobbying is neither the Cabinet Office nor the FCO in London, but the domestic lead department and the FCO's Brussels arm, UKREP.

4.1 European Policy-Making Departments in the Foreign and Commonwealth Office: Origins and raison d'être

When the UK joined the Community in 1973 the FCO immediately set up two European Integration Divisions, which were subsequently renamed European Community Departments (Internal and External) (Stack 1983). ECD(I) is concerned with monitoring and contributing to Community aspects of domestic policy-making; ECD(E) concentrates on external affairs and foreign policy. The

Foreign Office could always claim a specific expertise in negotiations with 'foreigners'. Consistency and good presentation abroad were thus part of the rationale for its selection as a main focus of EC activity. Whether the arguments still hold water in the changed world of European negotiations in the 1990s is a moot point. It is certainly true that officials in domestic departments dealing with EC affairs nowadays often have as much contact with foreigners and expertise in negotiating with them as many Foreign Office officials. They also have the technical sectoral knowledge required to make briefing more specific and negotiation more expert (Edwards 1992).

4.2 Functions of the European Community Departments of the FCO

In principle, the FCO's European Community Departments fulfil three functions. The first is the 'postbox' and monitoring function of receiving and distributing all material from Brussels, including Commission reports and proposals, telegrams concerning the day's meetings, etc. It also transmits material from Whitehall departments to UKREP for further handling, but it is important to note the caveat 'in principle'. Widespread use of facsimile machines throughout Whitehall and the increased proficiency of other Whitehall departments' efforts to co-ordinate EC developments in their own policy areas mean the FCO is increasingly bypassed.

The second major function of the FCO is the preparation of briefings for European Council Meetings and the General Affairs Council (the Council of Foreign Ministers). While individual departments could arguably prepare meetings in which their own minister takes part, each Council must be seen as one part of a complex pattern of ministerial meetings where trade-offs in negotiations can draw extremely diverse policy areas into package deals. The mere fact, also, that much of Council decision-making is settled by means of the 'A Point' procedure means ministers have an agenda before them with subjects, albeit not for discussion, completely outside their purview.[3] The Transport Ministers' Council of 30 October 1990 for instance, agreed by 'A Point', all the items except agriculture required for the Council's common position on the raft of legislative measures to incorporate the former GDR into the Community. Almost every area of Community policy was included.

A third function of the FCO is responsibility for European Political Co-operation. This lies beyond the scope of the present discussion, but it is important to note that one of the prime tools of an emerging European foreign policy remains the *acquis communautaire* and the relevant Treaty Articles necessary to enforce concrete measures such as economic assistance, sanctions, and changes in trade policy. While it was always true to say that economic policies were the tools of foreign policy, the Europeanization of domestic policies has made the process by which the tools are used far more transparent. If the UK wants to impose trade sanctions it cannot do so without a majority decision within the framework of Article 113 of the Treaty of Rome. So, while it is true to say that European integration has not totally removed the UK's ability to have an independent foreign policy (despite the constraints of European Political Co-operation) many of the tools of policy are now in the competence of the Community.

4.3 Lead Departments

EC legislative proposals and implementation measures come from the European Commission. Whilst Commission officials work closely with the Permanent Representations, they also maintain direct links with domestic departments concerned with competition matters, state aids, agricultural intervention, etc. As highlighted by Edwards (1985, 1992) Whitehall departments have evolved considerably in the years of British membership. Some departments such as MAFF and the DTI had begun the process of adaptation long before membership (Stack 1983). The general pattern for the evolution of European policy-making in domestic departments has been for European aspects of policy to be monitored by international divisions and subsequently, as the workload increases, for a co-ordinating European division to be set up. These European divisions do not themselves become involved in the day-to-day arrangements for specific technical negotiations or implementation of Community legislation. This remains the task of the functional division involved. The co-ordinating divisions come into their own when overlapping issues produce the need to co-ordinate the principles of policy as opposed to the detail.

The DTI's management of single market matters is a case in point. The Single Market Co-ordinating Division has oversight of the domestic implications of the internal market and manages the public relations campaign conducted in the UK. The co-ordination division is also present at most EQ(O) meetings as a matter of course, where technical officers in charge of specific legislation are brought into the process only when there is difficulty in reaching an agreed line or where the policy area has thrown up problems better dealt with horizontally. The co-ordination division works in close liaison with ECD(I) and ECD(E) in preparing for meetings of the Councils of Ministers and in ensuring that the UK's input into the Community's trade policy negotiations in GATT are coherently prepared. But negotiations on individual directives remain the responsibility of the specialized section concerned.

Thus, despite the prominent role played by the FCO and the European Secretariat, responsibility for EC policy-making rests to a considerable extent with departments. In theory at least, central intervention is only required in cases of disagreement or where there are complex horizontal complications. This means that individual departments are routinely allowed a high margin of man-œuvre in their Community dealings. The strength of the British system lies in the strong reporting and co-ordination mechanisms which ensure information flows, rather than in an all-pervasive centralized attempt to manage policy. If information flows according to agreed guidelines, the potential dangers of 'going it alone' are tempered by a series of trigger mechanisms which ensure other departments are brought into the process as and when required. The considerable independence of lead departments clearly calls into question the rationale of the European departments of the FCO. The role of the FCO might decline as home departments take on increasing responsibility for European affairs and as 'European policy' ceases to be regarded as 'foreign policy'.

5. THE UK PERMANENT REPRESENTATION TO THE EUROPEAN COMMUNITY

As the permanent contact point between Whitehall and the Community institutions, UKREP performs three general functions necessary to efficient government co-ordination of policy and to the defence of UK interests in negotiation with other Member States and the European Commission. First, it provides a Brussels base for Whitehall negotiators and a focus for advice, information, and co-ordination. Secondly, it monitors developments in the other

European institutions, and thirdly, it is the prime negotiator in most meetings in the Council.

UKREP numbers approximately forty-four senior officials including the Permanent Representative (a foreign office career diplomat of senior ambassadorial status) and his deputy (usually a senior DTI official). UKREP is similar in size to its German counterpart and larger than the French Permanent Representation which totals some thirty-five officials. Current figures for mid-1992 show an increase of one official per sector on 1990 staffing levels (*Vacher's European Companion*, cited in Edwards 1992). Thus, in addition to the Ambassador, his (DTI) deputy and the (MAFF) minister, there are five officials engaged in political and institutional affairs plus a temporary official taken on in 1992 to deal with the administrative implications of the UK presidency. Nine officials deal with external relations; six attend to economic, finance, and taxation matters; five handle food, agriculture, and fisheries; seven deal with social, regional, transport, and environmental policy; and six officials handle industry, energy, and the internal market. These desk officers constitute a vital link between UK lobbyists and the EC policy-making process.

5.1 UKREP's Co-ordination and Information Role

UKREP provides a central point in Brussels for departmental visits, whether at official or ministerial level. Indeed, it has been described as 'the hidden arm of Brussels in Whitehall' itself (Young and Sloman 1982: 73). Negotiators from Whitehall departments typically arrive shortly before a meeting, so as to liaise with UKREP desk officers, the Presidency, or the Council Secretariat and engage in last-minute pre-negotiations with other delegations. In principle, notice of meetings is transmitted by the Council Secretariat to Permanent Representations and the Commission. UKREP forwards notice and agendas to ECD and/or the relevant department concerned. Agendas are summary notices and departments often find it necessary to get UKREP to contact the Commission and the Council Secretariat to obtain a precise idea of the content of the meeting. Usually, individual working groups will continue to discuss issues unsettled at the previous meeting, but events and negotiating positions will have moved on in the meantime. If, on the other hand, discussing new initiatives is the real purpose of the meeting,

UKREP's preparation—information gathering and bilateral lobbying—is essential.

Since issues are constantly changing, departments may request UKREP to sound out other delegations in order to prepare discussions in Whitehall. On the whole, however, regular visitors to Council working groups will know their opposite numbers in the ministries of other Member States or in the Commission and will take direct soundings by telephone.

At COREPER level, co-ordination is highly formalized between Permanent Representations, the Commission, the Presidency, and the Council Secretariat by a regular weekly meeting of the so-called Antici group.[4] Two days before COREPER, the Anticis meet in the Council Secretariat to hear from the Presidency how it intends to run the next meeting of ambassadors. The order of points on the agenda will be discussed, as will likely new Commission positions or those of individual Member States. Typically, Anticis report to their colleagues that their ambassador is likely to make certain points on known agenda items. The Commission will also give the broad drift of its negotiating positions and national officials will announce any as yet unknown initiatives their ambassador is likely to mention. The advantage of the Antici meeting is that negotiators do not go naked into the negotiating chamber. Situations are thus avoided where ambassadors would be obliged to place a reserve on a particular issue and the Presidency can be assured that COREPER will be efficiently and sufficiently prepared. The UK Antici representative (the Head of Chancery in UKREP) will typically rush back to UKREP and telephone major points to his FCO contact. The written minute follows a short time after and provides a basis for a Whitehall round-up in case of need. In this way, government is able to avoid what Mazey and Richardson refer to as 'agenda uncertainty'—at least when avoidance is crucial (see Ch. 1).

Another weekly Antici meeting takes place in the Commission. Here, the General-Secretary of the Commission briefs the Anticis on the outcome of the weekly Commission meeting. This allows them to pose questions of national concern and to ask about the timing of coming proposals or Commission initiatives. In theory, the Permanent Representations are thus the first to know about matters arising. However, in the leaky Brussels system it is frequently the case that officials and interest groups have already been informed by commissioners' *cabinets* of the subject-matter involved and the likely outcome.

UKREP also maintains close links with the British and foreign press in Brussels and controls closely the information provided. Visiting delegates from Whitehall are instructed to leave press briefings with the UKREP press officer or the desk officer responsible for the relevant subject area. Much journalistic reporting concerns technical progress on specific legislation, but as the Community agenda becomes increasingly politicized, journalists vie for information from all sources. UKREP needs to keep a watching brief on this process, since leaking information to the press or sounding off about a delegation's reticence to compromise can affect the outcome of negotiations themselves. In practice, UKREP uses the press as a means of increasing the pressure on negotiators in London as well as in Brussels. As one former UKREP press officer remarked to the author, 'the press is part of the negotiating process here'.

5.2 UKREP's Monitoring Role

UKREP's second role is to monitor developments in all European institutions. It does this as an active participant in Council meetings and as a lobbyist of the other institutions—notably, the Commission and the Parliament. The Commission is the initiator of all Community legislation and executive for a large part of it, including the vital areas of agriculture, competition policy, state aids, and external trade policy. It also acts as mediator between the institutions and as 'guardian of the treaties'. This latter role often brings it into conflict with individual Member States over questions of implementation of Community legislation. UKREP is involved in monitoring the Commission's activities in all these areas and in maintaining close links with those Commission officials involved in them. Just as it feeds information to Whitehall, so it may be called upon to represent the UK's interests where the Commission's policies are thought to conflict with UK priorities. UKREP is thus a prime focus for the private-sector lobby as well as the lobbying arm of Whitehall departments.

In practice this means that all officials in UKREP maintain close contacts with their opposite numbers in the Commission, forming a kind of permanent UK lobby with the aim of influencing the

Commission's forward thinking and obtaining early warning of proposals or modifications to the Commission's negotiating positions. To be effective, UKREP needs to do this when proposals are mere 'gleams in the commissioner's eye' (see Ch. 5), long before. official notice to the Antici group. After consultation with Whitehall departments UKREP encourages those proposals which suit UK priorities and attempts to divert the Commission from those ideas which the government would find inimical to its own interests. It can do this by making its own ideas known to the Commission or setting out implications Commission officials might not have thought through. This key role underlines the importance of UKREP for the lobbyist.

UKREP also follows European Parliament affairs. Two UKREP officials monitor parliamentary committees and plenary sessions, reporting back to Whitehall departments on the handling of legislation affecting them. They also construct close links with MEPs from all Member States, so that in case of need UKREP can assist Whitehall departments in lobbying the Parliament on specific issues. UKREP maintains similar links with the Economic and Social Committee and, of course, with private-sector representatives whether Brussels based or on visits. In the changed world of Community law-making since the Single European Act and the Maastricht Council the pivotal position of UKREP, with its direct links to the European Parliament, Commission, other Member States, and lead departments in Whitehall has been considerably enhanced.

5.3 UKREP as National Negotiator in the Council

All senior UKREP staff are involved in the daily routine of negotiating in Council working groups and in the preparation of the two weekly COREPER meetings. The working groups are where detailed technical negotiations take place. Matters are 'put up' to COREPER either when they have been settled or when compromise at lower levels has proved impossible. Negotiators at lower levels provide back-up to the ambassador or his deputy in the more political deliberations which take place in COREPER in order that recondite points of detail, should they emerge, can be dealt with. Each of the (eighty or so a year) Council meetings are preceded by several weeks of negotiations at working group and

COREPER level. Though UKREP officials are the principal negotiators at all levels, they rely heavily upon briefings from the relevant Whitehall departments. It is also quite normal for department
officials to be present at negotiations in the Council working
groups, especially if the issue under discussion is highly technical.
However, it is the responsibility of the UKREP official to send a
summary note of the meeting to the FCO on the same day. The
rule of 'same day reporting' ensures that officials in Whitehall are
fully briefed by 9.00 a.m. the following morning.

6. CONCLUSIONS

The underlying argument of this chapter has been that British co-
ordination and policy-making arrangements are highly effective. But
it must now be clear that much of the machinery is inaccessible to
most private-sector lobbyists. Only the most senior business persons
and the best of the lobbying firms obtain access to the co-ordinators
in the Cabinet Office and the Foreign Office. Officials in lead
departments and UKREP are more accessible and constitute a vital
route of influence. Despite the fact that national governments constitute only one stage in the process of supranational decision-making, influencing national officials remains crucial. Indeed, given the
generally recognized strength of the UK's formal lobbying machinery and its ability to influence others in the process, the centrality
of UK Government machinery cannot be stressed enough.

It is thus worth drawing together some of the reasons for the
UK's achievement and underlining how knowledge of the machinery of government can shape the lobbyist's strategy. The first set of
reasons rests with the nature of the British political system itself.
UK Government is characterized by strong leadership, the absence
of open coalitions, and high-quality civil servants. Cabinet collective responsibility means the civil service can emulate this centralized and co-ordinated political system. In European policy-making
this is reflected in the successful co-ordination troika provided by
the FCO European Community Departments, UKREP, and the
European Secretariat of the Cabinet Office. As several commentators have remarked, the present system is as much a traditional
British response to new administrative challenges as it is a reflection of the changed nature of government business since British

membership of the Community (W. Wallace 1977; Central Policy Review Staff 1977; Edwards 1992).

Secondly, effective UK co-ordination rests on extremely tight and well-managed structures. The Berrill Committee concluded that the division of responsibility between the FCO and the Cabinet Office 'looks untidy but we believe it works reasonably well' (Central Policy Review Staff 1977: 5.36). As the Community has evolved, the 'untidiness' seems increasingly to correspond with new realities. Yet, if reality is untidy and complex, coping with it may require even greater administrative concentration on the part of the government and strategic thinking on the part of lobbyists. Given the exponential growth of Community business in the 1980s and 1990s, it will be interesting to see whether some of the options mentioned, but not adopted by the Berrill Report, find a new currency. Either the adage 'if it ain't broke, don't fix it' will apply, or the system could be streamlined under a co-ordinating European Ministry, thereby further increasing its effectiveness and providing a focal point for lobbyists.

Is such administrative reform necessary? Despite the general acclaim for British co-ordination of EC affairs, there remain two areas which are of long-term concern to the lobbyist where the system could, arguably, bear scrutiny and improvement. First, the small size of the European Secretariat and FCO European Departments is in one sense a positive feature of the system: responsibility for co-ordinating sensitive policy remains in the hands of a strictly limited number of officials who have close personal links with colleagues in Whitehall. However, the very small size of the Secretariat means that much time is spent on day-to-day co-ordination rather than on long-term strategic thinking. In short, both the European Secretariat and the FCO are better at 'issues' than at coherent, strategic analysis. In mitigation, it must be pointed out that since the Single European Act successive heads and deputy-heads of the European Secretariat have sought to shift the emphasis. British policy on the single market or on frontiers, for example, reflects this trend. In the last analysis, however, officialdom is dependent on political leadership. If the content of UK European policy remains largely based on response to others' initiatives, even the best strategists will be hard-pressed to affect the Community agenda.

A second criticism of the system is closely linked to the first. Much of what has been described here is a reactive rather than a proactive system. It corresponds to the nature of British policy in the Community until the mid-1980s, when the main aim could be described as damage-limitation. The main priorities lay in renegotiation of existing Community policies of particular high cost to the UK and in preventing the spread of Community competence (Edwards 1992). Mrs Thatcher's success in negotiating a British budget abatement and Mr Major's reticence at Maastricht were cases in point. While the outcome served the UK national interest as defined by the government with respect to the policy areas involved, it is doubtful whether the wider objective of achieving allies and long-term coalition-building were also attained. British policy-making has had an uncanny knack of antagonizing the UK's Community partners at all levels. The reasons are linked both to the content and style of the UK's approach. An important source of resentment is the very fact that the UK is so well co-ordinated and achieves UK aims so successfully—albeit not always tactfully. Britain's partners admire its negotiating skills, but reflect ruefully upon British dedication to changing the purpose of the Community itself. It is certainly true that for many years UK officials were obliged to run a policy of dualism—to come positively to terms with the problems of late membership on the one hand and to limit any further expansion of Community competence on the' other.

If the UK's partners see EC policy-making as being largely to do with furthering integration, the UK loses out when the Community's long-term goals are periodically revised. Examples of this abound. The surprise announcement by the French and the Germans at the 1985 Milan Council of a proposal on European Political Co-operation linked to the Single European Act negotiations is a case in point. The well-planned British position was designed to increase intergovernmental co-operation in foreign policy-making rather than strengthen the Community aspects. The British draft was revamped and presented as a Franco-German initiative with heightened Community content. Likewise, the various recent initiatives with regard to EMU and Political Union have often seen the UK in the guard's van running a security exercise rather than sharing the driver's seat of the locomotive. Since German reunification changed the stakes and accelerated the process of deepening the Community, the Italians, the Luxemburgers, and the Dutch have used their successive Presidencies to force a pace which UK negotiators have slowed with great difficulty. Until Maastricht, many people hoped Mr Major's new relations with his Community partners would prove to be a new period in UK policy. There were hopes that new attitudes might filter down to the level of those senior officials whose weekly routine includes participation in Council negotiation at the working-group level. There is some evidence that such a trend is underway, but the UK's isolation in Maastricht has doubtlessly reduced the UK's capacity to lead its Community partners.

But are these conclusions not restricted to a strategic high-political view of the decision-making process? Of what relevance are they to lobbying on specific issues? First, this analysis has hopefully underlined how complex the national input in any single decision can be. Lobbying the national official means participating in a chain of command with diverse political priorities, where the stakes might justify a compromise inimical to a particular private interest. However, where a lobby can persuade government of its cause, the efficiency and the strength of the machinery of UK European policy-making makes UK officialdom a very strong ally. Secondly, this chapter began with some generalizations about the dual role of national officials as lobbyists and as targets for the private-sector lobby. Individual firms, trade associations, or interest groups have similar complex steps to go through in ensuring their own policies are co-ordinated with other related interests. However, these interests are not part of a policy-making cluster as they are for government, where trade-offs can occur in the name of a higher good. It is thus vital not to focus solely on one's own national government as a target for lobbying. Thirdly, and most importantly, in European decision-making, the government's overall stance on Community affairs has a trickle-down effect on negotiations relating to specific items of private-sector concern. It may be that general government concerns are out of step with those of a given interest group. All the more reason to know how the system works, whom within it one can influence, and finally, where its limits lie.

Notes

1. The term 'British official' applies in this chapter to national civil servants employed by Her Majesty's Government (HMG).
2. In this case, the 1988 UK Merchant Shipping Act was overturned by a European Court ruling which found that the UK legislation amounted to a measure of equivalent effect to a ban on Spanish shipping companies registering ships in the UK.
3. 'A Points' (*Points agrées*) are agenda items agreed at Council meetings without discussion when agreement has already been reached at COREPER level.
4. The Antici group is named after its creator, a former official of the Italian Permanent Representation. It comprises one official from each Permanent Representation, the head of the Commission division dealing with the Council, and a delegate from the Council Secretariat's division for co-ordination with Member States. Seniority of the Anticis varies. In the British case, the Head of Chancery attends.

References

Bender, B. G. (1991), 'Whitehall, Central Government and 1992', *Public Policy and Administration*, 6 (spring): 13–20.

Carnelutti, A. (1988), 'L'Administration française face à la Regle communautaire', *Revue Française d'Administration Publique*, No. 48: 7–24.

Central Policy Review Staff (1977), *Review of Overseas Representation* (London: HMSO).

Donoughue, B. (1987), *Prime Minister* (London: Jonathan Cape).

Edwards, G. (1985), 'The Presidency of the Council of Ministers of the European Communities: The Case of the United Kingdom', in C. O'Nuallain (ed.), *The Presidency of the European Council of Ministers* (London: Croom Helm), 237–59.

—— (1992) 'Central Government', in S. George (ed.), *Britain and the European Community: The Politics of Semi-Detachment* (Oxford: Oxford University Press), 64–80.

Etzioni, A. (1963), 'European Unification: A Strategy for Change', *World Politics*, 16: 32–51.

Haas, Ernst B. (1958), *The Uniting of Europe: Political, Social, and Economic Forces 1950–57* (Stanford, Calif.: Stanford University Press).

Lequesne, C. (1987), 'Cordonner la politique européene da la France', *Projet*, No. 206 (July/Aug.): 42–54.

——(1988), 'Frankreich', *Jahrbuch der Europaischen Integration 1987/88*, 360–70.

Lindberg, L. and Scheingold, S. (1970), *Europe's Would-Be Polity* (Englewood Cliffs, NJ).

Metcalfe, L. and Zapico Goni, E. (1991), *Action or Reaction: The Role of National Administrations in European Policy-Making* (London: Sage).

Monnet, J. (1976), *Mémoires* (Paris: Fayard).

Seldon, A. (1990), 'The Cabinet Office and Coordination', *Public Administration*, 68/1: 103–22.

Stack, F. (1983), 'The Imperatives of Participation', in F. E. C. Gregory, *Dilemmas of Government: Britain and the European Community* (Oxford: Martin Robertson), 124–52.

Wallace, H. (1973), *National Governments and the European Communities* (London: Chatham House, European Series).

——(1985), 'Negotiations and Coalition Formation in the European Community', *Government and Opposition*, 20: 453–72.

Wallace, W. (1977), 'After Berrill: Whitehall and the Management of British Diplomacy', *International Affairs*, 54: 220–39.

Winham, G. (1977), 'Negotiation as a Management Process', *World Politics*, 20/1: 87–114.

Young, H., and Sloman, A. (1982), *No Minister: An Enquiry into the Civil Service* (London: BBC).

4

The Structure of the European Commission and the Policy Formation Process

MARTIN DONNELLY

1. INTRODUCTION

As the European Community's executive, the Commission plays a central role throughout the EC policy-making process. Those seeking to influence policy outcomes therefore need to understand the internal structure and functioning of the Commission. This chapter seeks to highlight the policy-making implications of the unique structural characteristics of the Commission; and to outline the important co-ordinating role played by the *cabinets* of the seventeen commissioners. The analysis underlines the extent to which the policy-making role of the Commission is shaped in particular by the absence of a single political ideology and the commitment to collegial responsibility within the Commission itself.

2. THE EUROPEAN COMMISSION: WHAT KIND OF EXECUTIVE?

There is a wide variety of internal and external influences on the policy-making process within the European Commission. Their operation needs to be understood in the context of the Commission's own organizational structure, which might be characterized as open but not transparent. What are the principal features which set the Commission apart from national public administrations?

The Commission works within a unique political context. National, regional, and local administrations in the Community are usually elected on the basis of a specific political programme. Even coalition governments have at least *de facto* agreements on priorities, work programmes, etc. They have a disciplined leadership and usually a single leader. Policy is determined centrally and then implemented more or less rapidly throughout the machinery of government.

In contrast, the European Commission is a fundamentally different type of organization. It has no ideology as most political parties on the left–right spectrum would understand the term. It has instead a formal position as guardian of the Treaty provisions, based around the 1957 Treaty of Rome and subsequent amendments, to ensure 'the proper functioning and development of the common market'. The Commission is also under a Treaty obligation of independence in its action.

Over the decades it has in practice acquired a general presumption in favour of measures at the Community level to resolve policy problems. The importance of the subsidiarity principle, that decisions should be taken and implemented at the lowest effective level of administration, has also been accepted by the Commission, and acts as a brake on excessive involvement in detailed decisions.

Within these relatively broad constraints the seventeen members of the Commission are free to set the direction of policy and priorities for Community action. The Commission only draws up proposals for primary legislation. It cannot implement them on its own authority. Their adoption requires the consent of the Council of Ministers and, in areas covered by the Single European Act, also of the European Parliament. To that extent the Commission's position is weaker than that of most national governments. The Community's legislative procedure does however ensure that the Commission plays a central role throughout the negotiation process.

The public statements of the Commission, its declared legislative and budgetary priorities, play a significant role in determining the course of political debate in the European Community. The Commission's ability to initiate carries with it real political influence, without all of the usual constraints of government executive responsibility.

The links of ideology, party organization, and political patronage which cement governmental cohesion at the national level are either weak or non-existent in the Commission. Members of the Commission have varying political affiliations which colour their approaches to issues. But there are no organized political groupings within the Commission. The guaranteed independence of each member would in any case preclude any significant moves in that direction. The Commission as a body does not have to seek a popular mandate, so there is no perceived electoral requirement to agree on a manifesto.

The lack of central patronage is perhaps the most important organizational difference. After the initial portfolio allocation each member can expect to retain the same responsibilities until the end of the Commission's four-year mandate. The power to move members of the administration between posts, or even to force their resignation, which is used by national leaders as a means of enforcing their authority, is not available to the President of the Commission. The President of the Commission does not control the agenda of the Commission, nor does he have more than one vote.

The Commission is therefore a genuinely collegial body. The practical implications of collegiality mean that each decision requires the support of an absolute majority of its members: nine out of seventeen votes. Debates in the Commission's weekly meeting influence both the detail as well as the general approach of proposals and mean that the process of persuasion required to achieve a majority needs to take place at all levels up to and including the Commission members, whatever their portfolio responsibilities. Any commissioner can insist that an item be placed on the agenda; and indeed is under no formal obligation to circulate the text of a proposed measure to his colleagues until shortly before the decision is to be taken.

The challenge therefore is how to combine this very high level of collegial functioning with the necessary consistency in policymaking. As well as the question of general policy direction there is within the Commission a need to take most of the normal decisions required on priorities to be found in any national administration. Issues involving tradeoffs between industry and environment, and the distribution of limited resources between policy areas, arise and need to be resolved. Budget proposals and a legislative programme must be agreed and presented to the European Parliament each year; and negotiations on an increasing range of issues undertaken with third countries.

National governments seek to deal with these issues through a mixture of political direction and administrative co-ordination. The Cabinet Office system of official and ministerial committees performs this function in the UK. In other Member States, governmental co-ordination is often handled directly by the Prime Minister's office.

Within the Commission much of the responsibility for achieving co-ordination falls on the President. He has responsibility for the Secretariat-General and the Legal Service, which cover the entire range of Commission activities. However, without the overall political discipline to be found in national administrations, decisions on policy priorities are inevitably reached rather differently.

The various DGs of the Commission, broadly equivalent to national ministries, function with considerable internal autonomy. The wide range of executive, supervisory, and legislative functions carried out by the different services inevitably lead to differing administrative styles. The structure most suited to preparing legislation on safe levels of additives in foods is likely to differ from that needed to implement the Community Merger Regulation within strict deadlines, or that required to supervise the application of Community fisheries policy.

The degree of informal communication between the DGs concerning work in progress also tends to vary. Formal procedures exist providing for consultation between DGs on the draft of any proposal before it can be put to the Commission. The comments of other DGs are then attached to the text circulated to *cabinets* so that the scope of any remaining disagreement is apparent. Tight working deadlines none the less mean that some parts of the Commission may be unaware, until a relatively late stage, of the detail of forthcoming policy initiatives relevant to their own work.

Inevitably therefore major decisions on policy priorities and part of the wider co-ordination of Commission activities are shifted upwards to the level of the commissioners' personal staffs, working in their *cabinets*.

3. POLICY-MAKING BY NEGOTIATION: THE ROLE OF CABINETS

Each commissioner has a *cabinet* of six or more members, of whom at least one is of another Community nationality. The *cabinets* tend to be a mixture of internal Commission staff and members of national administrations or others brought in by the commissioner. Thus several *cabinets* include members with trade-union backgrounds, while others have members with industrial experience. Generally at least half of each *cabinet* are likely to have come directly from the Commission services. Of the national civil servants in *cabinets*, many have worked in their country's Permanent Representation to the EC in Brussels and so bring experience of Council negotiation into the Commission's own structure.

Cabinet members work for the commissioner personally and are seen as his or her representatives. Each *cabinet* member will be responsible for following developments in a particular area of the Commission. Thus for example every *cabinet* will have members specializing in agriculture issues, competition cases, economic and financial policy, as well as those dealing with their commissioners' own direct portfolio interest.

Each week there are likely to be six or seven meetings of the seventeen *cabinet* members responsible for particular policy areas, to discuss legislative proposals or policy initiatives being prepared for the next meeting of the full Commission. When the Commission agenda is particularly full there may be as many as ten such meetings varying in length from several hours to the entire day on complicated or contentious subjects.

These *cabinet* meetings perform a double purpose. They offer an opportunity for points made by other DGs about a policy proposal to be considered and if necessary taken aboard—a horizontal co-ordination function which in less collegiate administrations would probably have been carried out at a lower administrative level. They also allow for the Commission's policy choices to be reaffirmed or where necessary reassessed from a political perspective.

Each meeting of *cabinet* members is chaired by the relevant member of the President's *cabinet*. The President's staff, relatively more numerous than the others, therefore plays a powerful role of political co-ordination at the *cabinet* level. Much effort can be expended in these meetings reassessing the continued applicability of earlier policy decisions which in a more rigid national structure tend to be set once and for all for the life of the Administration. The Commission structure means that the principles underlying decisions already reached can usually be reviewed. It can be necessary to reaffirm at the *cabinet* level that the same degree of political support remains over time for a policy position. Thus decisions, not only on budgetary priorities, but also on continuing policy concerns such as international trade negotiations, agricultural reform, or environmental protection, are always open for reconsideration and, in principle, amendment if a majority of the Commission so decide.

This policy co-ordination process is completed by a review of the entire weekly Commission agenda by the heads of each *cabinet*, known as the *Chefs de Cabinet*, under the presidency of the Commission's Secretary-General. This meeting normally takes place each Monday two days before the Commission itself meets on Wednesday. The *Chef de Cabinet* meeting is primarily concerned with isolating the political issues to be discussed by commissioners, confirming the more detailed decisions taken by the so-called 'Special Chefs' meetings on specific policy issues, and reaching agreement on the less controversial points so as to reduce the substantive agenda for the Commission itself.

The co-ordination process relies on *cabinets* liaising closely with their DGs and commissioner to ensure that the importance of a particular policy issue is registered by their colleagues. It is open to any *cabinet* to insist that a question is sufficiently important to be discussed during the Commission's weekly meeting, by placing a reserve on the conclusions of the preparatory discussions. Here again the primacy of collegiality is reflected in the procedure, although in practice if it is clear that one commissioner is likely to be isolated on a particular point there is usually little to be gained by pressing for it to be discussed by the whole Commission. None the less, the availability of this option allows any commissioner to ensure that the arguments are at least raised with his colleagues, and any point of principle or political sensitivity can be underlined in the full college of commissioners.

Thus the Commission itself receives issues for decision on which the DGs concerned will have at least exchanged views, commissioners' *cabinet* experts will have discussed at length, and commissioners' *Chefs de Cabinet* will have explored the scope for broader political agreement. The extent of the formal co-ordination procedure is an organizational reflection of the need to build and maintain a consensus within the college of commissioners across the range of its policy concerns.

At all stages in this procedure the policy-making process can be influenced by the provision of additional information or lobbying. There is a need for factual information on technical issues when legislation is being drawn up. But there may also be a need for the Commission to be made fully aware of any national or sectoral interests likely to be particularly affected by its decisions. In these areas external lobbyists, both from governments and the private sector, can play an important role in the policy-making process.

External policy input at the *cabinet* level depends very much on the relationship between *cabinet*, Directorate-General, and commissioner. The technical elements of a proposal are usually fairly clear by the time it is circulated at the *cabinet* level. Lobbying at this stage tends to focus on the wider political and economic issues, or individual technical points of importance to certain groups or industries.

Interest groups in Member States particularly affected tend to contact *cabinets* of their own nationality, and there can be a rerun at the political level of a debate on points already considered in a more technical discussion between the Commission's services. Depending on the observer's perspective, this can be considered a healthy check on the technicians, or a sign of excessive politicization of the drafting process. But as well as providing an occasion to raise obvious national or political sensitivities, *cabinet* discussion tends to be the point at which DGs and the relevant *cabinets* with a legitimate policy interest may seek to persuade other Commission members to support their concerns and amend a proposal accordingly.

4. REACHING DECISIONS

In general, discussion within the Commission itself (on Wednesdays) tends to focus on one or two salient issues of any proposal. If too many detailed points remain to be worked out the issue will tend to be pushed back into the *Chefs'* structure, so that the Commission discussion can take place without becoming bogged down in unnecessary detail. This procedure usually works effectively. External policy input is inevitably more difficult at this stage except at the very highest political or business level.

After the Commission has reached internal agreement on a proposal it can be published and where appropriate sent formally to the Member States and the European Parliament. At this point the relationship between the Commission and external pressure groups changes, as the non-governmental aspects of the Commission's role become more apparent. During the debates leading up to decisions by the Council and the Parliament, the Commission frequently needs to convince Member States and Members of the European Parliament to support its own proposals rather than the many variants which come forward. To that extent the Commission also has to play an important role of persuasion and lobbying in order to achieve agreement. Outside organizations concerned by the Commission's proposal can usefully lobby their own governments in support of the Commission's objectives; or in some cases help to cancel out the impact of other groups opposed to a proposal. It can therefore be in the Commission's interest to work during the legislative procedure with sympathetic lobbying groups which have influence in their own Member States or with MEPs.

Such co-operation may be more or less formal and involves an element of political judgement. In some cases the fact that the particular lobby is in favour of a measure will be seen by MEPs or even by some Member States as one reason for voting against it. And it would be wrong to see the Commission as masterminding a subtle campaign to achieve its own ends. The process of agreeing legislation in the Community usually includes some degree of confusion on all sides as to the effect of various often contradictory pressures on those involved in key negotiating decisions. Further compromises in the Commission's own position are often needed, and these too require the formal agreement of the college.

In the inevitably complex process of Community negotiation it is important to underline that the lobbying process is by no means simply one way. The Commission also needs external allies if it is to ensure that the policy proposals agreed through its complex internal co-ordination process are to be successfully translated into Community law.

5

Lobbying Brussels: A View from Within

ROBERT HULL

1. INTRODUCTION

I would like to look at the lobbying process and its effects on policy-making in the Community from a number of points of view. As
a Commission official for the last fourteen years or so, I have been
subject to lobbying and the work of pressure groups in a variety of
different forms and which from my point of view, have had a
widely varying degree of effectiveness. As far as I am aware, no
analysis has been produced of the attitudes, either of Commissioners or Commission officials, to the way they are regarded and
treated by those who lobby them. I suspect that very few of the
organizations or individuals seeking to influence the direction of
Community policies have any idea of the mentality of the key players in Brussels. My aim, therefore, is to try to provide a practical
guide to lobbying the Community system as seen by someone
inside that system. The views expressed are very much my own.

Lobbyists have come in many forms to my doorstep in the guise
of lawyers, public-relations firms, specialist consultancies, representatives of industrial federations, representatives of companies or
individual organizations, representatives of non-governmental organizations, and diplomats from non-Community countries. The
process has become much more professional in recent years particularly since the 1986 Single European Act. However, in most cases,
lobbyists come ill-prepared for their discussion and in general the
quality of their presentations is low. Most organizations think that
communication of any sort of case is better than the advocacy of a
good one. Where good lobbying takes place, it is the exception and
it tends to stand out very clearly.

I believe that the failure by most organizations to deal effectively
with the Commission stems from an inadequate understanding of
the Community decision-making process and in particular of the

way decisions are made on policy and legislation. The important thing is to know:

• the state of development of the policy process;
• what Commissioners and officials are trying to achieve;
• where the real decisions are made in the system;
• how it can be made to stick;
• who the key players are.

2. HOW TO INFLUENCE THE PROCESS

The good lobbyist or lobbying organization has to be seen to be honest but also aware of how the policy process works. They can virtually become part of the decision-making process if they choose to. Few successfully achieve this.

The Commission has to be the primary target of any lobbyist or pressure group. The early thinking on any proposal takes place usually in the office of one Commission official who will have the responsibility for drafting legislation. The individual who is responsible for the initial preparation process over a given period of time (first draft, consultations with the Commission, consultations with interested parties, subsequent drafts, navigation through the Commission) will find that when the final proposal is adopted by the Council it usually contains 80 per cent of his or her proposal.

At the beginning he or she is a very lonely official with a blank piece of paper, wondering what to put on it. Lobbying at this very early stage therefore offers the greatest opportunity to shape thinking and ultimately to shape policy. The drafter is usually in need of ideas and information and a lobbyist who is recognized as being trustworthy and a provider of good information can have an important impact at this stage. Thereafter, once the Commission itself has agreed a proposal and sent it to the Parliament and Council, scope for changing the proposal exists only at the margin, involving about 20 per cent of the total proposal. I suspect though, that if an analysis were to be carried out, 95 per cent of lobbying takes place at the stage after the proposal has been through the process of drafting within the Commission. This tends to be the point at which most people become aware that something is in the offing. This error can be avoided only if lobbyists develop a long-term relationship with the Commission so that the first stages of policy development are picked up early. Lobbyists also need to monitor the published work programme of the Commission which signals key directives in advance.

There are also possibilities for influencing the EC decision-making process at the *cabinet* or private office level within the Commission. This, however, is not a straightforward task. When approaching the cabinet of a Commissioner responsible for the preparation of a directive, a group may be reminded that it has already had its say via the usual consultation processes at the service level. Moreover, the Commissioner will have given a political steer to the directive which her or his *cabinet* is unlikely to abandon. In extreme cases, however, a group might be able to persuade other *cabinets* which it suspects shares its particular view or which contains members of the same nationality, to block proposals or introduce last-minute changes. This is a real opportunity, since a considerable amount of political horse-trading takes place between Commissioners. It is, however, a fairly unreliable way of influencing a proposal and can never guarantee results.

Once the proposal has been issued, there is scope for introducing changes at the European Parliament level through lobbying MEPs or even whole political groups. The role of the Parliament has certainly become more important as a result of the Single European Act (SEA) on issues relating to the single market. Its role is crucial at the first-reading stage where on these issues it has the power to block progress. The evidence is fairly clear that since the SEA the Commission has been forced to take on board an increasing proportion of parliamentary amendments. These do tend however, to be technical amendments rather than fundamental changes. Lobbying input here needs to be made at the level of the respective Committees, which discuss proposals and prepare draft opinions for approval by the monthly Plenary Session. Effective lobbying needs to take the form of detailed briefing at a technical level and often the best point of input can be the secretariats of the political groups from which MEPs take advice.

Input of new ideas through sympathetic MEPs is a route a commissioner may use on an informal basis when he or she wishes to make minor amendments to a proposal without doing so formally. The Commission would then in due course take the amendment on board as its own. This speeds up the decision-making process by avoiding the necessity to resort to the formal Commission decision-making process where the amendment is likely to be uncontentious.

At the Council level there are opportunities for groups to talk to national officials in the Council working groups involved in the discussion of proposals in an attempt to influence Member States. However, the scope for influencing them is limited and their voice is one in twelve in the working group. Here too the risks are substantial, given majority voting and the pressures for compromise in the Council itself. Contacts are best made with those national officials directly involved in the policy sector or with members of the Permanent Representations. Groups should note that they probably stand a better chance of success once the discussions have started, not prior to them, and once the position of other Member States has begun to become clear; in other words when there has been a first-reading discussion in the group and before any decisions have begun to crystallize.

The best practical advice throughout this process would be to stay in contact with the Commission official who drafted the initial proposal and who is likely to continue to navigate it through the various shoals to final adoption. He or she is often influential in determining the acceptance or rejection by the Commission of parliamentary and/or Council proposals for amendment.

The best lobbying is built on a clear understanding of this process. The situation is not like Washington, and US organizations which have attempted to follow the US process, where the White House machine provides a clear focus, have not been very successful. The important difference which they fail to realize is that power in the Community is even more dispersed than in the USA. Lobbying and pressure-group activity therefore needs to be built upon a sophisticated understanding of, and connection to, each of the Community institutions and Member States. Only on this basis can an effective lobbying strategy be developed.

3. WHO ARE THE MOST EFFECTIVE LOBBYISTS?

Lobbyists and pressure groups come in many guises. As a result of the fact that Commission staff resources are limited, with a consequent lack of time, Commission officials tend to appreciate a representative lobbyist or interest group which can speak on behalf of a cross-section of interests throughout the Community rather than the interest of an individual company or organization. On the other hand, groups which do have a wide representative role, for example, some of the European industrial federations, will often be able to present only a lowest common denominator approach, which because of its nature carries little weight. In such cases a Commission official may well find it useful to have an input from individual companies with specific interests and representing opposing sides of the case.

Public-relations firms on the whole are not well regarded. They tend to be perceived as glib purveyors of a tale which they have prepared for a particular meeting. They are normally unable to get involved in any kind of detailed discussion of an issue because they do not understand it fully once the discussion strays outside their brief. Lawyers are increasingly involved in lobbying for clients, but with rare exceptions this is a difficult role for them and only the Italians and Spanish seem to be effective. In the latter cases there is a national tradition of lobbying by lawyers: few other types of lobbyist exist. As a result lawyers tend to be more politically aware and astute than their counterparts in other Community countries.

Apart from particular interest groups ready to build a long-standing relationship with the Commission (although here there are dangers of too cosy a relationship developing), the future, I suspect, lies with professional lobbying firms. These can offer a composite lobbying service based on accurate, comprehensive, and up-to-date information about issues of concern to a client, be it a company or group of companies or even a federation. This kind of lobbyist is perceived by Commission officials as being more professional and is in a position to build up permanent relationships with the Commission so long as he or she makes clear the interests he or she is representing. Users of lobbyists and pressure groups should choose their lobbyist well, since many have a bad reputation which is obviously counterproductive when a case has to be presented. There are lobbyists too, who over-estimate their importance and their ability to influence Commission officials. Good professional lobbyists are attracted to Brussels because they perceive that the future lies with the Community and that important decisions are now taken at the Community level rather than at the national level.

Those who are most successful are those who have perceived that the policy-making in the Community is at the same time diffuse and yet more open than in most national administrations. As a result those individuals who have political awareness together with the necessary technical expertise tend to be the most appreciated. Former diplomats tend to be unconvincing and recently departed former Community officials are treated with some suspicion. The most effective lobbyists will begin their contacts on an issue when legislation is little more than a gleam in an official's eye. Timing of the input is therefore of the essence; effective lobbying requires sufficient investment in time and effort to ensure that the gleam in the eye is understood and acted upon at the earliest possible moment through the provision of useful information.

The lobbyist or interest group in presenting a case needs to be clear on his or her objectives, even if it is only to establish a dialogue and provide a sympathetic ear in some cases. The most successful are those who have:

- developed a clearly defined strategy;
- researched well the input they want to make based on sound and accurate information;
- prepared well for their meetings—including tailoring the case according to the nationality or the language of the person to be lobbied;
- presented their case with brevity and clarity and recognized that their view is only one part of the argument and that there is another side to their case;
- left a position paper behind;
- already established themselves as a useful source of information;
- appreciated the limits of what the lobbying process can achieve.

Whilst working-level officials should probably be the priority targets and are usually ready to talk, the higher the officials' position in the Commission hierarchy, the more open to discussion the individual is likely to be. Those at the middle level are more likely to see talking to lobbyists as a greater risk. At all levels officials will naturally insist upon knowing why they are being approached on an issue and will not appreciate being bombarded repeatedly in an oversell process. Having said that, it is nevertheless true that the 'nag factor' does help from time to time.

Bear in mind too, that rivalry between DGs with different

approaches to an issue which overlaps competences can provide openings to influence the decision-making process. Nationality factors can also have an influence; a Brit talking to a Brit or a Frenchman talking to another Frenchman may often produce more effective results than is generally appreciated. It is important too to realize that officials of some nationalities are likely to be more open to lobbying than others.

4. SECTORAL DIFFERENCES: FINANCIAL SERVICES AND THE ENVIRONMENT

Generally, lobbying in the financial services sector tends to be much more professional than is the case on the environment. This is perhaps not unexpected given that the environment is a less well-established policy area.

Lobbying on financial services issues during the four- or five-year period when the single market legislation was being prepared with the Commission tended to be targeted towards very specific points. It was carried out essentially by practitioners rather than by lobbyists acting on behalf of a financial institution or group of institutions, although there were an important number of exceptions. The professional associations, whilst assiduous in commenting on proposals once they had been made, rarely sought to influence proposals in the preliminary stages of preparation and thus missed the opportunity to make an important input. As part of the normal process of preparing proposals, DG XV officials would seek advice and input from consultations with bodies such as the European Banking Federation, the European Stock Exchange Federation, the various insurance federations, and others, but these bodies failed to seize the initiative early enough in the process. As a result, because of the problems of getting a consensus and because of the time constraints involved, comments tended to arrive at a stage too late to be of use. Subsequent debates with these bodies were, therefore, perhaps more conflictual than were strictly necessary. It must also be said that European federations face a major problem in trying to reach a consensus from among the views of their constituent, national bodies.

The most efficient lobbyists tended to be the British, but it has to be said that they too were very late in arriving at DG XV's door. They had been preoccupied with Big Bang and were slow to realize the implications of the single market programme in the financial services sector. By this time the Japanese financial institutions had already been knocking at the Commission's door to glean information to allow them to make their own assessments but did not try to influence the decision-making process. When the British did come, they tended to be persistent.

In the environment sector the lobbying process is more diffuse and less mature and of a more general nature, though the situation is changing very rapidly. This change reflects a recognition of the perceived importance of environmental policy. Until recently the process of lobbying on environmental issues was very much a process of pricking the conscience of the Commission to push it into taking a more environment-friendly approach. On this basis the Commission has reacted to complaints about filthy drinking water, complaints about bathing water, and to the possible destruction of natural habitats.

Many of the environmental pressure groups still see their roles as acting primarily in this way. There are a large number of environmental pressure groups, and this has created a problem in itself, since it has been very difficult for them to present a coherent position. This has changed to some extent with the advent of the European Environmental Bureau (EEB) which brings together the greater proportion of environmental pressure groups and with which (together with Friends of the Earth, Greenpeace, and the World Wildlife Foundation) the Commission has developed a kind of institutionalized dialogue based on regular consultations.

The problem is that the EEB tends to play a role as a 'pricker of the Commission's conscience' rather than recognizing the real issues. It has tended to be reactive rather than proactive. In some cases its input has been counter-productive. For example, over the European Environment Agency the EEB argued against the Commission's proposal in an attempt to persuade the European Parliament that what was being proposed did not go far enough and should be rejected. However, in the case of car emissions the pressure for a more fundamental approach than originally proposed by the Commission came from the Parliament where the strength of the environmental lobby was important.

Given the lack of necessary resources within the Commission, the work of environmental research bodies and think-tanks is becoming an increasingly important input into DG XI thinking. Similarly, with the movement of environmental policy closer to central economic decision-making in the Community, lobbyists and pressure groups from particular sectors of the economy have now started to come to DG XI directly rather than seeking to influence environmental policies through the DGs perceived as being more fundamental to their particular interests such as industry, agriculture, or energy. They now approach DG XI directly with specific objectives in mind.

For example, contacts between the car industry and the Commission on environmental issues tended in the past to be channelled exclusively through DG III which was seen to be a useful buffer and in many ways a kind of internal lobbyist. Now the contacts on issues like emissions are directly with DG XI and this pattern is being repeated in other industrial sectors as realization grows of the importance of environmental concerns for industry in the future. Discussion with industry, either directly or through lobbyists, has tended to be confrontational rather than constructive up to now, with environmental standards being seen as a threat rather than an opportunity. That situation is changing rapidly.

5. CASE-STUDY

It is interesting to analyse one particular case where the lobbying process worked well. It relates to the vexed question of what became known as the 'reciprocity clause' in what is now the Second Banking Directive. It involved a group of US banks established and with substantial interests in the Community, but who had little confidence in the capacity of bodies like the European Banking Federation or their own national government or any other body to articulate their case efficiently. They had a particular point to put across.

The US administration had taken a high-profile approach on the overall reciprocity clause issue, which they saw as a symbol of a move towards a kind of 'Fortress Europe'. US officials argue that their approach won the battle whereas in reality it had little influence and may indeed have been counter-productive. This high-profile approach was followed by other US banks who made a lot of general noise about what they saw as a fundamental question of principle but were not very constructive in their thinking.

The banking group in question appointed a specialist adviser from a professional lobbying firm to work with them. On the basis of his advice they decided on a discrete low-profile approach which allowed them to get much closer to the Commission and to Member States.

• They drew up a factual report on the effects of reciprocity which set out to compare the relative rights and opportunities of US and EC banks in their respective countries. The report threw into relief some of the effects and dangers of the Commission's approach for Community financial institutions.

• They realized however that deletion of the 'reciprocity clause' from the proposal was not viable politically and they therefore decided on realistic objectives. They realized too, that it would be difficult to engage in a dialogue on such a sensitive issue and that it was important to appear constructive rather than destructive.

• They therefore pursued a change in the relevant clause by putting forward detailed drafting proposals. These were then pursued with the Commission and with a number of interested Member States most directly concerned. The end-result was that the drafting proposals were in the end not dissimilar to what appeared in the final text.

When the legislation was finally adopted, there was a positive reaction by the group of banks in question—not an over-reaction. They did not seek to claim any public credit.

The whole affair was managed very professionally and with great discretion. The fact that European advisers were used rather than US nationals, who would probably have had a counter-productive effect, was important. What was perhaps also important was that the banks were used to operating in a multinational framework. They saw how best they could influence the process and where the most appropriate input points were and approached these on a systematic basis.

6. CONCLUSION

Officials are subject to an increased amount of lobbying and are themselves becoming demanding in their reaction. Given the increased pressure they work under, especially in areas where new policies are developing and where there is intense activity, they look increasingly to lobbyists to provide useful and objective information. In these circumstances the lobbyist himself has to become much more professional. The lobbyist will have to recognize that lobbying involves a two-way traffic in which the lobbyist is not only a recipient of information but also a provider. Successful lobbying firms will have to become more systematic in their approach and operate on a more regular basis, probably establishing themselves in Brussels. What is vital to bear in mind is that the Community is *sui generis* and not to be approached as if it were a national administration or the US White House.

PART II

SECTORAL STUDIES

6

Europe of the Regions: Territorial Interests and European Integration: The Scottish Experience

SONIA MAZEY AND JAMES MITCHELL

1. INTRODUCTION

The Treaty of Rome refers only to nation-states and national governments; regional and local authorities are not mentioned. Nor is there any provision in the founding Treaties for the formal representation of regional and local interests at the European Community (EC) level. In reality, however, subnational levels of government throughout the EC (with the notable exception of Britain) have acquired important new policy-making and legislative powers, especially in the field of socio-economic development. Within Britain, Scotland with its own legal system, separate administrative structures, and nationalist aspirations qualifies as an important regional entity. As their policy-making powers have expanded, regional authorities have become increasingly subject to and constrained by EC legislation. In this context, the ratification of the 1986 Single European Act and the establishment of the 1 January 1993 deadline for the completion of the Single European Market constituted an important turning-point. Regional authorities have been quick to react to these changes: since the mid-1980s there has been a sharp increase in the EC lobbying activities of regions eager to secure EC funds for economic-development programmes and a more prominent role in the formulation of Community policies. Meanwhile, the European Commission, anxious to minimize regional disparities within the single market, now recognizes the need to consult not only national governments, but also regional and local authorities. The fact that the latter are frequently responsible for implementing and monitoring EC legislation further explains the Commission's commitment to the regional level.

The result of these simultaneous trends (regionalization and European integration) has been regionalization of EC policy-making in two senses of the word. First, regional authorities are becoming integrated into the EC policy-making process and are developing direct links with the Commission. Secondly, the European Commission believes that an effective EC regional policy (formally referred to as 'economic and social cohesion') is necessary for the successful functioning of the single market. These developments combined with the increasing assertiveness of regional authorities within the EC have prompted fresh demands from regional politicians for a European assembly of the regions and given new hope to regionalists eager to establish a 'Europe of the Regions'. Indeed, one commentator has suggested that the development of regional policy in the EC is no less than a 'staging post on the path to federalism' (A. Adonis, in *Financial Times*, 20 Dec. 1991).

The purpose of this chapter, therefore, is twofold: to examine in detail the reasons for and the growth of the regional lobby in Brussels, and to highlight the wider political and constitutional implications of this development. This discussion is divided into two parts. The aim in the first part is to provide a general overview of the extent to which regional interests have become incorporated in the EC policy-making process. The second looks specifically at the case of Scotland. This case-study highlights the difficulties which sub-state territorial entities have in articulating their interests in supranational institutions. As with the concept of 'national interest', definitions of 'regional' and 'local' interests are highly subjective and thus subject to dispute. Determining who should articulate these interests is, in consequence, a controversial political issue. There is also the question of the means by which this should be achieved. The noted openness of the European Commission provides numerous opportunities for regional lobbyists and recent reforms (see below) have created a Committee of Regions specifically designed to incorporate regional interests into the consultative process. The European Parliament offers another target for territorial lobbying. Apart from these openings at the supranational level, the regions are able to lobby the governments of their respective state. Indeed, since the Council of Ministers remains the most important EC institution, lobbying at this level will continue to be extremely important. However, as highlighted below, the growing assertiveness of regional representatives within the context of EC policy-making has created tensions between regional and national level authorities. The debate surrounding the opening of Scotland Europa, a lobbying/information office in Brussels, offers interesting insights into issues involved in sub-state territorial articulation of interests in the European Community.

2. THE REGIONS AND EUROPEAN INTEGRATION

2.1 The Emergence of Regional Government in the European Community

The 1970s and 1980s in Western Europe were years of territorial reform. Apart from the UK where the cumulative impact of recent local government reforms has been to weaken the powers of inter-mediary levels of government, the overall effect of these reforms has been to strengthen the economic and political importance of the regional authority. Nevertheless, it is important to note that notwithstanding the existence of regionalist pressures (e.g. in France, Italy, and Spain) during the 1970s, regional reform was perceived by national governments everywhere primarily in func-tional terms—as a means of restructuring and modernizing the national politico-administrative system in order to render it more effective. This pragmatic motivation is reflected in the type of pow-ers and responsibilities typically accorded to regions by national governments in the 1970s. Without exception, regional authorities are primarily responsible for the preparation and implementation of regional economic-development programmes. Typical areas of policy competence include: land-use planning; management of public utilities; public transport and the maintenance of trunk roads, ports, and navigable waterways; provision of vocational and professional training (usually within the context of a regional employment policy); the maintenance and administration of hospi-tals, schools, and colleges; tourism and culture.

2.2 Regions and the EC Policy Process

The founding Treaties of the European Community make no pro-vision for the formal representation of regional and local interests at the EC level. Instead, it is up to each Member State to decide how best to protect the interests of regions in the context of EC policy-making. In recent years, however, regional and local interests have gradually become institutionalized within the EC's decision-making processes. Regional policy in the European Communities was also slow to develop despite the provision in the preamble of the Treaty of Rome stating that Member States were:

anxious to strengthen the unity of their economies and to ensure their harmonious development by reducing the differences existing between the various regions and the backwardness of the less favoured regions.

The accession of the UK, Ireland, and Denmark to membership in 1973 marked a watershed in the development of EC regional policy. The expanded EC Commission included a commissioner for regional policy. Following a report produced by George Thomson, the first Regional Policy Commissioner, the European Regional Development Fund (ERDF) was established in 1975 (see Wallace 1977). The later accessions of weaker economies—Greece in 1981, Portugal and Spain in 1986—gave added impetus to the development of an active regional policy. As part of the negotiations leading to the passage of the Single European Act, agreement was reached to increase the structural funds to strengthen 'economic and social cohesion' within the Community. This was the price that Irish and Southern European Members extracted for this support for market liberalization.

Criticisms of the ERDF have, since its inception, focused upon the size of the fund and the manner in which it has been distributed among the Member States. Insufficient resources combined with the use of the quota system (which until 1988 allocated the bulk of the ERDF to national governments to be used as they saw fit), ensured that the impact of ERDF was negligible. The EC regional policy was, as with that of the Member States, ameliorative rather than primary. It attempted to alleviate problems in the poorer regions rather than fundamentally alter the imbalance which existed. Antonio Giolitti, Regional Affairs Commissioner in the late 1970s, described the policy as an 'accompanying measure' (Mawson, Martins, and Gibney 1985). As indicated above, however, the situation is now changing; since 1986 the Commission has sought to increase the effectiveness of EC regional policy. Pressures for a 'Europe of the Regions' have thus been increasing at both the subnational and EC levels.

Within the Council of Ministers, regional and local interests are indirectly represented by national government ministers and national COREPER officials. In the UK, for instance, the Scottish Office is responsible for co-ordinating the representation of Scottish interests within EC affairs. In France, the Ministers for European Community Affairs and National Economic Planning are frequently called upon by regional authorities to defend their interests in Brussels. The French Permanent Representation also includes a *sous préfet* whose primary role is to monitor regional affairs. The European Parliament provides the principal forum for the direct representation of regional interests and has for several years demanded that regional interests be given a bigger say in EC policy-making. An EP Resolution on EC regional policy adopted in 1988, for instance, included a 'Community Charter for Regionalization' which advocated that elected regional governments be granted statutory representation within the EC (*OJ* C326/296, 19 Dec. 1988). There is also a European Parliamentary Intergroup (all-party committee of MEPs) who also hold local and/or regional elective mandates and who seek to establish a common position on legislative proposals affecting local and regional authorities (Romus 1990).

Regional interests have also been institutionalized slowly (albeit only on a consultative basis) within the European Commission. Following the creation of the ERDF in 1975 a Regional Policy Committee was created to comment on EC regional policy and ERDF allocations. The committee was, however, composed of national rather than regional officials. The British delegation included silent observers from the Scottish, Welsh, and Northern Ireland Offices. This committee was replaced in January 1989 by the Committee for the Development and Reconversion of Regions. Its role is essentially the same as that of its predecessor. Significantly, Germany (a federal state) and Belgium (a quasi-federal state) include regional representatives in their delegation to the committee. Regional interests are also represented within the Commission by the Consultative Council of Regional and Local Authorities. Created by the European Commission in 1988, the council must be consulted over any matter relating to regional economic development and all aspects of regional policy. It comprises forty-two members nominated by the three European regional associations: International Union of Local Authorities (IULA),

European Assembly of Regions (ARE), and Council of European Municipalities and Regions (CEMR) (Romus 1990).

Pressure for greater opportunities for sub-state levels of government to have access to EC decision-making mounted. The German *Länder* were most active in this respect in exerting pressure on urban Brussels and their own national government. The fear that European integration would diminish the powers and competences of the *Länder* without major institutional changes has been documented by Rudolf Hrbek (Hrbek 1987, 1988, 1991). As debate on political union leading to the Maastricht summit in December 1991 focused on the powers of the EC's quadripartite institutional structure, little attention was paid to institutional reforms which would facilitate a greater role for the regions. At the first meeting of the newly constituted Bundestag which included the five former East German *Länder*, a resolution was passed unanimously demanding that the *Länder* be given a formal say in the drafting and operation of EC policies and spending programmes for the regions (*Frankfurter Allegemeine Zeitung*, 10 Nov. 1990).

The draft Treaty on European Political Union which emerged from Maastricht in December 1991 included provision for a Committee of Regions consisting of 189 members with the UK, France, Italy, and Germany each having 24 representatives; Spain, 21; Belgium, Greece, Portugal, and the Netherlands, 12; Denmark and Ireland 9; and Luxembourg 6. It is to be consulted on matters which have a major impact on the regions. This development, though potentially significant, fell far short of demands—now widespread among MEPs and regional politicians—for a second chamber of the Nations and Regions to replace the existing Council of Ministers (*EP News*, 18–22 Nov. 1991). As highlighted below, who should represent the regions in the new committee has been a matter of debate in Scotland.

2.3 The Regional Impact of the Single European Market

Since the mid-1980s all regional and local authorities have been increasingly affected by EC legislation and—more specifically—by the '1992' programme. The latter covers a number of policy sectors which come under local or regional authority competence including local economic development (and the attraction of external investment), vocational training and language teaching, local transport (both public and private), the supply of public utilities, environmental health policies, anti-pollution control, health and safety in the workplace, and consumer protection law.

A key area of EC legislation of direct concern to regional and local authorities includes rules governing regional aid (Art. 92 of the Treaty of Rome). The development of a more effective EC regional policy since the mid-1980s has helped reduce the degree of autonomy enjoyed by national and regional authorities in this area (Auby 1990). In December 1990, for instance, the French Government was forced by the European Commission to withdraw development grants from twenty departments which did not qualify under EC law for regional aid. The European Commission also threatened to take legal action against the French Government over industrial restructuring grants awarded by the latter to six public companies, Électricité de France, Elf-Aquitaine, Thomson, Pechiney, EMC, and Rhône-Poulenc (Le Monde, 25 Dec. 1990; Le Figaro, 21 Dec. 1990). This single example highlights the degree to which EC Member States are now constrained by EC regulations in the area of regional policy. Awareness of this fact has prompted more concerted EC lobbying on the part of the French Planning Minister and regional governments anxious to ensure that EC rules governing regional aid are favourable to their interests (Le Figaro, 10 Mar. 1989; Le Monde, 18 July 1989). As is the case with other groups, in order to be effective EC lobbyists, regions must liaise closely with central government.

EC legislation which came into force on 1 January 1989 designed to open up public procurement markets to outside competition also has far-reaching implications for local authorities which have traditionally relied upon their own direct labour organizations and in-house suppliers. All supply contracts valued at 200,000 ECU and all public-works contracts worth 7m ECU or more must now conform to EC rules. Contracts must be advertised in the Official Journal of the EC and must not discriminate against non-national firms (e.g. by specifying national rather than EC technical norms). Further legislation adopted in 1990 extended the above procedure to the previously 'excluded sectors' of energy, water, transport, and telecommunications.

As major employers, local and regional authorities also have a direct interest in single market legislation designed to establish the free movement of labour within the EC. Of particular concern to all such authorities is the Commission's determination to prevent the abuse—hitherto widespread within public administrations—of Article 48 of the Treaty of Rome which permits the closure of certain public-sector posts to non-nationals. More generally, local and regional authorities will have to comply with the legislative provisions of EC social policy (e.g. on equal pay and training) and the 1988 EC Social Charter, intended to improve the working conditions and social rights of employees.

In reality, EC intervention in any sector has multiple implications for regional authorities. The Commission's desire to establish a common transport policy (deemed to be necessary for the effective functioning of the internal market) is a case in point. In this sector alone, issues of current concern to regional authorities include the harmonization of the weight of heavy goods vehicles and speed limits (and the environmental impact of these changes), the prohibition of subsidies paid to ports and airports and EC proposals to introduce VAT on public transport (Cini 1990).

The above are but a few examples of the legislative impact of the '1992' programme upon regional authorities. More generally, however, the creation of the internal market will variously affect regional economies in the EC and may well compound existing regional disparities. Obviously, this is of great concern to regional authorities, particularly those peripheral regions within the Community such as Scotland which fear they will lose out to the golden triangle delineated by London, Berlin, and Milan. The primary concern of peripheral authorities is that investment capital will (in the absence of adequate regional policy incentives) be drawn to the wealthier regions within the single market. Recognition of this problem on the part of the Member States is reflected in the 1986 Single European Act which commits the signatories to the maintenance of 'economic and social cohesion' within the EC. More specifically, the Single European Act strengthened the EC's own regional policy and structural funds designed to assist poorer regions within the EC. The possibility of obtaining additional EC finance is undoubtedly what attracts regional and local authorities to Brussels.

There are three categories of aid available to regional and local authorities: grant aid, loans, and miscellaneous sources. Grant aid is provided by the European Regional Development Fund (ERDF), the European Social Fund (ESF), and the Guidance Section of the

Agricultural Guidance and Guarantee Fund (EAGGF). As part of the '1992' programme the amount of resources devoted to these structural funds is to be increased from 7.2 billion ECU (19 per cent of the EC budget) in 1987 to 14.5 billion ECU (25 per cent of the EC budget) in 1992 (Commission of the European Communities 1990: 6). The ERDF, created in 1975, is the largest of the funds and provides non-repayable grants for investment in infrastructure and industrial development. The ESF, established in 1961, provides financial assistance for training projects, particularly among groups such as women, young people, and migrants, who are disadvantaged within the labour market. The EAGGF (Guidance Section), set up in 1964, provides grants for agricultural restructuring and rural development. The main source of EC loans is the European Investment Bank (EIB) and the Coal and Steel Community which provides assistance for coal and steel workers affected by industrial restructuring (pit closures, etc.). Other miscellaneous sources of EC finance available to local authorities include grants for scientific research and development and Local Employment Initiatives (LEIs) (Cini 1990).

In 1988 the rules governing the allocation of the structural funds were changed in an attempt to maximize their impact. The funds are now concentrated upon five objectives defined by the European Commission (see Table 6.1). Up to 80 per cent of the funds are reserved for the first objective and are targeted exclusively to the poorest regions (Southern Europe and Ireland). Since 1984 the Commission has sought to channel the structural funds into pluri-annual programmes rather than individual short-term projects. This has entailed encouragement of Integrated Operation Programmes (IOPs) and National Programmes of Community Interests (NPCIs). These typically involve a co-ordinated set of policy objectives funded over a period of years by national, regional, and local sources, backed up by the EC structural funds (Celemine 1991).

The reforms also introduced two new operational principles: 'additionality' and 'partnership'. The principle of 'additionality' requires that EC funding be additional to aid provided by the Member State (either by the national or regional authorities). This principle favours those EC Member States such as France which have established regional development policies and interventionist governments (at the regional and national level). In contrast, the European Commission recently withheld £600 million for

Table **6.1.** *ERDF Objectives*

Objective	Criteria
1. To aid less-developed regions	Per capita less than 75% of EC average Council of Ministers determines list Northern Ireland only area in UK
2. To promote Industrial Conversion Areas	Average unemployment rate above EC average % share of industrial employment above EC average An observable fall in industrial employment Council of Ministers decides criteria, Commission decides eligibility
3. To combat long-term unemployment	Promote occupational and social integration Provide employment subsidies, assistance, and (re)-training for women, disabled people, and migrants All local authorities eligible
4. To integrate young people into the job market	Basic training leading to a recognized qualification; higher skills training All local authorities eligible
5. To reform the CAP by (a) adapting agricultural production processing and marketing structures; and (b) promoting development of rural areas	High share of agricultural employment in total; low level of agricultural income; low level of GDP per capita; Council of Ministers decides criteria peripherality; low population density Commission decides eligibility

Source: Audit Commission 1991

run-down coal-mining communities in Britain because it feared that the UK Conservative Government (which is ideologically opposed to regional policy) would not provide matching funding (*Guardian*, 14 Nov. 1991). In January 1992 the Commission withheld a further £900 million allocated to UK regions under Objective 2 (Industrial Reconversion) on the grounds that the UK Government intended to use the aid for areas other than those specified by the Commission (*Observer*, 26 Jan. 1992). The new regulations also stress the need for closer collaboration (i.e. partnership) between the Commission and those regional and local authorities involved in the implementation of the funded programme.

2.4 The Regional Lobby in Brussels

In recent years there has been a sharp increase in the amount, levels, and different types of 'contact' between the EC and regional authorities. Many regions have either opened or sponsored the creation of a Brussels office—often to the irritation of their respective national governments. The Spanish regional governments of the Basque country, Canary Islands, Galicia, Murcia, and Valencia have set up offices in Brussels with the legal status of limited trade companies. In Catalonia, the Patronat Català Pro-Europa, a public consortium established in 1982 brings together representatives of Catalan public and private sector bodies with an interest in EC affairs. In 1986 the Patronat opened a Brussels office to liaise between the Commission and Catalan interests (Morata 1991). Many of the 26 French regional governments including Rhône–Alpes, Île-de-France, Alsace, Franche–Comté, Aquitaine, Languedoc–Roussillon, the Midi–Pyrénées, Bretagne, Pays-de-la-Loire, and Nord–Pas-de-Calais are represented in Brussels. There also exist a number of interregional associations within France whose *raison d'être* is to secure regional funding for infrastructure programmes which cross regional boundaries. For example, the regional governments of Aquitaine, Corsica, Languedoc-Roussillon, the Midi-Pyrénées, and Provence–Alpes–Côtes-d'Azur set up the association of the Grand Sud in 1986. This association maintains a permanent Brussels office which defends the interests of individual authorities and campaigns for funding for joint programmes such as the Integrated Mediterranean Programme. This example was followed by the regional governments of Alsace, Bourgogne, Champagne–Ardennes, Franche–Comté, and Lorraine which grouped together to form the association of the Grand-Est (Luchaire 1990). Most German *Länder* have permanent delegations in Brussels. Moreover, due to the federal nature of the German political system, the *Länder* have since 1959 had an official EC observer (*Beobachter*) for the *Länder*. The observer, appointed by the Conference of Economic Ministers of the *Länder*, attends meetings of the Council of Ministers and the Committee of Permanent Representatives

(COREPER), reports back to the *Länder* and participates in meetings of the Bundesrat. The *Länder* are entitled to representation in EC matters which are exclusively their responsibility and send delegates to various Commission committees such as the Regional Committee, the ERDF Committee, and the Standing Committee on Agricultural Subsidies. Belgium, now a quasi-federal state, has also appointed an EC observer and sends regional government representatives to these committees.

2.5 Regional Associations

Equally important in terms of EC lobbying are the various European associations of regional and local authorities. These include the International Union of Local Authorities (IULA) established in 1913 and based in the Hague; the Council of European Communes (CCE) established in 1951 and based in Paris, which became the Council of European Municipalities and Regions (CEMR) in 1984; and the Permanent Conference of Local and Regional Authorities established in 1957 by the Council of Europe. Since September 1986 there has been a Permanent Representation of local and regional authorities in Brussels, jointly funded by the IULA and CEMR. Finally, the Council of European Regions was established in 1985. Renamed the Assembly of European Regions (ARE) in 1987, this regional lobby which is based in Strasbourg represents 107 regions including eleven non-EC regions (Swiss Cantons and Austrian *Länder*) (Chauvet 1989).

In addition to the associations listed above there has been a proliferation since the early 1970s of transfrontier regional associations and Euro-regions within the Community. For the most part, these

TABLE 6.2 *Local and Regional Offices in Brussels*

Country	Local and regional offices
France	Brittany
	Grand Est[a]
	Grand Sud[b]
	Nord–Pas-de-Calais
	Pays-de-la-Loire
	Picardie–Essex
	Rhône–Alpes

Country	Local and regional offices
Germany	Baden Wurttemburg
	Bavaria
	Berlin
	Bremen
	Hamburg
	Hessen
	Lower Saxony
	Nord-Rhein-Westphalen
	Rheinland-Pfalz
	Saarland
	Schleswig-Holstein
Spain	Andalucia
	Catalonia
	Galicia
	Islas Canarias
	Murcia
	Pais Vasco
	Valencia
Belgium	Brussels
	Flanders
	Wallonia
Denmark	Alborg
	Arhus
	Odense
United Kingdom	Birmingham
	Cornwall
	Essex–Picardie
	Greater Manchester
	Highlands and Islands
	Kent
	Northern Ireland Centre
	Scotland Europa
	Strathclyde
	Welsh Bureau

[a] Lorraine, Alsace, Burgundy, Champagne–Ardennes, Franche–Comté
[b] Aquitaine, Corsica, Languedoc–Roussillon, Midi–Pyrénées, Provence–Alpes–Côte-d'Azur
Source: Audit Commission (1991), 35 (amended to take account of recent developments).

have been set up on the initiative of regional authorities either because they are neighbouring authorities or because the participating authorities, though geographically scattered, share common socio-economic problems. By joining forces in this manner, individual regional authorities hope to increase their influence over EC decisions and secure additional EC funds. Associations of this nature include the Association of European Frontier Regions founded in 1971; the Conference of Peripheral Maritime Regions of the European Community established in 1973; and the Community of Industrial Regions set up in 1984, based in Lille. The last brings together the regions of Nord–Pas-de-Calais, Rhineland Westphalia, Strathclyde, and Wallonia. Probably the best known Euro-region is Nord–Pas-de-Calais and Kent, set up and funded by the Commission to develop a transfrontier regional development plan in the light of the channel tunnel project (Luchaire 1990). In some cases the European associations do little more than co-ordinate the EC lobbying activities of individual authorities. In other cases, however, co-operation extends to the implementation of regional development programmes (funded jointly by the EC). What is clear, however, is that the concept of a region is extremely flexible and within the Single European Market often transcends national frontiers. In order to be effective EC lobbyists, regional authorities have quickly learnt to co-operate with their EC counterparts.

3. SCOTLAND AND THE EUROPEAN COMMUNITY

3.1 Scottish Office and EC Affairs

Scotland has a unique position within the UK which has been recognized by successive governments. In institutional terms this is expressed through the existence of the Scottish Office, a territorial department headed by a Secretary of State who by convention sits in the Cabinet. Additionally, there are four other junior ministers. Set up in 1885, it has gained responsibilities over a wide range of functions covering the equivalent of about eleven different Whitehall departments (Rose 1982: 118). The Office is organized internally on a functional basis with five principal departments:

Scottish Office Education Department (SOED)
Scottish Office Agriculture and Fisheries Department (SOAFD)

Scottish Office Environment Department (SOED)
Scottish Office Industry Department (SOID)
Scottish Office Home and Health Department (SOHHD)

The European Community impinges most on the work of SOAFD and SOID. In addition to the statutory responsibilities of the Scottish Office, ministers are assumed to be answerable for almost any area of public policy with a Scottish dimension. The consequence of this has been, as a previous Scottish Secretary remarked, that 'power limps lamely behind responsibility' (Ross 1978: 9).

As part of the UK Government, the Scottish Office has no independent existence and therefore cannot conclude international treaties or agreements other than in the capacity as a branch of the UK central government. The Scottish Office is a fairly minor department in the UK Government and has rarely been headed by a significant political figure. In negotiation with Brussels it is far more likely that the equivalent functional department will act as 'lead', for example the Ministry of Agriculture, Fisheries, and Food (MAFF) rather than SOAFD. There have been few exceptions. In the late 1970s, at a time of intense sensitivity to Scottish interests caused by the rise of the Scottish National Party, the Scottish Office played a more significant role in discussions with the European Community in fishing issues, an industry of greater concern to Scotland than the UK as a whole and affecting constituencies where the Nationalists were making gains. Through membership of the Cabinet, the Scottish Secretary will have access to the forum in which key issues in EC politics are discussed. Given the central role of the Council of Ministers this is potentially the most significant means by which Scottish interests will be articulated. However, this depends on what the full Cabinet discusses, whether the Scottish Secretary is a member of the relevant Cabinet committees and the calibre of the incumbent.

Scottish Office attendance at meetings of the Council of Ministers in the EC have been few: five attendances out of 151 in the two years to the end of 1988 and then in a junior capacity dealing with fishing. None of the 95 major ministerial speeches made over the same period on EC topics were made by Scottish Office ministers (Hansard, *Written Answer*, 7 June 1989). The Scottish Office also plays a minor part in legislative procedure in this country in introducing EC policies. In the year up to June 1989, only one item of primary legislation was sponsored by the Scottish Office—recognition of the professional qualifications of teachers obtained elsewhere in the EC was contained in a controversial piece of legislation on Scottish education (Hansard, *Written Answer*, 7 June 1989, col. 177).

A European Funds Division (EFD) came into existence in 1988 as a separate division having formerly been part of the same division dealing with urban funding. The EFD has responsibility for the Scottish Office's side regarding the European Regional Development Fund (ERDF). The head of this unit was later charged with responsibility for leading a European central support unit. Similarly, SOAFD administers the European Agricultural Guidance and Guarantee Fund (EAGGF). A survey of work undertaken in the 117 management units and divisions of the Scottish Office in late 1991 revealed that 89—over three-quarters—were involved in EC work and over one-quarter rated their EC work as 'crucial' or 'major'. One-fifth of Scottish Office staff were involved in some way with this work (*Scoop: The Scottish Office's Own Paper*, Sept. 1991).

The intention within the Scottish Office has been to raise the number of civil servants working on secondment in Brussels each year, to increase the European dimension of training and encourage trainee EC officials to spend time working with the Scottish Office. Training sessions for staff to increase awareness of the European Community has become a standard part of the development of the Euro-profile of the Scottish Office. All of this has, in itself, gone some way to further the primary objective of the European Commission to develop a European outlook.

A number of quasi-autonomous public bodies in Scotland are of relevance to a study of EC–Scottish relations. The Scottish Development Agency (SDA), founded in 1975, and the Highlands and Islands Development Board (HIDB), founded in 1965, had fairly tenuous links with the EC with the bulk of work passing through the Scottish Office. The HIDB shared an official who was based in Brussels with Grampian and Borders Regional Councils and the Mid-Wales Development Board and benefited considerably from EC structural funds, largely expenditure on infrastructure. The HIDB, the local MEP, and others were involved along with others from rural parts of the EC in lobbying for an additional objective to be added to the revised European Regional Development Fund (ERDF). Their efforts were not in vain: Objective 5(*b*) of the

ERDF gives the Highlands and Islands, the Scottish Borders, Mid-Wales, Devon, and Cornwall special status within the Community permitting them access to ERDF funds.

The SDA and HIDB were replaced in 1991 by new organizations—Scottish Enterprise (SE) and Highlands and Islands Enterprise (HE)—meeting the demands of the Conservative Government for a less interventionist style and more entrepreneurial approach to local economic generation. The idea had been proposed by Bill Hughes, former chairman of the CBI (Scotland) and chairman of the Conservative Party in Scotland. The White Paper introducing the idea of new agencies noted new challenges awaiting Scotland in the 1990s including the completion of the Single European Market (Scottish Office 1988).

SE took over the training responsibilities of the Training Agency in Scotland and has sought to decentralize its activities, paralleling proposals for England. In key areas—economic development, training, and the environment—the responsibilities of Scottish Enterprise and the EC coincide. Two main themes in the Commission's programme emerging in the 1990s which have been identified as of greatest significance for Scottish Enterprise have been the external relations of the Community, particularly the GATT negotiations, and the reform of the structural funds.

The external relations negotiations of the EC on the Multifibre Arrangement (MFA) and the Common Agricultural Policy (CAP) are recognized to be of great significance to the Scottish economy. The MFA will have particular relevance to the Scottish borders where the textile trade is concentrated. The CAP negotiations have wider implications. Additionally, industrial restructuring funds will be of interest to Scottish Enterprise.

Changes in structural funds have led to a need for greater co-ordination. Within Scottish Enterprise there is a view that the role of Scottish local authorities is likely to diminish as its role increases, a view not shared by the authorities themselves. This view is based on the shift from infrastructural projects to productive-capability projects within the ERDF, the need for greater co-ordination and the increased emphasis to be placed on training as Scottish Enterprise has assumed responsibility for applications under Objectives 3 and 4. Concern amongst local authorities that Scottish Enterprise and the local enterprise boards might infringe on their well-established territory has been recognized inside the

Scottish Office, but the absence of details in the government's consultative paper on local government reforms has fuelled local authority fears (Scottish Office 1991).

Another area targeted by Scottish Enterprise is non-defence related research and development where Scotland lags behind the rest of the UK which, in turn lags behind its major EC competitors. Transport policy also has obvious implications to a geographically peripheral part of the Community such as Scotland. The adoption of a proposal to upgrade rail networks within the Community in February 1991 had a mixed reaction in Scotland. While the upgraded lines specified included such important links as Glasgow–Edinburgh, Glasgow–London, and Edinburgh–London, there was concern that rail lines north of the Scottish central belt, and particularly to Aberdeen, had not been included. Overall, the EC impinges on a wide range of areas of importance to the Scottish economy. Given the range of responsibilities of the Scottish Office and the nebulous but important function of the Scottish Secretary representing Scottish interests in government, it is not possible to draw up a list of responsibilities as might be attempted with other statutorily created and defined institutions such as local government.

3.2 Scottish Local Authorities and the EC

An Audit Commission report on local authorities and the EC noted three main ways in which the EC affected local authorities:

i. *Euro-regulation* imposes unavoidable obligations to implement, enforce and monitor EC legislation;
ii. *European economic integration* creates new opportunities for (and pressures on) the local economic base; and
iii. *Euro-funds* offer potential support for the local economy and for a range of local authority projects (Audit Commission 1991: 7, para. 9).

Discussion of the implications of European integration and '1992' in particular have already stressed the importance of developing European networks in order to take advantage of opportunities and to be forewarned about dangers which lie ahead (see also Bongers 1990; LIGB 1989).

There has been a variety of responses to the 'European challenge' from local authorities. Strathclyde Regional Council, the largest local authority unit in Europe, has a full-time official based in Brussels (as do Cornwall, Greater Manchester, Highlands and Islands, Birmingham, Kent, and Essex in conjunction with Picardie). Lothian Regional Council opted for a policy of second-ment of officers to and from the Commission in Brussels while the other ten island and regional authorities were more *ad hoc* in their approach. Towards the end of the 1980s, Scottish regional authori-ties have attached an increased priority to the European dimension with 'Europe weeks', formal links with local business to help pre-pare for '1992', attendance at EC conferences and training events, and involvement in European associations such as Strathclyde's involvement in the Conference of Peripheral Maritime Regions.

A survey of Scotland's 9 regional, 3 islands, and 53 district coun-cils by the Convention of Scottish Local Authorities was conducted in 1989 and again in 1991 (COSLA 1991a). From the nine regions, 45 districts, and two islands that replied it was discovered that all regional and islands authorities had discussed the Single European Market but only 36 per cent of district councils had done so. All regional councils, one of the islands councils, and 19 districts had an officer co-ordinating the authorities response to '1992'. Finally, all regions, two islands, and 12 districts had European Liaison Officers. There was a marked increased in awareness of and activi-ties related to EC matters amongst councils compared with an earlier survey published in 1989. Generally speaking, islands coun-cils, as all-purpose authorities, and regions which are responsible for major strategic matters were more aware and prepared for EC challenges.

The range of issues which authorities saw as facing them with regard to the single market in 1989 had included: development, public procurement, harmonization of standards, freedom of move-ment (including harmonization of qualifications), language skills, the social dimension, and structural funds. Less than two years later, other issues were raised in addition to those mentioned in 1989: environment, rural development and particularly the effects of the reform of CAP, equal opportunities, personnel issues, peripherality, transfer of citizens' rights over national boundaries and consequent problems regarding welfare payments, increased tourism, financial management including opportunities for short-term borrowing, technical directives particularly in environmental health and food. Given that a primary aim of the Commission is to heighten awareness of the European dimension and thereby encourage the Europeanization of local and regional politics, it would be fair to say that the Scottish local authorities have been responding as intended.

Relations between central and local government in Scotland in the 1980s deteriorated and one of the few areas where co-operation appeared genuine and constructive was in EC affairs. This was hardly surprising as central and local government had a common goal which necessitated a co-operative approach in applying for funding from the Commission. Arguably, the skills required for 'grantsmanship', to use Brigid Laffan's term (Laffan 1989), were those which the Scottish Office and local authorities had developed throughout their existence. However, even here relations have not always been good. One of the most controversial issues affecting the local authorities has been 'additionality'. In this area, the local authorities have joined forces with the Commission to put pressure on the UK Government. In September 1991 the finance committee of COSLA made this clear in submissions to both the Scottish Office and the Commission (COSLA 1991b).

3.3 Scotland Europa

The idea of establishing an office in Brussels to lobby on behalf of Scottish interests had been discussed for some time before the SDA formally considered its viability and value. The coincidence of three developments encouraged the SDA to consider the idea. First, there was the 1992 Project of the European Communities and the propaganda campaign encouraging businesses and government agencies to 'think European'. Secondly, debate on Scotland's constitutional status had taken on a novel form when the Scottish National Party adopted a policy of 'independence in Europe' which forced other parties to set their policies in a European context. The European and Scottish dimensions had taken on an importance again and were perceived to be linked (Keating and Jones 1991). Thirdly, the changes which the SDA had undergone brought about a changed perception of its relations with the EC. The new agency, Scottish Enterprise was to be a more decentralized, private-sector led organization with a strategic and enabling role rather than being an interventionist, centralized organization. The initial steps involved the Board of the SDA visiting Brussels, followed by a consultant's report on the idea of opening an office there. The consultant's report concluded that there was strong support for the establishment of an office in Brussels and discussed existing models based on offices for German *Länder* and Spanish regions in Brussels.

This was considered by Scottish Office civil servants whose deliberations were later leaked to the press. These leaked papers offer an interesting view of the thinking which led to the decision to establish Scotland Europa and the nature of the body. The view of the official with overall responsibility for urban policy, European funds, and new towns in the Scottish Office was that Scottish Enterprise and Highlands and Islands Enterprise should between them hold at least 51 per cent of the equity. This would ensure that Scottish Office agencies would have a controlling influence and the government would not be at the mercy of hostile interests in Scotland. What was clearly envisaged was not a Brussels office for the Scottish Office but an office which would facilitate contact with European Community institutions and officials for those willing to become clients.

The question of permitting the COSLA and the Scottish Trades Union Congress (STUC) to be involved was discussed and the civil-service view is worth quoting at length here as it shows the major issue of controversy:

One issue is that both COSLA and the STUC have expressed interest in the concept and would probably be willing to take an equity share. Clearly we would not want them to be in a position to press Scotland Europa into lobbying against Government policy. One option would be to allow them to subscribe for services but not to hold equity (although they could indirectly wield influence through the Scottish Council). On the other hand excluding them might weaken the lobbying power of the body, given the Commission's corporatist ethos. Scottish local authority delegations go out very frequently to Brussels, and Mr Campbell Christie [STUC Gen. Secy.] currently spends 3 days a month in Brussels on the Economic and Social Committee. It would be unfortunate if COSLA or the STUC sought to undermine the credibility of Scotland Europa when on such visits. On balance officials think it may be best to tie these bodies in through allowing them a small equity stake, if the SDA wish to do so, but would welcome Ministers' views on this point. (Weeple 1990)

The papers passed between Scottish Office civil servants and ministers reveal the concerns as well as the attractions which a Brussels office had for the Scottish Office. There were a number of attractions in having a Brussels office:

i. Scottish economic and business interests would have a more powerful and effective lobby with a full-time presence than the previous fragmented efforts permitted
ii. Scotland's profile in Brussels would be raised and would have a different character than that projected by the Scottish local authorities, predominantly Labour controlled, who were most active in lobbying the Commission
iii. it would provide a flow of information about opportunities and threats to Scotland's interests
iv. *Scottish Enterprise* could be more active in the European context than the SDA had been and for which it was frequently criticised. (Weeple 1990)

However, a number of dangers were envisaged which the Scottish Office was particularly sensitive about:

i. While it was hoped that such a body could 'complement and reinforce' Government policy there was an awareness that it might 'cut across' the Government's position
ii. on the other hand it was appreciated that other Government Departments such as the Foreign and Commonwealth Office, UKREP and the Cabinet Office would not want a body representing the Scottish Office in Brussels though they would have no difficulty in a lobbying/intelligence gathering body so long as it was identified with *Scottish Enterprise*
iii. there was concern that the office would be an 'excuse for unnecessary foreign junkets' particularly by public bodies. (Weeple 1990)

The idea emerging within the SDA towards the end of 1990 was a private limited company to be called Scotland Europa Ltd with initially seven staff based in Brussels whose funding would come from equity held by a small number of bodies, from subscriptions paid by a wider range of bodies for services, and from trading income (mainly from EC 'orientation' training). A core group of organizations was envisaged including:

Scottish Enterprise
Highlands and Islands Enterprise
Scottish Council (Development and Industry)
Scottish Financial Enterprise
Law Society of Scotland
Institute of Chartered Accountants of Scotland

Local authorities and trade unions in Scotland were dissatisfied with these proposals and suggestions were made amongst the local authorities that they should establish a separate office in Brussels themselves.

In May 1991 Scottish Enterprise issued a paper outlining proposals along the lines that had been discussed with the Scottish Office. It estimated that the annual cost of a small permanent office in Brussels would be in excess of £120,000. Clients would be offered different levels of representation: a subscription service with a small number of executives who would pursue issues on behalf of subscribers; and direct representation for those requiring a greater presence in Brussels. It was expected that between these two levels of participation a number of other options would be made available. Scotland Europa was envisaged less as a territorial lobby than as a lobbying office for whichever bodies—commercial and business in the main—based in Scotland were willing to pay for the service. The role of public bodies would be central to its nature. The involvement of public bodies would probably provide it with the scope of interests which would make it more than a consultancy unit for Scottish interests in Brussels.

The typical activities of participants listed in the Scottish Enterprise paper were:

i. EC Policy Development: ensuring that Scottish interests were fed into decision-making in Brussels
ii. Intelligence: gathering information on emerging thinking in the Commission
iii. European Community Funds: attempting to increase funds from the EC for individual projects particularly in research and development, education and training and rural development
iv. Networking: making contact with other regional representative offices in light of Commission's propensity to support transnational collaborative projects. (Scottish Enterprise 1991)

The appointment of the former chief economist for the Royal Bank Group, Grant Baird, in September 1991 as chief executive of Scotland Europa gave the body a formidable head. Despite his banking background, Baird's appointment was generally welcomed across the political spectrum in Scotland and was seen as offering hope amongst local authorities and the STUC that they might yet find a role in the scheme. Baird's view of the role of the organization was clearer than that of those who appointed him. However, by early

1992 agreement had not been reached with local authorities as to whether they would be involved and a number of east-coast local authorities were preparing to establish a lobbying office of their own in Brussels.

The key problem that has afflicted Scotland Europa, and is central to the political debate in Scotland, is determining who has the right to speak for Scotland. Territorial politics and territorial lobbying must resolve the central question of what the interests of the territory are. As there will be different and conflicting interests within any territory the battle to speak on behalf of it is an important first step. Even before the doors of Scotland Europa have been opened in Brussels this has proved difficult to resolve. The Scottish Office and its agencies claim this right as part of central government, the local authorities equally claim this right as the only elected institutions representing Scotland. In other words, conflicting mandates have given rise to difficulties.

4. CONCLUSION: TOWARDS A EUROPE OF REGIONS?

The interests of a particular region will be the subject of intense debate with different sectional interests within the region claiming to speak on its behalf. Without some elected body formally articulating the interests and views of a region, the government of the state as a whole will be in a strong position to ensure that its view is taken as that of any region. This, of course, entirely contradicts the notion of regional interests which can be expected to differ on some issues at least with the government at the centre. In the absence of directly elected regional government, an intense debate as to who has the right to speak for the area—whether institutions of central government, the collective voice of local government, or functional interests such as business and trades unions—is bound to ensue and perhaps dissipate the effort made in lobbying externally.

Rhodes (1974) noted the ambiguity in the term *regionalism*: it is possible to distinguish between regional administration, regional economic planning, regional government, and regional devolution. Further confusion arises from the fact that regionalist loyalties and conflicts are inevitably linked to socio-economic problems typically associated with peripherality. A regional policy and institutions offering subnational levels of government representation in EC decision-making have slowly been emerging but the Community remains very firmly tied to its quadripartite institutional structure. A regional policy has been emerging largely because it has been in the interests of certain Member States who, in terms of the Community, are themselves classified as regions with claims on the structural funds. Additionally, the Commission sees regional policy as a necessary adjunct to the Single European Market. Regional policy has, therefore, in large measure developed because it is in the interests of those operating within the existing institutions. In 1974 Rhodes concluded that the idea of a 'Europe of the Regions' was a non-starter though an active regional policy may develop. Since then, however, regions have asserted themselves more forcefully in the European arena.

The proliferation of European regional associations and transfrontier regional co-operation reflects the growing Europeanization of regional policy. Within the single market, national boundaries are no longer relevant for the purpose of regional development. Increasingly, EC structural funds are allocated to medium-term transfrontier regional development programmes. The policy has been established, but the institutional nexus has yet to be adequately catered for. At present, all such programmes have to be approved by the Member States which, for the moment at least, remain the constitutional partners of the European Commission. Moreover, national governments are without exception reluctant to relinquish overall control of regional policy. The above developments have, however, changed the balance of power between national governments, regions, and the European Community. In short, the development of powerful regional government throughout the EC has created a situation in which 'sovereignty' is now shared between two tiers of government. Not unreasonably therefore, regional authorities are now demanding a much greater role in the EC decision-making process.

Since the adoption of the 1986 Single European Act, debates and negotiations over the future development of the European Community have been permeated by references to the principle of 'subsidiarity', defined by a British Foreign Office Minister as 'the principle that things should not be done at Community level unless they cannot be done at national level' (Adonis and Jones 1991). Regional governments have, in turn, invoked the concept of subsidiarity in support of their demands for a bigger say in EC affairs and autonomy from national government. In practice, however, the principle of subsidiarity is effective only when understood within the framework of a particular conception of the common good. As illustrated above, no such consensus exists with regard to the definition of Scottish interests. For nationalist parties 'the Community is now seen as a mechanism for circumventing a British State committed to political centralisation and the sway of unrestrained market forces' (Keating and Jones 1991). Thus, the development of the regional lobby in Brussels has potentially far-reaching implications for the development of the Community. Whereas other groups seek to secure their interests within the context of specific EC policies, many subnational governments wish to change the political and institutional balance of power within the European Community itself.

References

Adonis, A. and Jones, S. (1991), *Subsidiarity and the Community's Constitutional Future* (Discussion Paper No. 2; Centre for European Studies, Nuffield College, Oxford).

Auby, J.-F. (1990), 'L'Europe des Régions', *L'Actualité juridique: Droit administratif*, 20 Apr.: 208–16.

Audit Commission (1991), *A Rough Guide to Europe: Local Authorities and the EC* (HMSO, Dec. 1991).

Bongers, P. (1990), *Local Government and 1992* (Harlow: Longman).

Celimene, F. (1991), 'La Réforme de l'action des fonds structurels européens', *L'Actualité juridique: Droit administratif*, 20 Apr.: 251–66.

Chauvet, J.-P. (1989), 'Participation des collectivités territoriales aux décisions européenes: Le Role des lobbies locaux et régionaux', *Après-Demain*, May–June: 8–12.

Cini, M. (1990), *Local Government and the EC* (European Dossier Series No. 16; London: PNL Press).

Commission of the European Communities (1990), 'The New Structural Policies of the European Community', *European File* (June–July), 7.

COSLA (1991a), *Update Report on Local Authorities and the 1992 Single European Market*, July 1991.

COSLA (1991b), *EC Capital Grants: Additionality*, Finance Item 4.5, 17 Sept. 1991.

Duchacek, I. (1986), *The Territorial Dimension of Politics: Within, among and across Nations* (Boulder, Colo.: Westview Press).

Hrbek, R. (1987), 'The German Länder and the European Community', *Aussenpolitik*, 2/87: 120–33.

——(1988), The German Länder and the European Community: Towards a Real Federalism', in W. Wessels and E. Regelsberger (eds.), *The Federal Republic of Germany and the European Community: The Presidency and Beyond* (Bonn: Europa Union Verlag), 215–30.

——(1991), 'German Federalism and European Integration', in Charlie Jeffrey and Peter Savigear (eds.), *German Federalism Today* (Leicester: Leicester University Press), 84–162.

Keating, M., and Jones, B. (1991), 'Scotland and Wales: Peripheral Assertion and European Integration', *Parliamentary Affairs*, 44: 311–24.

Laffan, B. (1989), ' "While you're there in Brussels, get us a grant": The Management of the Structural Funds in Ireland', *Irish Political Studies*, 4 (1989), 43–57.

LGIB (Local Government International Bureau) (1989), *Introductory Guide for Local Authorities on 1992.*

Luchaire, Y. (1990), 'Les Régions et l'Europe', *Annuaire des collectivités locales* (Paris: Libraires Techniques).

Mawson, J., Martins, J. R., and Gibney, J. T. (1985), 'The Development of the European Community Regional Policy', in M. Keating and B. Jones (eds.), *Regions in the European Community* (Oxford: Clarendon Press), 20–59.

Morata, F. (1991), *Spanish Regions and the 1993 Community Challenge* (Working Paper No. 34; Institut de Ciencies Politiques i Socials, Barcelona).

Rhodes, R. (1974), 'Regional Policy and a "Europe of Regions": A Critical Assessment', *Regional Studies*, 8: 105–14.

Romus, P. (1990), *L'Europe régionale* (Brussels: Editions LABOR).

Rose, R. (1982), *Understanding the United Kingdom* (London: Longman).

Ross, W. (1978), 'Approaching the Archangelic?', *Scottish Government Yearbook 1978.*

Scottish Enterprise (1991), 'Scotland Europa: Discussion Paper', May 1991.

Scottish Office (1988), *Scottish Enterprise: A New Approach to Training and Enterprise Creation* (Scottish Office, Dec. 1988, Cm 534).

——(1991), *The Structure of Local Government in Scotland: The Case for Change, Principles for the New System* (June 1991).

Wallace, H. (1977), 'The Establishment of the Regional Development Fund: Common Policy or Pork Barrel?', in H. Wallace, W. Wallace, and C. Webb, *Policy-making in the European Community* (London: Wiley), 137–63.

Weeple, E. (1990), 'Internal Scottish Office Papers on Scotland Europa' (Nov. 1990).

7

The Rationality of Lobbying in Europe: Why are Euro-Groups so Numerous and so Weak? Some Evidence from the Car Industry

ANDREW MCLAUGHLIN AND GRANT JORDAN

1. INTRODUCTION: THE LOGIC OF EURO-GROUPS?

The emerging literature on European lobbying suggests that groups are responding to the EC's political development by organizing themselves into supranational federations. In recent years there has been a proliferation of Euro-groups. Furthermore, empirical studies have indicated that EC decision-makers prefer to consult via such federations (Pryce 1973; see also Ch. 1). However, this preference for consultation by the Commission appears to have been made difficult by fundamental weaknesses within the Euro-groups. Drawing on evidence from the car industry, our analysis considers three main themes: the service that the Euro-group provides for participating members; the weaknesses of these groups; and the rationale for participating in such organizations. This chapter notes the widespread assumption that because Community institutions are increasingly important, there is inevitably a growth in Euro-group activity. Some kind of mechanical link between the influence of the EC and the mobilization of interests is commonly asserted. Kirchner and Schwaiger, for example, postulated that 'the newly created European Monetary System will most likely be an impetus for affiliates to delegate an additional competence or transfer more authority to UNICE (Union of Industries of the EEC) and thereby increase its effectiveness' (1981: 5).

Indeed the level of Euro-group development is sometimes used as an indicator of the extent of Community interest in an area. Sidjanksi (1967) has been quoted by Kirchner and Schwaiger, as follows: 'the development of the power of the EC has given rise to a

reaction from those interests which are most directly affected'
(1981: 397). This assumption rests on two premises which need to
be examined. First, it is possible that increased Community policy-
making could stimulate increased activity of national interest
groups: that the response among competing national interests need
not be to develop transnational groupings (see Ch. 2).

Secondly, there is the important argument by Mancur Olson in
The Logic of Collective Action (1965). Olson argued that rational
behaviour was not to subscribe to organizations which sought collective benefits available to both subscribers and non-subscribers
alike, but to free ride. Olson argued, 'Indeed, unless the number of
individuals in a group is quite small, or unless there is coercion or
some other special device to make individuals act in their common
interest, *rational, self-interested individuals will not act to achieve
their common or group interests*' (emphasis in original) (1965: 2).
Olson often challenged the pluralist view that groups sprung up
more or less automatically to reflect shared interests. He suggested
that groups were difficult to mobilize as potential members would
attempt to have the benefits without the investment. He argued,

Consider a hypothetical, competitive industry, and suppose that most of
the producers in that industry desire a tariff, a price support program, or
some other government intervention. To obtain any such assistance from
government, the producers in this industry will presumably have to organize a lobbying organisation. . . . *(But) Just as it was not rational for a particular producer to restrict his output in order that there might be a higher
price for the product of his industry, so it could not be rational for him to
sacrifice his time and money to support a lobbying organization to obtain
government assistance for the industry.* (emphasis in original) (1965: 10)

In Olson's perspective there is no automatic emergence of groups
to reflect collective concerns. Group membership is based on selective benefits available only to members rather than accessible to
members and non-members alike. The argument presented below is
that participation is motivated by the selective benefits Olson
identified, by a particularly narrow private concern not shared by
other members, and by a desire to influence the group's own position. Despite the abiding weaknesses of the Euro-group, the individual company cannot afford to free ride, since participation
offers the necessary opportunity to influence group destination.
Olson thought group mobilization for collective action was irrational and he argued against the likely proliferation of groups. The

proliferation of groups in Europe can thus be seen rather as non-Olsonian. However Olson is relevant in that he is directing attention to the motivation of participation ˙ in these proliferating groups. Arguably, it is not based on automatic response to shared attitudes and concerns but because there are specific benefits for each participant. We argue that the selective incentive is not simply a material benefit in the style of cheap insurance for members but a selective policy benefit—that participation can shape the organizational agenda in a way that is favourable to the member organizations. Participation allows an opportunity to influence group goals.

Olson's model is based on the assumption that companies act as profit maximizers: they will make rational calculations of cost when taking decisions. This assumption, based on a belief that companies behave with 'pure' rationality, has been challenged in economic theory by behavioural models (see Cyert and March 1955; Simon 1958). Simon argued that companies acted with a 'bounded' rationality as opposed to a 'pure' rationality of the nature Olson assumes. This model offers a redefinition of the rationality concept which argues that in an uncertain world it is rational for the company to adopt 'satisficing' behaviour as opposed to 'maximizing' behaviour. In their earlier study Cyert and March had already questioned the premises underpinning Olson's hypothetical example above. They argued that in order to minimize business uncertainty, it was in fact rational for companies in an industry to seek 'negotiated environments'. Thus, they would enter into tacit collusion with their competitors by joining trade groups. Therefore it makes sense for the company acting with a bounded rationality to join the group. The argument presented below notes the relevance of this increased sophistication in the theory of company behaviour to the non-Olsonian proliferation of Euro-groups.

Yet, Olson's pointer to under-mobilization of interests does seem to give some clues to the apparent paradox that Euro-groups are both numerous and weak. Is the under-supply of lobbying caused by the free-rider phenomenon? Does the policy-shaping motivation for participation lead to a rather tokenistic level of organization?

Our study both confirms Olson's stress on the need for selective benefits—and dissents from his belief that lobbying for collective ends is quite as irrational as he presents.

2. EURO-GROUPS IN THE CAR INDUSTRY

Prior to 1990 the car industry was represented in Brussels via two organizations: the Liaison Committee of the Automobile Industry of the Countries of the European Communities (CLCA) and the Committee of Common Market Automobile Constructors (CCMC). CLCA was the peak association for the EC's seven national automobile trade groups representing the 'general, economic, legal, fiscal and technical interests common to all manufacturers' (CLCA 1990). CLCA was established in the early 1960s as a satellite of the Organisation of International Automobile Constructors (OICA) set up in 1955 to lobby the United Nations Economic Commission for Europe (UN-ECE) in Geneva. The creation of CLCA was an early recognition of the emerging policy-making function in the EC. Moreover, the UN-ECE's Working Party 29 (Transport) has remained an important market for ideas for EC officials seeking to formulate vehicle regulations. However, since its creation in 1972, CCMC had remained the industry's most prestigious group. CCMC was in effect a 'club' of European producers established following dissatisfaction with the lack of direct company participation in CLCA.

CCMC's founding members were also concerned to create a group which could respond to a perceived clash of interests with American subsidiaries in Europe. In the early 1970s the EC began to deal with technical issues it had previously ignored such as engine emissions. European producers feared that under pressure from American companies in Europe the EC would seek to implement proposals similar to those already implemented in the US. In the event, this did not materialize as the Americans developed a completely different model range for their European operations, but it was an important factor in the formation of CCMC (Interview information, 7 Oct. 1991). Membership of CCMC was restricted to those firms whose corporate headquarters were located within the EC (see Appendix 1 for a note on the respective memberships of the groups). For most of the post-1972 period the two groups worked together in monitoring the relevant policy area. This included the monitoring of national agendas for developments which might impact on EC policy. For example, in 1984 CCMC protested to the Commission against efforts by the national government of West Germany to introduce unilateral engine emission standards. This was upheld on the grounds that such a move would represent a technical barrier to market entry, and thus contravene the Treaty of Rome.

Co-operation between the two secretariats (they shared the same office floor in Brussels) ensured that each could assume responsibility for representation in their respective areas of strength. Thus, CCMC tended to concentrate on technical issues, while CLCA became the dominant group on legal and fiscal matters. However, the EC's political and economic development, and in particular the momentum of the Single European Market programme, led to increased policy-making activity and the distinctions between the two groups' areas of expertise became blurred.

The primary function at formation of CCMC was to respond to a welter of EC technical regulations. By the mid-1980s the group's Administrative Committee, composed of the legal and public-affairs executives of member firms, had assumed a major function within the group. This committee was responsible for the increasingly time-consuming and burdensome task of 'advising' the industry's presidents on political and economic aspects of policy in order to assist them in their dealings with the Commission. CLCA—under pressure from its US and Scandinavian members who were excluded from CCMC—also became increasingly involved in technical issues. While on some issues the two groups continued to find some common ground, they had also begun to cover the same issues—even competing for representation—and it became increasingly evident that to arrive at shared positions required the creation of a new unified group. By the autumn of 1990 these developments had stimulated widespread support within the industry for the disbandment of CCMC and CLCA.

Despite these problems, we can gain some measure of the importance that firms attached to the groups by considering the resources they committed. At the most obvious level, the groups' members had to fund permanently staffed offices in Brussels. National groups and companies also staffed the specialist committees whose work was co-ordinated by these permanent secretariats. One smaller specialist car-maker suggested that so frequent had the meetings of some committees become, that dispatching 'experts' was an increasingly costly exercise (Interview, 7 Mar. 1991). Furthermore, the heads of the European industry had to take on the task of a one-year stint as CCMC president on top of their primary responsibilities as chairmen of their respective companies. Though one-year arrangements tend to weaken elected officers, company chairmen rarely sought immediate re-election because of the sometimes burdensome nature of the task. However, it would be incorrect to interpret the one-year tenure simply as a reflection of the workload involved. In such a competitive sector the companies are reluctant to allow an individual a longer term presidency for fear that they might acquire a disproportionate influence over group policy. Hence the custom evolved in CCMC of each of the four major EC manufacturing industries—France, Britain, Germany, and Italy—taking on the presidency of the group in rotation for a period of two years. For example, France's two-year period of tenure would be divided between Renault and Peugeot.

The latter part of our analysis focuses on group membership because of the Euro-group's role in the policy process; groups also provide some services for their members. While subscriptions represent an initial membership cost, they are usually dwarfed by the costs of active participation in the group. It might be useful therefore to identify some of the 'potential' benefits that a participating company would seek.

2.1 The Benefits of Participation

An important reason for joining the Euro-group is its ability to stay abreast of developments at the European level. This is a cost-effective incentive. The group will alert its members to emerging political developments. This is increasingly the case, since not only is the pace of change so rapid but also the EC political agenda is far wider and less predictable than at the national level. But company size can be a factor here. It appears that larger companies will want to do in-house monitoring of their own core areas (while perhaps receiving general advice on matters such as health and safety).

This early warning function appears to have assumed great significance in relation to the European Parliament (EP). Of particular relevance is the EP's ability to propose amendments to Commission proposals in certain areas. For example, in 1989 the EP made a number of amendments to the Commission's directive on emission standards for small cars, effectively tightening the original requirements (COM 89 257–final, 11 May 1989). The Commission apparently agreed to these changes within the new co-operation procedure because it was unwilling to unravel the complex directive should the EP have rejected it unamended. In this instance the changes provided an eleventh hour bolster for environmental groups who felt the original standards were not stringent enough. The managing director of a lobbying consultancy group, Powerhouse Europe, in the *EP Review* (No. 1, 1989) cited the Council of Ministers' acceptance of tougher exhaust controls as a parliamentary success. He said, 'These measures, and many other less publicised ones, have earned parliament new respect. In earlier years, all too often, those who aimed to influence decisions would concentrate their efforts on the Commission and the Civil Servants of the member states. In 1989 these efforts will no longer suffice.' The article did nevertheless concede that the Commission and the Council still predominate in decision-making. Indeed, the EP's right to reject a Commission directive has proved something of a blunt instrument. This is mainly because a rejection prevents short-term progress of any kind on an issue. As a result, the EP often fails to reach an agreement on a contested document and the process continues into the Council. In a recent internal document, General Motors' (GM) Brussels office reported: 'Following the recent failure by the EP to reach agreement on the further tightening of the EC Commission proposal (on engine emissions) the Council can now go ahead with the final approval of the EC Commission directive' (GM 1991: 6).

The car industry has in recent years devoted considerable extra resources to lobbying the EP. Several of our respondents confirmed that this was an area which they readily delegated to the Eurogroup. There are a few practical reasons for this. By the time proposals reach the EP there is more likelihood that a common position has been reached between the industry and the Commission. The Euro-group can be entrusted to press this position in Strasbourg during parliamentary debate. Furthermore, while groups realize the emerging significance of the EP, they may again simply lack the resources to maintain a high profile there. One legislative affairs executive commented: 'The German flavour of the Parliament on environmental issues is something of a problem . . . But we cannot commit further resources to it. Within the proper context of decision-making it remains relatively weak and as the emissions debate illustrated there are no guarantees of a return for your efforts' (Interview, 15 Feb. 1991). Companies have quite naturally skewed their resources towards the Commission, since most proposals are formulated in this bureaucratic arena. Some groups have unilaterally adopted measures to deal with the EP's new role. For example, the Society of Motor Manufacturers and Traders (SMMT) external relations department has established an EP information service for MEPs akin to the service it provides at a national level. Most groups have however relied on the Euro-group as a conduit for their views in Strasbourg. Thus, the Euro-group may be better placed to respond to the EC's institutional development. The CCMC's last activity report underlined this factor. 'In the past few years CCMC has strengthened its relations with the EP. The increased powers accorded to the Parliament under the new procedure for collaboration instituted by the SEA, mean that the EP is an even more important discussion partner' (CCMC 1990). The report also stressed this development in relation to the Economic and Social Committee and the Permanent Representatives of Member States.

An example of the need for 'early warning' is the re-emergence of the debate surrounding the industry's cross-national pricing policies. A report by the European Bureau of Consumers' Union (BEUC) published in 1990 has alleged that some companies are charging different prices for the same product in different EC markets with prices in Britain amongst the highest in the Community (BEUC 1990). Less than five years ago following a previous investigation, the Commission had laid down the basic rules under EC competition law for the distribution of vehicles in a bid to prevent such car price differentials. These regulations stipulated that if the price for a similar car sold in different national markets should reach an 18 per cent differential at any one time, or exist at 12 per cent for more than a twelve-month period, then this may justify a further investigation by the EC. The latest BEUC report suggests that these safeguards have not been observed. The Commission has responded to this new evidence with a formal investigation into price differentials. The BEUC report has also prompted an investigation in Britain by the Monopolies and Mergers Commission.

As Mazey and Richardson have noted: 'one characteristic of Brussels decision-making (compared to the relative predictability of, say, UK decision-making) is that ideas and proposals can emerge from "nowhere" with little or no warning, simply because the Commission has seen fit to consult a particular group of experts' (1990: 15). Thus, to borrow a phrase, participation in a Euro-group may be part of an exercise to 'minimize surprises', as member companies cope with a changeable and unstable policy agenda.

It is precisely because of the uncertainty involved that Olson's discussion of a rational calculation of membership is unrealistic. Membership has to be taken out as an insurance principle: it may be wasted but the potential benefits in managing to pre-empt or avert some future policy are such that major players cannot afford not to pay. In this sense the insurance provides advanced protection rather than compensation after the event. In Olson's language the monitoring service of Euro-groups is a selective benefit which encourages membership. The 'bulk buying of European information' means the company has access to information that would not be economically available to non-members. This gathering of 'intelligence' is essential in the Brussels lobbying game.

2.2 The Euro-Group as Discussion Partner with the EC

The participating company may envisage potential benefit from a group whose permanent secretariat has established personal contacts throughout the EC bureaucracy. Groups place a high premium on such contact in Brussels. This function may be particularly desirable to the smaller company or national group which does not have the resource of a Brussels office or permanent representation in Brussels. Despite maligning CLCA's inability to reconcile the interests of its divergent membership one SMMT director emphasized that 'the CLCA is nevertheless a very effective body . . . picking up signals in and around the Commission' (Interview, 17 Jan. 1991). This was an extremely important factor for the SMMT which has found the Commission at times very unreceptive to bilateral overtures. In this respect the competence of the group's secretariat is an important factor. As we shall see later, CCMC's secretariat lost credibility with the Commission and this severely damaged its ability to represent the sector in the policy process.

But again we see that participation may be governed by a concern to benefit from an 'early warning system'. Moreover, UK firms which do not have a Brussels office, often use the Euro-group and other facilities such as the CBI's Brussels staff to gain 'introductions' to relevant officials when they intend to make a bilateral overture (see Ch. 11). This again is a facility only available to members.

Clearly, a company would prefer to build its own specialist service and personal links to policy development. It is cost-effectiveness that pushes it to the 'second best' solution of activity via a group in which the company's special concerns may be diluted. However, we should not see the group as always necessarily a 'second best' solution. If a common view can be agreed in a group which adequately covers the company's interests, then considerable weight may be added to the position presented. As one interviewee put it: 'In such circumstances the group is a very effective mechanism for pursuit of a company's special concerns and, indeed, a better alternative than individual action' (Correspondence, 21 Aug. 1991). Therefore it is true that the group has some advantages over even a well-financed DIY approach. The company will be keen to act through the Euro-group if the Commission gives preferential access to Euro-groups. Such a policy helps simplify the consultation map for the Commission and makes sense in terms of an ideology of integration.

3. THE SYMBIOTIC REWARDS OF CONSULTATION

Most academic interest in groups has been concentrated on 'insider strategies' (Peters 1977) or in 'bureaucratic accommodation' (Jordan and Richardson 1982). In fact, despite his prominence in the literature, Olson is not an empirical interest-group author. There is quite a different flavour to his account based on principles of public-choice theory from those who have tracked practice.

The orientation of empirical accounts is well captured in Averyt's early essay on Euro-groups in terms of what he called (following La Palombara) 'clientela' relations between groups and the relevant bureaucracy. He claims that a group will tend to become a 'natural representative' of the bureaucracy when the following features are found on both sides of the relationship:

Agency Characteristics
1. the vertical nature of the administrative agency: it is concerned with one social sector (business, labour, etc.);
2. a regulatory activity is modal: the job of the agency is to regulate the sector; the agency has to depend on the group it is supposed to regulate for co-operation and information;
3. the agency is perceived by itself and by the clientele group as serving the interests of the regulated;
4. the agency needs more than its own initiative to regulate: it needs the co-operation of those who are to be regulated;
5. the agency lacks full control over information: the regulated groups possess a better technical staff or better information than the agency;
6. the agency–group relationship is reciprocal: both want to know and influence the actions of the other.

Group Characteristics
1. the bureaucracy prefers to deal with *representative* group clients;
2. the group must be respectable: it must not embarrass the agency;
3. the group must be an *effective* instrument of contact between the agency and the clientele group; it must therefore be well organised;
4. the group must be authoritative: it must be able to make binding rules on its own constituent sub-groups;
5. the interest group must be physically close to the agency, i.e. it must maintain offices in the city where the agency headquarters are located. (1975: 956)

Within this second list we can identify the typical weaknesses of the Euro-group from which CCMC and CCLA suffered (particularly point 4). However, the recent reorganization of the industry's lobby, which we discuss below, may be interpreted as an attempt to move towards these 'ideal' type characteristics which Averyt identified. In this perspective the relationship is not an Olson type one where interest groups attempt to extract advantage from a monolithic administration but is a symbiotic relationship between the administrators and the regulated. As Hull (Ch. 5) observes, the staff in the DGs are often looking for advice rather than responding to external pressure. Car-makers have recognized the importance of participating at this early stage in the policy process. One interviewee told us: 'The key to successful lobbying is in the writing process. EC drafts are like rolling stones . . . The further down the process you go the opportunities to make an input decrease, it is therefore vital to get in early. Early on he [the official] is looking for advice and you are in the ideal position to be effective because you can make suggestions and no one has to lose face value' (Interview, 23 July 1991). The same interviewee also emphasized the need to be constructive and avoid presenting a subjective company view.

If this is the spirit of the relationship that operates, then the calculation of participation is likely to be skewed much more in favour of membership than Olson presented. For little investment, companies can expect to get the bureaucracy to act as their advocate; the bureaucracy is predisposed to assist. These factors surely push the logic towards participation in the Euro-group. Olson may be correct to say that theoretically non-membership has the potential to gain something for nothing, but membership can mean that there is a selective benefit in which policy-makers are 'sensitized' by the group to the problems of participants. Moreover, there is a special kind of benefit which is the opportunity to influence group policy. The selective benefit is negative: the possibility that non-friendly policies can be pushed if one does not participate. Participation can then be a defensive strategy: ensuring that the group does not seek collective benefits that would be disadvantageous to the potential member.

3.1 Intra-Industry Contact

While the Euro-group often may not provide the forum for intra-industry agreement, its members still see a use for maintaining regular contacts with colleagues. As one car-maker put it: 'Everyone likes to know what everyone else is thinking' (Interview, 15 Feb. 1990). This is particularly important in an industrial sector such as the motor industry where one British minister discovered, 'there is a remarkably developed grapevine' (Lord Young 1990: 288). The concept of a network of personal contacts within a sector was explored by Grant, Paterson, and Whitston in their study of the chemical industry. They concluded that a 'policy community' had developed amongst public-affairs managers in the industry (1988: 204–5). While they found the propensity for differences of interests to be high, they suggested that the managers had developed shared values which they sought to defend. A similar pattern of relationships can be assumed in the motor industry where personnel meet regularly at motor shows, conferences, and so forth. Also, within Brussels itself, there exists a highly developed network of personal relationships between group secretariats and the staff in the various company offices. Lord Young's experiences tend to confirm this. His comment above was made after the Rover Group chairman had discovered that the Volkswagen chairman had made an informal overture to a junior trade minister about the possibility of purchasing the British company.

Participation in this type of network could also reflect the more calculated career ambitions of the personnel involved. Therefore the benefits of participation could be more marginal to the firm in some cases than they are for its public-affairs managers. This tends to support the behavioural model's distinction between company ownership and company management. While the owners (shareholders) may seek profit maximization, large companies are run by managers who will have a different set of goals. Simon (1958) has argued that managers will have a number of non-economic goals such as prestige, status, consolidation, and so forth. There may therefore be a push towards participation created by the desires of company management. Also, as MacMillan (1991) discovered, companies have had to be wary of personnel in their Brussels operations 'going native'. Thus, a system of shared values may develop amongst personnel in the policy community which do not necessarily correspond with the interests of the company. For this reason most of these Brussels operations are closely linked to the companies' national public-affairs divisions.

3.2 Non-EC Discussions

It should not be assumed that the sole business of the Euro-group is to interface with the Commission. Former British Leyland chief and CCMC president Sir Michael Edwardes recalls the group was at its most effective when representing the EC car-makers in negotiations with its Japanese counterpart. The harsh economic environment of the 1970s had contributed to an unprecedented decline in the European motor industry. Of increasing concern to all European producers at the time was the import penetration achieved by Japanese producers. In response to this, CCMC under Edwardes set up a series of high-level negotiations with the Japanese Association of Automobile Manufacturers (JAMA). CCMC had decided in the first instance to try and obtain a 'gentleman's agreement' with JAMA over the need for Japanese prudence before taking the matter up with the Commission. Though the negotiations broke down acrimoniously, Edwardes is in little doubt that CCMC's actions produced the desired outcome, 'their export drive gradually eased during 1981. I suspect that this was influenced by the often sharp exchange with CCMC and by the way in which the disparate personalities of the leaders of the European Industry complemented each other, showing a united front and lobbying their national governments' (Edwardes 1983: 273).

This was the Euro-group at its most effective, reaching a common position and binding its members to that position both within the group and in their national lobbying efforts. The importance of the issue undoubtedly pushed the group towards unity. However, as we shall see below, the industry was rarely able to achieve such internal cohesion as the 1980s progressed. This episode was very much the exception rather than the rule.

To summarize this first part of the chapter, it is clear that participation in the Euro-group can provide substantial benefits to members. These benefits may be the non-economic goals of status and prestige, or reflect a company desire to tap a potentially useful resource rather than the provision of collective goods. Participation of the 'good corporate citizen' type may be passive and token: active membership will be aggressive in pursuit of sectional and company ends. Therefore, activism becomes a key factor in analysing group participation.

4. THE COHESION ISSUE

The EC's accelerating political development in the 1980s has placed an increased demand on Euro-group functions. In its efforts to create a single market in vehicles the Commission has assumed increased responsibility for technical and environmental regulation of the sector, the regulation of financial assistance, and international trade. A member of the CCMC's Administrative Committee suggested to us that the group's internal decision-making structures became antiquated in the face of these developments. The group was apparently ill-equipped to respond to the Commission's demand for responses to proposals.

In the mid-1970s CCMC formed a political wing at the instigation of the Commission. It was not an original function. The Commission was attracted to the group because it represented all the European-owned producers and brought together their respective chairmen. Our original statutes were not designed to create cast-iron policy positions. As the push for harmonization started, most technical issues became political and we encountered enormous difficulties trying to achieve a common position within the voting system. (Interview, 15 Feb. 1991)

There is some evidence here that the Commission 'sponsored' internal changes in the group. The group represented a prestigious and potentially invaluable discussion partner. There is wider evidence that the Commission, like any bureaucracy, has attempted to organize or reorganize groups in a sector where the constituency lacks organization. For example, Cawson (1990) found that DG XIII had sponsored the establishment of the twelve-member Roundtable of the European Electronics Industry. This may overstate the Commission's ambitions, but we shall proceed with this assumption before considering the issue of sponsorship again later. Were CCMC and CLCA to have fulfilled roles as policy-formulators consistently, then they would have had to maintain a disciplined degree of internal cohesion. This is something they proved unable to do.

It is generally assumed that interest groups are out to secure benefits that will enhance the lot of their member companies. Sidjanski argued that

In principle, for a group to be able to act, it must have a clear view of the desired goal and it must be able to count on the support of its members . . . Indeed, the European organisation generally takes a confederal form, which provides the best guarantee for the protection of the particular interests of its members. And yet this confederal form acts as a brake on the efficient functioning of a European group; COPA, for instance, was paralysed during discussions of the question of the uniform price for lack of unanimity. (1967: 414)

In short, the group must know what it wants and be able to deliver this position. CCMC collapsed in late 1990 because it was unable to maintain internal consensus on major policy issues. We must be careful here not to over-generalize however. For example, Greenwood and Ronit (1991: 23–4) have suggested that a greater degree of cohesion had been achieved in the European pharmaceutical lobby. However, both of the car industry's Euro-groups suffered from the abiding weakness of such confederal organizations:

reconciling conflicting national and product interests without producing lowest common denominator policies. A comparative example
of the politics of relative strengths within a confederal body is the
contested process of change in the Confederal Council of Engineering Institutions in the 1970s (see Jordan 1992). Again, the issue was
that equal voting rights of members did not recognize the highly
unequal strengths of members.

This was a fundamental weakness in CLCA. The group was
composed of eight national trade associations. At this level it
encountered quite marked differences of interest reflecting different
industrial structures. For example the SMMT represented only a
small British-owned car industry, the American multinational
subsidiaries, and uniquely, Japanese car producers. Somewhat
inevitably this group's views clashed on a range of issues with
some of its sister federations. Most notably the French trade group
which was completely dominated by the two French-owned producers Renault and Peugeot. Both these companies were outspoken
critics of the British Government and the SMMT for allowing the
Japanese to establish car production inside Europe. In fact, clashes
of national economic interests over the Japanese presence in
Europe led to the bizarre circumstance where CLCA excluded the
issue from its discussions. One CLCA director told us: 'The Japanese presence in Britain undoubtedly influences the other members'
view of them. We do not even discuss the Japanese anymore. The
French and Italian spokesmen represent very important national
interests, they are simply not allowed to agree to anything' (Interview, 17 Jan. 1992). As a result of such divisions the group often
reached common positions so innocuous that they were of little use
to decision-makers.

Furthermore, the position adopted by each national group in
CLCA was itself a form of common denominator. (An obvious
exception would be the French and Italian groups which are dominated by their national manufacturers.) For instance, the SMMT
had fourteen vehicle-producing members which it represented at
CLCA meetings. This potentially disparate national membership
interest had all to be distilled into a common position within the
SMMT before being carried to Brussels (though we must be careful
not to over-exaggerate the frequency or nature of such differences).
At the European level this national denominator was likely to be
further altered during negotiations to achieve a common position

there. There is an obvious danger that the original position of any one firm is likely to have been diluted or altered beyond recognition during this process. It was precisely because of this dilution process in CLCA that EC car-makers formed CCMC in the early 1970s. Clearly, it would have been irrational for any company to rely on the CLCA as the main conduit for its views at the European level. Therefore companies are forced to adopt simultaneously Euro-group, national group, and DIY approaches. CCMC suffered from similar forms of impotence. The group's problems were compounded more than anything by its internal voting system. One participant in its administrative committee outlined the nature of the group's dilemma: 'It could have been quite an effective body. The difficulty was that the common denominator was dependent upon the unanimity rule. One extreme position tended to bring the system down' (Interview, 8 Mar. 1991).

These difficulties led to the group's collapse in November 1990. Throughout the autumn the secretariats of CCMC and CLCA had initiated several studies to revise the situation of dual representation and examine the need for a new organization. This would have entailed forming a new group from the antecedents of a narrower and much wider organization. Whilst CCMC excluded non-European members, the national trade groups in CLCA had among their members American, Japanese, and Swedish companies. These 'advanced' discussions were jeopardized at a Paris meeting of CCMC when the Peugeot-Citroën (PSA) president used his veto to prevent the group from adopting a system of qualified majority voting (requiring a 75 per cent threshold). The PSA group insisted that CCMC should retain the unanimity requirement. Following this veto, eleven of the other twelve member companies resigned *en bloc* from CCMC and it subsequently emerged that CCMC's members had become so disillusioned by the repeated use of the veto that they had anticipated the need to create a new group prior to this last incident. The use of the veto had prevented the group from taking a stance on a range of issues such as, Japanese imports, vehicle specifications, and environmental and safety regulations (*Financial Times*, 29 Nov. 1990).

This does lead us to an extra reason for participation in groups noted above. Group membership might be worthwhile in that participation in the group will provide an opportunity to veto proposals that might be disadvantageous for the member company. This does appear to be a possible motivation for larger firms with established bilateral contacts in Brussels.

Yet it appears that the principal motives behind the creation of a new unified group were the desires by some companies to allow the US multinationals full membership rights and, more importantly, to end the inefficiency that had accompanied dual representation. The existence of two lobbying groups had increasingly been seen as detrimental to the industry's relations with EC officials. The last Executive Secretary of CLCA (and holder of that position in the industry's new group) had lobbied vigorously within the sector for the creation of a new body. In his study of economic adjustments in the European motor industry, Wilks identified the CCMC as playing a marginal role in the process of restructuring the sector: 'On the grand issues of restructuring, however, the CCMC can simply register disagreements' (1990: 36–7). He further suggests that far-reaching reforms are needed to make the industry's lobby a 'more effective body', since the Commission regarded CCMC 'with a degree of derision'. A DG III official outlined the bureaucracy's frustration: 'The unanimity rule can be effective if it is handled with sufficient political skill . . . But they were unable to come up with anything meaningful on the major issues and we became exasperated'. (Interview, 24 July 1991)

Despite the group's waning reputation, the PSA president, M. Calvet, does not appear to have regarded CCMC as quite such a mechanism for policy-making. In fact both groups suffered because participating firms viewed them as merely one option in a multilateral lobbying strategy.

It is important here to stress the crucial role that is played by the group's secretariat. A further problem for CCMC was that several of its members felt that the group was too 'reactive', responding to issues after they had become a problem. Moreover, some car-makers felt that the secretariat had fallen too much under the influence of protectionist car-makers such as the PSA group (Interview information).

5. MULTIPLE STRATEGIES

Above it was noted that companies have favoured the adoption of multiple strategies in attempting to exert influence in Europe.

When Daimler-Benz opened their 'corporate representation' in Brussels they specifically argued, 'The Brussels corporate representation is a manifestation of the desire of Daimler-Benz advanced technology conglomerate to *use all possible channels* to foster the dialogue between the economy and politicians, against the background of growing economic integration and the creation of a single market in Europe' (1989: 27). They, somewhat ingeniously, argued, 'Quite clearly, this has nothing to do with what is usually known as "lobbying". It is much more a question of ensuring mutually advantageous cooperation between officials with their political duties and obligations and the company with its many years of experience' (1989: 27–8).

As long ago as 1977 Averyt set out the 'Orthodox Strategy' for a national interest group (see Fig. 7.1). This was an approach approved by the Commission in which Euro-groups co-ordinate the concerns of national interest groups. Averyt showed that the orthodox model had in fact been supplanted in agriculture by a 'national strategy' that saw national groups use their national governments as a conduit for their views (see Fig 7.2). This tendency for groups to use a national government strategy is not surprising. At the EC level, supreme decision-making power still resides in the Council of Ministers. One car-maker told us: 'If you lose something in the drafting process you go straight away to COREPER and the national department in a bid to build up some opposition there . . . Usually this means sending it back to the Commission for a review' (Interview, 22 July 1991). In addition, the Commission is generally dependent on the co-operation of national governments to implement its directives.

In at least one sense the EC has enhanced the tendencies for national policy communities between departments and domestic client groups. As this interviewee concedes, the national strategy is

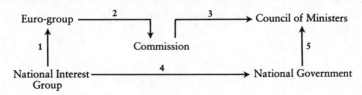

FIG. 7.1.   *Averyt's Orthodox Strategy*
Source: Averyt 1977: 102.

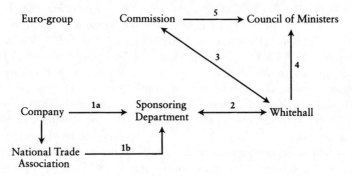

Fig. 7.2. *Averyt's National Strategy*
Source: Developed from Averyt 1977: 108.

mainly a defensive mechanism used to minimize losses incurred in the initial drafting process. The EC budget and legislative procedure is a joint target. Success will benefit the government and its partner groups. Therefore, groups will quite naturally seek to lobby via their established contacts at a national level in a bid to influence the government's position in relation to EC policy. Though this strategy is by no means foolproof—within the Council decisions are usually reached through a complex process of bargaining and trade-offs between Member States—it does reinforce the nation-state bargaining character of the EC (Jordan 1980). Clearly, national departments remain important allies for national groups in the European policy process (see also Chs. 1 and 2).

The degree to which groups can be over-dependent on the national strategy was illustrated during the proposed sale of the state-owned Rover Group to British Aerospace (BAe) in 1987. Under EC competition law the national department was obliged to inform DG IV (Competition) of the proposed terms of the sale. In this instance the Commission requested radical changes to the deal agreed between the government and the two companies. A BAe spokesman confirmed to us that during the EC's investigations the company relied solely on the national strategy. 'We dealt solely with HM Government and did not initiate or become involved in any discussions with the European Commission' (Interview, 21 Nov. 1990). In fact, the DTI had instructed the groups involved to allow them to handle the negotiations with the Commission via ˙

UKREP. The DTI minister responsible for negotiating the deal recalled in his memoirs just how frantic the government's efforts to gain EC approval for the deal had become. The DTI's Vehicles Division and UKREP were in almost daily contact with DG IV officials, the minister had six personal meetings with the Directorate Commissioner over a two-month period (over and above telephone conversations), and both the minister and the then Prime Minister, Mrs Thatcher, raised the issue with the President of the Commission, M. Delors. Despite these national efforts the original deal had to be substantially altered. Indeed, the conditions imposed by the EC proved so unacceptable to the groups involved that the government had to offer an eleventh hour package of financial 'sweeteners' to secure a deal. These too were discovered by the Commission and BAe was ordered to repay them (Lord Young, 1990: 296–302). However, BAe has since contested and won its opposition to the repayment in the European Court. Nevertheless, the episode highlighted a basic failure by the national groups involved and the government to fully comprehend the EC's political authority in this area.

Despite the prevalent use of a 'national strategy', Averyt's 'orthodox strategy' does imply that a particular company will attempt to advance its interests in Euro-groups of companies such as CCMC or a Euro-federation of national interest groups such as CLCA. But the sorts of positions a company might favour are not by any means areas where there will be a collective interest among the members. For example, we saw earlier that CCMC's Technical Committees were regarded as the group's main area of strength, yet two detailed analyses of the EC's attempts to set engine emission standards—the largest single area of EC technical regulations—indicated that CCMC's role in the policy process was no more than marginal (Turner 1988; Arp 1990).

Both studies showed that at each stage of the policy negotiations between 1985–90, the car industry's lobby was fragmented along nationalistic and product lines. Moreover, the issue was of substantial political significance in a number of EC Member States whose governments adopted very strong positions. As a result of these national priorities and divisions within CCMC itself, the group's role in the policy process was greatly diminished. National groups concentrated on national strategies and the issues were largely resolved after lengthy negotiations in the Council of Ministers. Arp suggests that the outstanding issue of small car standards was finally resolved in 1989 partly because those firms most affected— PSA, Renault, and Fiat—failed to secure intra-industry solidarity for their opposition. He concluded:

Although an industry-wide 'common denominator' existed (most firms were opposed to further regulations) manufacturers were affected in different ways by regulation-induced changes, and their responses to proposed standards varied accordingly. Individual car companies targeted their national governments to ward off damage to their interests, and the Governments brought these interests to bear in the EC framework. (1990: 31)

The use of multiple strategies by companies and national groups, which produces a much more complex environment for the Commission, has made the task of policy formulation more difficult for EC decision-makers to 'manage'. This has been illustrated during recent efforts to formulate an EC policy on Japanese car imports. It is important to note that in attempting to develop an EC policy, officials have been constrained by their negotiations with the Japanese Government and JAMA. Indeed, the EC's Japanese policy has been negotiated through the External Affairs Directorate-General and not DG III. In addition, the Japanese producers also export vehicles to the EC from their American plants and both the US Government and US groups participated in the debate at various stages. However, although the Commission did not have to cope with non-EC lobbying, it faced greater difficulties trying to agree a common policy with the European industry as CCMC was unable to present such a coherent view. The Japanese issue saw the industry's lobby fragmented as a result of different national and product interests. Once again these interests were influenced by differences between national policies on the same issue. In June of 1990 the Commission reached a preliminary agreement with MITI. This entailed the Japanese continuing to implement a policy of self-prudence on a common export restraint. National governments would also monitor this for their own national markets over an agreed five-year period. These proposals met with opposition from a number of leading manufacturers.

Again the most outspoken critic was the PSA group which had been excluded from the June negotiations between the Commission and the car-makers apparently because of the intransigence of their position (*Financial Times*, 3 Oct. 1990). In a vitriolic speech to the

Paris motor show the PSA president described Britain as 'a Japanese aircraft carrier just off the coast of Europe'. He went on to highlight the pressures that Japanese successes in the American market had placed on indigenous producers there (*Independent*, 3 Oct. 1990). M. Calvet, presenting the group's own more protectionist policy document, demanded the suspension of talks between Brussels and Tokyo until the Europeans had debated the issue more fully. The incident demonstrated a willingness on the part of a large company to carry its position directly to the Commission. But, although the PSA group's position was the most extreme, general opposition from the other producers to the June proposals brought the negotiations to a standstill.

Faced with this problem the Commission formally extended its consultations to bilateral dealings with selected companies. The four largest European-owned manufacturers—PSA, Renault, Fiat, and Volkswagen-Seat—were invited in late September to submit joint proposals on the issue. In the event, the paper which was submitted in December 1990 was not signed by PSA who felt it was not stringent enough. The group, known as the 'European Generalists', suggested similar measures (albeit diluted) to those of PSA. Most notably, they demanded reciprocal access to Japanese markets and the maintenance of restrictions for a ten-year period and not five as the Commission had suggested. The Fiat president Umberto Agnelli stressed: 'It is impossible to think of less than ten years as the period we need to acquire technological credibility' (*Financial Times*, 3 Dec. 1990).

The intractability of this issue illustrates the complexity of the consultation process when it extends beyond Euro-groups to bilateral contacts. This perhaps helps to explain the Commission's general preference to consult via Euro-groups. The failure of CCMC to produce a position led to the resultant consultation cacophony and officials proceeded no further with the issue in 1990. But though the Commission might have preferred the 'Orthodox Strategy'—confirming as it does a sort of Euro-consciousness—and simplifying the administrative task by building up strong authoritative umbrella groups at the European level—the national strategy and use of bilateral contacts appears to have been resilient. Moreover, the use of bilateral channels appears, in this sector at least, to have become an accepted part of the consultation process.

Eight European car-makers have opened Brussels offices with the main intention of developing personal links to policy development. This is practical because on some issues such as state aids there will be no group discussion of individual cases—such sensitive issues are simply kept off the group's agenda. But clearly companies have utilized direct contacts on a number of broader issues such as engine emissions. Though most groups realize the need to use these contacts discreetly and sparingly, such is the importance of EC decisions that where debate in the group has gone against a company, they have not felt sufficiently constrained to accept the collective view. The policy network has not assumed the cohesiveness or stability normally associated with a national 'policy community'. Furthermore, it is also clear that where the Commission is sceptical of a group view, it will often test that position by seeking the opinions of individual group members. Almost against their will the officials have had to accept the limitations of the Euro-group and the need for a more complex consultation process.

6. EURO-GROUP REORGANIZATIONS

In February of 1991 the car industry finally agreed upon the statutes for a new unified industry representation: the Association of European Automobile Constructors (ACEA). The new group has adopted two major differences in internal structure from either of its predecessors. It has extended its membership to include the American and Swedish manufacturers—but not the Japanese—and it has adopted a system of majority voting. It also has more resources than either of its predecessors with a full-time staff of eighteen personnel (see Appendix 1).

We might identify four motivations for extending the membership of the industry's lobby group. First, the legitimacy of the CCMC was always affected by the fact that it did not represent Europe's third and fourth largest car producers. Between them Ford and General Motors account for over one-quarter of the EC car market. Therefore EC officials invariably had to conduct bilateral consultations with these firms over and above anything agreed with CCMC. Secondly, there was support within the industry for inviting the American and Swedish firms to join. Throughout 1990, CCMC's German members made proposals to this end. One industry official told us: 'We felt that it was divisive and unhelpful not to incorporate the Americans into our decisions . . . After all, most of us had worked with them at a national level for years' (Interview, 17 Jan. 1991). Thirdly, the lobbying resources of both multinationals made them attractive to the reformed lobby. For example, Ford and GM, as well as having their own well-staffed offices in Brussels, are members of three national trade groups, allowing them to deploy three national-level strategies, and are active members in a network of American business groups in Brussels, e.g. the American Chamber of Commerce. Such resources are important, since as Mazey and Richardson (Ch. 1) reveal, the open nature of the EC bureaucracy and the unpredictability of the EC political agenda means that those groups which wish to keep abreast of developments must commit an often prohibitive level of resources to monitoring. This tends to confirm Mazey and Richardson's point that American groups are amongst the most effective lobbyists in Brussels. This fortification of the Americans' lobbying operations in Brussels was encouraged from an early stage by their exclusion from several Euro-groups (see Bates 1990). Finally, the Americans managed to negate their exclusion from CCMC to some extent by becoming particularly active in CLCA. By utilizing their membership of several national trade groups and by establishing close links with CLCA's secretariat the Americans became the federations' most active members (Interview information, 23 July 1991). But, as we have seen, the representation of company interests via CLCA was far from ideal and it too was often paralysed by sensitive issues. In an internal document dated November 1990 GM noted: 'The (CCMC's) uncompromising stance [on US membership] has been softened and on several *non sensitive* issues such as transport policy and recycling, joint CCMC–CLCA work groups have been established' (1990: 3).

Earlier we suggested that participation in the Euro-group provided the opportunity for an active member to veto from within. However the repeated use of the veto frustrated some CCMC members to the point of resigning from the group. ACEA has adopted a majority voting system requiring a 75 per cent threshold with decisions reached on a one member one vote basis. Though its members insist that the new group will continue to strive for unanimity, we shall proceed on the assumption that the move is intended to improve the decision-making capabilities of the lobby.

Our working assumption is that a body with a majority voting system would be better able to avoid lowest common denominator responses and thus be able to engage in a higher level of policy-making dialogue with the Commission. But at the same time an organization that too regularly goes against even a minority of the membership will develop internal pressures. For cohesion there has to be a political skill to keep disgruntled members 'in' with the promise of long-term benefits that will balance temporary disappointments. Therefore a lack of political skill on the part of the group activists could rupture the federation. This is partly what happened when Peugeot's repeated use of the veto led to eleven of the CCMC's twelve members resigning from the group. Here again the role of the group secretariat can be significant. They will have the responsibility for drafting policy papers prior to a meeting and often face the delicate task of balancing competing member interests. But it is important to stress that the group generally goes to extraordinary lengths to avoid having to take a vote at all, in a bid to avoid such internal frictions. For example, ACEA has yet to use the new majority system. Indeed the group's Executive Secretary stressed that the system is only seen as a 'disciplinary instrument' should the need arise (Interview, 26 July 1991). There might also be some special characteristics of the policy area. Are the problems 'zero-sum' with 'winners' and 'losers' or can all participants be 'paid off'? There often needs to be a policy of self-denial in which groups informally agree not to examine policies whose review is bound to be divisive—but for some groups to do so in their particular circumstances would be to opt out of the game.

Within ACEA, voting power resides with the fifteen member companies in the Board of Directors (see Appendix 1) and there has been a marginalization of the role of trade associations. The distinctive characteristics of CLCA as the peak association of such groups has been all but subsumed in the new structure. The new group's Liaison Committee is in fact the CLCA in miniature. Its members are the eight national trade groups but it has no voting power and can only make an input into working groups when invited to do so. One ACEA member indicated that the group would cater more for company views than those of national groups when he outlined the ambitions for the new organization:

It will be responsible for primary interfacing with the Commission. The more success it has here the more encouragement there is for producers to use it as their main route to Brussels. We felt it was time to establish a group that matched our economic status . . . Within this new approach the trade associations will increasingly be tied to dealing with local conditions. (Interview, 8 Mar. 1991)

Therefore the individual firms are the decision-takers. If some semblance of consensus could be maintained within the new group it would clearly be an important 'discussion partner' for the Commission. Clearly, the European industry remains unwilling to allow the Japanese any direct participation in decision-making. Though the Japanese remain outsiders, this exclusion is only likely to lead them to fortify their own lobbying operations in the EC. JAMA already has an office there and along with the individual companies they have over 120 officials working in Brussels. (Interview information, 24 July 1991.)

As we saw earlier, the trade groups tended to present a very diluted view of the specific company interest. Though the development of these company-specific 'clubs' at the European level will present the Commission with a much more complex map of groups, the orthodox expectation of group aggregation through a European federation of national federations has often proved to founder on the breadth of the business to be discussed (leading to elaborate internal specialization) and national disconsensus.

ACEA has commenced lobbying on behalf of the industry almost immediately. Recent examples of its activities include a high-profile initiative on the issue of automotive waste management including proposals for the recycling of car plastics. ACEA has submitted several draft recommendations (including a transcript policy) advocating a system of recovery of used plastic parts and continued research into the problem. This reflects the concerns of the new group to adopt a higher EC lobbying profile and to be more proactive than CCMC. The *European Report* (25 May 1991) reported: 'ACEA underscored that car makers are capable, through self-regulation, of finding a solution for the recycling of plastic parts, as they did for metal parts, provided that the research is not nipped in the bud by EC regulations'.

ACEA's attempts to draft constructive policies does correspond closely with the process of 'looking for partners' which Hull described earlier. Indeed, one Commission official told us he was 'taken aback' by ACEA's initiative on the recycling issue, since DG XI had not even begun to draft proposals on the subject (Inter-

view, 23 July 1991). However, the group's most significant achievement to date has been on the vexed issue of Japanese imports. One
British official described it to us as the 'classic example of an issue
that cannot be Europeanized' (Interview, 14 Jan. 1991). A CCMC
member also described to us how efforts to reach a position on the
issue broke down within the group.

Within CCMC we needed to establish core positions around which
national positions could be accommodated. If the group ever achieved a
core position it gave the Commission some comfort. They expect the
group's members to carry that core view back to their national governments. The Japanese issue is an example where we could not develop a
workable core view. When that happens it makes life very difficult for the
Commission. (Interview, 8 Mar. 1991)

Yet, within two weeks of its formation ACEA produced a united
policy paper on this seemingly intractable issue. Clearly the new
organization was an expression of a pre-negotiated position on
Japan. It did not decide a policy on Japanese imports: its creation
furthered a pre-agreed position.

The ACEA document reflected a compromise between the Commission's position and that of the 'European Generalists'. The
manufacturers retained their requests for continuing national controls and reciprocal access to Japanese markets. However, they
compromised in three important areas. First, they increased from
10 per cent to 15 per cent the EC market share they felt that the
Japanese should be 'allowed' during a transitional period. Secondly, they reduced their demands for a ten-year transitional
period to seven years (the Commission had been insisting on only
five years in its June 1990 proposals). Thirdly, and for the first
time either jointly or individually the producers accepted in principle that the market should be completely free of restrictions after a
transitional period. The document also requested that any growth
or downturn in the EC market should be shared by 'agreed principles' between Japanese and European producers (*Financial Times*,
21 Mar. 1991). The document provided an early indication that
ACEA had overcome some of the disorganized inertia that had
afflicted CCMC. As one ACEA member put it: 'We succeeded in
moving away from the lowest common denominator towards a
policy package which accommodated the various industry positions' (Interview, 24 July 1991).

However, this was undoubtedly facilitated by the decision of the PSA group, not to participate in the new group. It had been PSA's intention to pursue a more protectionist policy via national channels. However, this appeared to be undermined when the French Government publicly supported the ACEA position on the eve of a Council of Ministers session to discuss the issue. The French industry minister commented, 'I hope the Commission will agree on a proposal not much different from what the European car producers have put forward'. (*Financial Times*, 30 Apr. 1991)

The policy finally agreed between the EC and MITI in late July of 1991 corresponded very closely to the main elements of the ACEA document. The transitional period was agreed at seven years and Japanese EC market share should only increase from 12 per cent in 1991 to 16 per cent by 1999. Moreover, the agreement allowed the more protected EC car markets gradually to expose their domestic industries to greater Japanese competition by informally implementing sub-ceilings. The EC and MITI have agreed to discuss the issue formally every six months and, in addition, the situation will be reviewed following a downturn or an upturn in the EC market (for full details, see *Financial Times*, 2 Aug. 1991). However, in a reflection of the problems officials have encountered gaining a consensus, the fine detail is highly complex and the document is characterized by opaque language, inexactitudes, and discretionary powers. Thus, the policy—aptly entitled 'Elements of a Consensus'—is characterized by differentiation and the continuing recognition of the need for diversity of practice between Member States. In this sense, it is typical of the trend in EC policy-making identified by Kastendiek (1990: 77), which saw officials make strenuous efforts to ensure co-operation in policy development rather than pursue full integration and the attendant risks of national disconsensus.

The most significant difference between ACEA's position and the final agreement is over the question of Japanese transplants in the EC. The EC had been under intense lobbying from the UK Government to provide guarantees that cars from British transplants were granted free circulation in the EC. Despite opposition from other EC states and ACEA's suggestion that transplants be included in the overall quota, the Commission has met the UK Government's demands—but in a roundabout fashion. In order to partly meet the concerns of the UK Government, the Commission, to the dismay of the Japanese producers, has reduced the increase in direct Japanese imports in the next seven years to a trickle. By not directly limiting transplant production the policy is also pragmatic, insomuch that it keeps production in the EC. Nevertheless, the British success on this vital issue is further evidence of the continued importance of nation-state bargaining in the EC policy process.

But clearly, the Commission has also gone to considerable lengths to negotiate a policy that reflects the positions eventually agreed by the industry in ACEA. In this instance, the agreement of a policy in the group arena was crucial to the resolution of the issue. Thus, companies may now be seeking more from the Euro-group than its monitoring functions and the fraternal benefits outlined at the outset. If these were principal motivations for reorganization, they do suggest a major non-Olson argument for participation in the Euro-group. Whereas Olson suggests that an individual company can rationally decide to free ride and obtain the benefits of collective action, our perspective emphasizes that the acceptability of the outcome cannot be assumed: the company must be active in the group to ensure that the destination is acceptable. A free rider cannot expect to steer the vehicle.

In this respect, the non-participation of the PSA group in ACEA is somewhat irrational given the potential losses involved. Even within a majority voting system the potential for partial veto exists. For instance, a coalition of four members would be sufficient to prevent ACEA's 75 per cent threshold being reached. Therefore group membership makes sense not because it helps ensure the adoption of policy by the EC but because it helps shape the policy demand by the group and it helps inform a sympathetic bureaucracy of specific needs. Since it has not joined ACEA, Peugeot may have decided to pursue its lobbying via alternative channels. However, while other options exist, our emphasis would be that there is no adequate substitute for participation in the sectoral group. Not to participate in the group is to discard one of the cards and such is the importance of the issues at stake to company interests that such a strategy would involve unwelcome risks. In fact, it appears that Peugeot's continued non-participation has been caused by the dogmatic views of M. Calvet who opposed the creation of ACEA, rather than a failure to realize the group's importance.

Finally, Olson and other collective-action theorists assume that demands by groups are self-evident. This may be true for some kinds of cause groups; one will join them or join some other group. But for business groups there tends to be only one group to join hence it is vital that it is not allowed to ignore the special interests of the company in these circumstances. Thus, even a multinational such as Ford with a well-developed lobbying facility of its own, cannot afford the potential risks of non-participation in the Euro-group.

This point is itself perhaps artificial and theoretical where it assumes that companies have positions that they wish to advance. For example, in 1984 a House of Lords Select Committee scrutinizing EC efforts to harmonize EC car prices was told by the SMMT president that the group's position had been derived from that of the Euro-group. CLCA and CCMC had prepared a joint paper which specifically questioned the Commission's legal authority to regulate prices. In their evidence to the committee SMMT stressed the importance of these legal arguments. The SMMT president told the Lords: 'I think our stance is being taken quite clearly, and it has come straight out of the CLCA document, that we believe it is not the business of the Commission to try to impose a price clause and a price regulation on a competitive industry' (HL 302 1984, para. 37, p. 61). Thus in real life the company may use the group view to help define its own position: in other words membership allocates attitudes rather than reflects them (see Bauer, de Sola Pool, and Dexter 1964: 398).

7. THE EURO-GROUP AS POLICY-MAKER

Empirical studies have shown that participation in groups is not governed by the sort of mercenary calculation that Olson believed to underpin rational action. For instance, Marsh (1976) concluded that because the cost of membership is relatively low, medium and large firms spend little time considering membership as an issue. We have argued that a concentration on subscriptions would also misjudge the real costs of participating in Euro-groups. What perhaps needs to be clarified is the degree to which participation is governed by the motivation to be part of a coherent policy-making federation.

As we saw earlier, during recent negotiations on the issue of

Japanese imports the Commission bilaterally consulted four manufacturers. Their consultations in this instance were clearly skewed towards the large European-owned car companies. One legislative affairs executive of a small car company told us that his group envisaged ACEA as their primary route into the EC bureaucracy. If the consultation process is skewed in the above manner, then this firm's strategy is quite rational. However, we might question whether the large firms—the 'European Generalists'—with greater access to decision-makers view the Euro-group in quite such a central role. Critical mass is perhaps an even more important factor at the EC level than it is nationally. Thus, small European car firms such as Rover and Jaguar who enjoy direct access to national officials—notably the DTI's and the DTp's respective vehicles divisions—may be minor actors in the pan-European consultation process. Greenwood and Ronit suggest that 'for the European bureaucracy, there may be a preference, where individual liaison is necessary, to relate to firms which have experience in operating in politico-economic environments in a number of EC states' (1991: 22). This implicitly suggests large European firms and multinationals. Small and large firms may therefore view certain Euro-group functions with different degrees of emphasis. This is certainly the case in terms of the monitoring function. Large firms have far more substantial lobbying resources at the EC level. For example, BMW, Daimler, Ford, Fiat, General Motors, Peugeot, and Renault–AB Volvo all have Brussels offices. Over four years ago Grant suggested that running such an operation cost in the region of £100,000 per annum (Grant and Sargent 1987). These operations attach a high priority to developing and maintaining personal contacts in the small bureaucracy. Therefore it would appear that larger firms are less dependent on the services of the Euro-group. Also, for multi-product companies like Daimler-Benz, there is no group that can adequately cover all their product interests and it has been essential to develop sophisticated in-house operations.

How then can all this be reconciled with attempts in the motor industry to improve the internal policy process of the Euro-group? On some issues group members will see benefits in speaking with a collective voice in the hope that the Commission will 'buy' the argument. For example, with the Japanese issue now resolved, ACEA is focusing its lobbying activities on the so-called 'Volet Interne', which will identify areas where the Commission can assist the industry with its restructuring efforts during the transitional period, e.g. R & D, regional aid, etc. This will be the subject of a forthcoming ACEA submission to the Commission. But also, while larger firms such as ICI, Fiat, and Volkswagen realize a need to create groups better placed to respond to EC developments with common positions, we should not assume these efforts signify a major shift in strategy. Empirical evidence clearly indicates that companies do seek to represent their interests via alternative channels. Therefore companies participate in umbrella groups that might be dominated by conflicting interests for two main reasons:

1. the group is one option (albeit an important one) in an overall lobby strategy: efforts in the Euro-group can always be supplanted by bilateral contacts and national strategy;
2. active participation in a group is necessary to prevent the group from pursuing unwelcome policies.

This is particularly the case when it is the Commission which is very often in the market for ideas. There is universal consensus in the literature that the Commission prefers to work via such groups. Thus there is a functional logic of consultation (Jordan and Richardson 1983: 259) from the perspective of the European bureaucracy but national interests have a choice of strategy to adopt. Companies do perceive a sense of efficacy in the Euro-group, but it is evident that Euro-groups are weakened because their members sometimes prefer to concentrate on national strategies. Very often this results from irreconcilable national interests. Indeed Mazey and Richardson remind us: 'one should not underestimate the enduring strength of nationalist sentiments and their capacity to undermine the formulation of stable transnational policy communities'. (1990: 10)

8. WAS OLSON RIGHT FOR THE WRONG REASONS?

A basic Olsonian model would suggest that in the absence of selective incentives, there is no reason to suppose that interests shared by a number of rational companies will be organized politically. The costs to one actor of working to establish an organized group may be greater than the benefits perceived by the actor from the organization of that interest. This balance may be reversed if the organized group offers selective incentives over and above the generally shared interest. If the group does not do so, there is an incentive for the individual actor to free ride. However, Olson's premises concerning the under-mobilization of group activity can be countered by a series of ideas.

1. As he argued, there are selective benefits in membership.

2. The mechanistic link between the level of subscription and degree of success that permeates Olson's approach is inappropriate. Subscriptions are a gamble about future needs not a calculation about known costs and benefits.

3. Potential members have a 'bounded' rather than 'pure' rationality (Moe 1980). The fact that the companies feel membership is rational makes it rational to join. Thus, Koutsoyannis (following Simon) has argued, 'Some objectives (of the company) may even take the form of wishful thinking, that is, they are unquantifiable goals, of a non operational form; for example, the goal of "serving best the public", or "keeping a good public image", or being "progressive" and "pioneering" and so on' (1985: 389). If companies are constrained by a sense of participation because they wish to be 'a good corporate citizen' it is rational to respond to that non-economic incentive.

4. Olson's approach is based on individual membership as a central model. The logic for a company may be different. Walker (1983) shows that many US groups are dependent on patronage rather than individual subscriptions.

5. Euro-groups might be 'permitted' by Olson in his (vague) account of the logic of small number groups where in special circumstances, he says, 'in some small groups . . . There are members who would be better off if the collective good were provided, even if they had to pay the entire cost of providing it themselves, than they would if it were not provided' (1965: 34).

6. Olson defines a selective incentive as 'selective' only to those in the organization (1965: 51). He discusses negative and positive incentives. We are underlining that a negative selective incentive is that non-participation can produce unwelcome group decisions. Participation in the definition of the collective demand is a selective benefit. Olson sees selective benefits as less necessary for small groups (1965: 134), but we are arguing that it is the selective benefit that is particularly viable in the small group setting where the effects of participation are more obvious.

7. Olson presents lobbying as a cost-sensitive issue but companies might themselves see it as a profit-centre activity. In other words, the benefits are not fixed but can be increased.

Moreover, it is argued that Olson neglects the atmosphere of modern policy-making that sees policy development in group/bureaucratic networks as normal and necessary. Olson misunderstands the nature of the outputs required by business concerns. It is not just the big collective good that can be delivered to the free rider but marginal changes of policy that can be best put on the agenda by the active company. This, and the encouragement given to groups by clientelistic DGs, perhaps accounts for the proliferation of group activity that challenges Olson's conventional wisdom of low mobilization. And yet, there is the contradictory conventional wisdom of group weakness that seems more compatible with Olson. The underfed 'Euro fed' seems a common species.

Our argument is to try to redefine and redraw the relationship between interests and the policy-making process. The impression given by Olson is that the group puts forward agreed collective demands to a bureaucracy which will then 'buy' the argument if the pressure is sufficient. If instead the group activity is put in a less formal policy-making context in which the bureaucracy (relevant Directorate-General) is engaged in constant marginal (and less often radical) policy adjustments, then the need to be in the group is enhanced. The bureaucracy will want to make use of group resources. It is looking for partners not opponents. It is not 'safe' to allow that group/bureaucratic process to run on uninfluenced: it might decided on outputs which in their particulars do not suit the potential member.

Participation in the group is one means to participate in the policy network which will attempt to make policy. It is not sensible to free ride because the collective benefits might be unacceptable. The group cannot be relied upon to seek acceptable benefits without 'inside steering'. In this light the participation in the group is quite compatible with participation nationally or on a bilateral basis with the Commission. Each avenue of influence will be utilized: not to do so would be to throw away a potential advantage.

None the less participation in the Euro-group often appears tokenistic—a 'Just Enough' membership. Subscriptions are generally low given the consequences of possible policy changes. We do not think at these levels of cost there is much by way of cost/benefit analysis of membership by larger firms. They can, however, perform a second calculation about level of activity. The costs of active membership (travel, executive time) are much larger than subscription costs. It is perhaps at this level of participation that cost may become a significant factor in its own right. Thus it is likely that companies will use the level of activity as a reflection of the potential reward of membership.

Arguably, the Euro-group weakness does not stem from interests economizing on representation but from the intra-organizational political difficulties. Groups often become paralysed because they cannot maintain internal consensus amongst conflicting interests. If we see a weakness in the volume and the quality of Euro-organization the flaw seems to lie in this area rather than in the Olson-type pronouncement. This study suggests that the fundamental weakness of groups in Europe is that members are unsure about the process of aggregating their interests rather than that they fail to participate in a belief that they should free ride. Thus, individual members may alternatively participate in specialist groups where the problem of agreement is simplified. For example, GM may act via the American Chamber of Commerce if a specific American interest is involved. Or alternatively, companies will initiate their own efforts through in-house staff or commercial consultants.

Finally, from the top down we can identify a central problem in the EC bureaucracy's consultation process. The Commission goes to extraordinary lengths to establish constituencies of Euro-groups around each Directorate-General—practically 'sponsoring' their formation. These groups occupy a potentially pivotal role in the EC policy process. They are the bridge between the agency and the regulated. Clearly the structure of the bridge is, in most cases, too weak to support the volume of traffic passing over it. Consultation will often break down along nationalist and product lines, group cohesion is lost, and the dominant mode of contact can become bilateral. Thus, to echo a point made earlier, while the Commission is drawn into a quasi-clientelistic 'dependency' relationship with the Euro-group, most group members view the group as merely one option in a multilateral lobbying strategy.

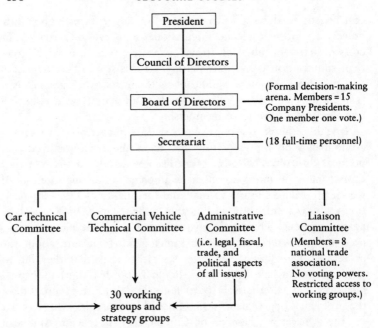

FIG. 7.3. *ACEA Internal Structure*

Appendix 1

CLCA Membership (National Trade Groups)

ANFAC (Spain), ANFIA (Italy), BIL (Sweden), CCFA (France), FEBIAC (Belgium), RAI (Netherlands), SMMT (United Kingdom), and VDA (Germany)

CCMC Membership (National Companies)

France: PSA Group, Renault (RNUR); Germany: BMW, Daimler-Benz, MAN, Porsche, Volkswagen-Seat; United Kingdom: Rover Group, Rolls-Royce Motor Cars; Italy: Fiat; The Netherlands: DAF, Volvo BV.

ACEA Membership (Companies)

Renault, BMW, Daimler-Benz, Fiat, MAN, Porsche, Volkswagen, Rover Group, Rolls-Royce Motor Cars, DAF, Volvo Car BV, General Motors Europe, Ford Europe, AB-Volvo, Saab-Scania

Notes

The authors are members of the ESRC–funded 'British Interest Group' project at the University of Aberdeen. The authors are grateful to members of the European motor industry and the European Commission for their co-operation throughout the research and for their comments on earlier drafts of this paper. In particular Mr D. C. Lindley (Rover), Dr H. Glatz (Daimler-Benz), and Mr. R. Beger (ACEA).

References

Arp. H. (1991), 'Interest Groups in EC Legislation: The Case of Car Emission Standards', a paper prepared for presentation to the workshop on 'European Lobbying towards the Year 2000' at the ECPR joint sessions, University of Essex, 22–28 Mar. 1991.

Averyt, W. F. (1975), 'Euro-Groups, Clientela, and the European Community', *International Organisation*, 29: 948–72.

——(1977), Agropolitics in the European Community (London: Praeger).

Bates, E. J. (1990), 'Outsiders Inside', *European Management Journal*, 8/4: 526–8.

Bauer, R.A., de Sola Pool, I., and Dexter, L. A. (1964), *American Business and Public Policy* (New York: Atherton Press).

BEUC, 'EEC Study on Car Prices and Progress Towards 1992', BEUC/10/89, a report prepared for the Directorate-General for the Environment, Consumer Protection, and Nuclear Safety.

Cawson, A. (1990), 'Modes of Policy-Making and Patterns of State/Interest Group Relationships: The EC, 1992 and the Consumer Electronics Industry', a paper prepared for presentation at the 'New Europe' conference of the ECPR, Rimini, Italy, 26–29 Sept. 1990.

CCMC (1990), *Objectives, Structure and Operation* (Brussels: CCMC).

CLCA (1990), *Activities Report* (Brussels: CLCA).

Cyert, R. M., and March, J. G. (1955), 'Organisation, Structure, and Pricing Behaviour in an Oligopolistic Market', *American Economic Review*, 45 (Mar.): 129–34.

Daimler-Benz (1989), *Towards a New Horizon* (Brussels: Daimler-Benz, no. 1).

EATP (1990), *Poly-News* (Paris: EATP, no. 1).

Edwardes, M. (1983), *Back from the Brink: . . . an Apocalyptic Experience* (London: Collins).

GM (General Motors) (1990), *Government Relations Brief* (Brussels: Nov.)

——(1991), Government Relations Brief (Brussels: July).

Grant, W., with Sargent, Jane (1987), *Business and Politics in Britain* (London: Macmillan Educational).

——Paterson, W., and Whitston, C. (1988), *Government and the Chemical Industry: A Comparative Study of Britain and West Germany* (Oxford: Clarendon Press).

Greenwood, J., with Ronit, K. (1991), 'Organized Interests and the New Transitional Challenge: Europe and the Associated Dimension', a paper presented to the Politics/Business panel at the XVth colloquium of the International Political Science Association, Buenos Aires, 21–25 July 1991.

House of Lords Select Committee on the European Communities 27th Report, *The Distribution, Servicing and Pricing of Motor Vehicles*, HL 302 session 1983–4 (HMSO).

Jordan, A. G. (1980), 'Scottish Local Government in Europe', in C. Archer and J. Main (eds.), *Scotland's Voice in International Affairs* (Hurst/McGill Queens/RIIA; Oxford: Clarendon Press).

——and Richardson, J. J. (1982), 'The British Policy Style or the Logic of Negotiation?', in J. J. Richardson (ed.), *Policy Styles in Western Europe* (London: Allen & Unwin), 80–110.

——(1983), 'Overcrowded Policy-Making: Some British and European Reflections', *Policy Sciences*, 15: 247–68.

——(1992), *Engineers and Professional Self-Regulation* (Oxford: Clarendon Press).

Kastendiek, H. (1990), 'Convergence or a Persistent Diversity of National Politics?', *Political Quarterly*, Special edn.: 'The Politics of 1992'.

Kirchner, E., and Schwaiger, K. (1981), *The Role of Interest Groups in the European Community* (Farnborough: Gower).

Koutsoyannis, Anna (1985), *Modern Microeconomics* (London: MacMillan Educational).

Lord Young of Graffam (1990), *The Enterprise Years: A Businessman in the Cabinet* (London: Headline).

MacMillan, K. (1991), 'The Management of European Public Affairs', a paper prepared for presentation to an ECPA/Conference Board Meeting, Brussels, 30–31 May 1991.

Marsh, D. (1976), 'On Joining Interest Groups: An Empirical Consideration of the Works of Mancur Olson', *British Journal of Political Science*, 6: 257–72.

Mazey, Sonia, and Richardson, J. J. (1990), *British Pressure Groups in the EC: Changing Lobbying Styles?* (London: Brunel Papers in Government).

Moe, T. M. (1980), *The Organization of Interests: Incentives and the Internal Dynamics of Political Interest Groups* (Chicago, Ill.: Chicago University Press).

Olson, M. (1965), *The Logic of Collective Action* (Cambridge, Mass.: Harvard University Press).

Peters, G. (1977), 'Insiders and Outsiders: The Politics of Pressure Group Influence on Bureaucracy', *Administration and Society*, 9/2: 191–218.

Pryce, R. (1973), *The Politics of the European Community* (London: Butterworths).

Sargent, Jane (1987), 'The Organization of Business Interests for European Community Representation', in Grant and Sargent (1987), 213–35.

Schmitter, P. (1990), 'Organised Interests and the Europe of 1992', unpublished paper.

Sidjanski, Dusan (1967), 'Pressure Groups and the European Economic Community', *Government and Opposition*, 2: 397–416.

Simon, H. A. (1961), *Administrative Behaviour: A Study of Decision-Making Processes in Administrative Organisations* (New York: Macmillan, 2nd edn.).

Turner, I. (1988), 'Environmental Policy in Europe: Uniformity or Diversity: A Case Study of the EEC Car Emissions Decisions', Cambridge, CEED Division Paper No. 7.

Walker, J. L. (1983), 'The Origins and Maintenance of Interest Groups in America', *American Political Science Review*, 390–405.

Wilks, S. (1990), *Restructuring of the European Motor Industry in the 1990s* (Research Unit for the International Study of Economic Liberalisation, University of Exeter).

8

Groups and the Process of European Integration: The Work of the Federation of Stock Exchanges in the European Community

JEFFREY KNIGHT, SONIA MAZEY, AND
JEREMY RICHARDSON

1. INTRODUCTION

Elsewhere in this volume (Ch. 1) it was argued that there is an inherent 'logic' which drives the European Commission to consult Euro-groups and to attempt to integrate them into the policy process within the Community. It was also argued that there are inherent weaknesses in the organization and structure of Euro-groups. These weaknesses force the Commission, despite its 'procedural ambition' (Jordan and Richardson 1982: 80) of managing the consultation process via Euro-Groups, to consult national associations and individual firms directly, thereby undermining the work of Euro-groups. At least two fundamental problems face Euro-groups. First, the structure and organization of particular industries may differ markedly cross-nationally, producing different representative institutions and different relationships with national governments. Secondly, competitive forces (often encouraged by recent national and Euro-legislation) set practical limits to the degree of co-operation that can be achieved at the European level. The integrative processes set in train by the Single European Act may themselves render the formation of Euro-groups that much more difficult.

In this chapter we analyse the Federation of Stock Exchanges in the EC as an example of a Euro-group trying to develop and maintain a degree of co-operation, in the interests of Europe as a whole, whilst representing a membership which is subject to rather strong disintegrative forces brought about by increased competition.

Despite these forces, however, the Federation appears to be a good example of an interest group attempting to play the role predicted for groups by the neo-functionalist theorists of European integration. Neo-functionalist theories have dominated analyses of European integration, although the empirical evidence to support one of the central features of this theory—'spill-over'—is not uniform (Lintner and Mazey 1991: 9). Two kinds of spillover are said to exist—'functional spillover' and 'political spillover'. The former suggests that 'because modern industrial economies are composed of interdependent parts, it is impossible to isolate any particular policy sector; integration of one policy sector will succeed only if contiguous areas are also integrated' (Lintner and Mazey 1991: 8). The latter involves a build-up of political pressures in favour of further integration. Ernst Haas, writing in 1958, noted that when national governments join regional economic organizations, this tends to lead to the defensive grouping of commercial interests fearful of no longer being able to lobby effectively at a national level (Haas 1958: 318). He argued that, in varying degrees of intensity, this pattern has become a general one in Europe. Furthermore, he argued that 'despite ideological differences, the institutional and political logic of supranationalism has brought with it the formation of trade associations in *all* relevant fields of endeavour' (Haas 1958: 323). His general conclusion was that groups would play a central role in European integration, as these groups would turn to supranational means when this course appears profitable to their members. The actions of groups in pressing for further European integration would not be based upon a highly principled commitment to Europe—they would emerge as tactical co-operation, as organized employer groups in a pluralistic setting outgrow dependence on and loyalty to the national state (Haas 1958: 354). We will return to what Haas called a 'lack of ideological cohesion' in Section 5, after describing the Federation's activities and its rather mixed fortunes in bringing about even the tactical co-operation predicted by Haas.

2. THE NATURE OF THE FEDERATION AND THE IMPORTANCE OF MARKET STRUCTURE

The Federation of Stock Exchanges in the European Community is a lobbying group, but not solely or even primarily so. In practice, the Federation is striving to bring about a real integration of the European market in a particular sector, the securities market. The Federation was founded in 1974 and comprises the stock exchanges—which in the case of Italy and Germany means the national association of exchanges—of the twelve Community countries. (Individual firms cannot be members of the Federation.) The membership reflects the interest of the stock exchanges in the legislative measures proposed by the EC Commission over the last twenty years, and the existence of the Federation is regarded by the EC authorities as serving a useful point of reference and opinion. The Federation's membership has recently (1991) been extended to include non-EC exchanges such as the Helsinki, Oslo, Stockholm, and Vienna exchanges, and the Association of Swiss Stock Exchanges. The Federation has also opened corresponding relationships with a number of exchanges from the emerging markets of Central and Eastern Europe. It is, therefore, typical of many Eurogroups in representing interests across Europe as a whole, not just within the twelve EC nations.

The Federation's objectives are simply stated. They are:

1. to contribute . . . to the attainment, in the field of securities and financial markets, of the aims of the Treaty of Rome;
2. to promote exchange of views and closer co-operation between member stock exchanges . . . to promote the development of the securities markets of the Member States . . . to promote closer co-operation in . . . trading, clearing, settlement, and deposit of securities and in relevant regulatory matters, so as to facilitate achievement of the Single European Market in the securities industry;
3. to act as a representative voice of stock exchanges . . . in matters of concern to the European securities industry;
4. to facilitate co-operation with other organizations concerned with the creation of a more integrated European and international securities market.

This chapter, however, concentrates on ways in which the Federation is attempting to achieve the second of those objectives— namely, its role in the creation of a single market. That objective has little to do with the lobbying process, as such. Indeed, it is a much more difficult and complex task, as changes in market structure following deregulation have meant that the members' original interest in collaboration and co-operation is now increasingly offset by their need to compete with each other. This competitive environment was sparked by Britain's process of deregulation, starting in 1983, itself in part a response to international competitive pressures on London as a centre for financial services. The process of deregulation helped to allow London to compete internationally and this in turn produced innovation in exchanges in many parts of the world. Once London had been deregulated, other European exchanges had to follow suit. The end-result of this 'domino-deregulation' is that there is now a radically changed market structure in Europe. Moreover, since the extreme bull conditions of 1986 and 1987, there has been less business available and much fiercer international competition for it—both between European exchanges and between exchanges throughout the world.

Even without these more recent changes, the Federation is not as homogeneous in its membership as its name might suggest. There have been long-standing structural differences in the national securities markets in Europe and the stock exchanges have for historical reasons played different roles in their national economies and regulatory structures. In Germany, for example, membership of a stock exchange is restricted to banks, and the exchanges—there is one in each *Land*—are very much part of the banking system. In the countries which adopted the Code Napoléon—France, Italy, Spain, Belgium—the exchanges are very much official bodies, membership of which is, or until very recently was, open only to private individuals, who were officers of the state, and operated in an official cartel. In those countries the exchange played a central role as a regulator and was the only permitted market, *de jure*. In Britain the stock exchange until 1986 had no statutory authority, but in the British tradition of self-regulation, assumed a leading role as a regulator of virtually the entire capital and securities markets.

The long period of deregulation, involving radical structural change, was designed to make the exchanges each more competitive in a world where the one commodity which flows very easily across national boundaries is capital. At the same time there has been a process of re-regulation in the form of statutory regulation, much of it emanating from Brussels, and the introduction of regulation where in many cases none had existed before. Thus, many of the exchanges have given up their own regulatory capacities and have seen them replaced by new statutory agencies.

The most startling case is that of Britain, where the Stock Exchange acting as a voluntary regulator, has been replaced by statutory bodies at several levels, including the Securities and Investments Board and the SROs. In Spain, Belgium, and Portugal new state bodies have taken over from the stock exchanges the regulation of investment firms. Perhaps most significant of all, the European Community's Investment Services Directive will be based upon the authorization by national authorities of investment firms. Moreover, the existence and extensive powers of these state or semi-state bodies, regulating the business and the capital adequacy of authorized firms, makes it more difficult for the exchanges to co-operate—for example, by sharing or exchanging information—in the regulation of their members. In almost every case the exchange remains responsible only for market regulation.

So, having ceased to be regulators, having seen their monopolies fractured, and having in most cases ceased to be trade associations acting on behalf of their members, the exchanges—the members of the Federation—have turned themselves into commercial enterprises. They seek to defend their national territory, in the shape of the market in their own domestic stocks, and to win as much as they can of the business in international stocks, which at least in theory can be transacted anywhere in the world. The Federation is, therefore, comprised of organizations which until very recently carried out a national role (generally operating in protected markets) which made their participation in a European trade association relatively straightforward. Of course, European associations comprised of companies which are in competition with each other are by no means unusual. In essence this is no different from the problems faced by a national association of competing firms. But competing organizations trying to find a basis on which to collaborate via a Euro-group in building infrastructure systems essentially concerned with European integration present a different order of difficulty for a representative association.

The shift, almost brutally abrupt, in the role of the stock exchanges is the response to competitive conditions which have not merely dislocated the conventional geography of the capital markets but have raised the fundamental question of what a stock exchange really is in the modern world. The exchanges are fighting each other on a number of fronts. They are concerned primarily to retain the trading in their own domestic securities, and hence to

THE FEDERATION OF STOCK EXCHANGES

offer the most liquid market in those securities. In this ambition the Continental exchanges are ranged, jointly and severally, as it were, against London, which through SEAQ (Stock Exchange Automated Quotations) International offers an alternative to the domestic market in professional size transactions. The exchanges also seek to attract listings of non-domestic stocks, and most of all of US and Japanese equities, and hence to affect trading in those stocks. And each exchange seeks to be a vital part of an effective concentration of financial services in its own capital.

Those are the things the exchanges do independently. But they nevertheless have a collective interest in attracting international business to Europe, so that the wider Europe, not confined to the Community countries, can offer a range of services for raising capital and trading in financial instruments, which is capable of being the rival of Wall Street and the Far East. Despite the new pressures to compete with each other, the Exchanges do, therefore have a common European interest, in order that the European time zone can compete effectively with the rest of the world. The financial markets, for currencies, bonds, and shares, tend to be congregated in or operating in relation to three time zones. These are, starting in the Orient, in South-East Asia—which is of course dominated by Tokyo; in Europe—which is dominated by London; and in the east coast of the US—dominated of course by Wall Street. The three overlap in their operations. More importantly, a large number of the types of business, indeed even individual transactions, can be carried out in any well-organized financial centre. Under these competitive conditions, Europe tends to be looked at as, at least potentially, a single financial market. Thus it is that there is an underlying logic which should lead to collective action in the form of a Euro-federation, in addition to the practical need for the European industry as a whole to respond to proposals emanating from the Commission.

3. THE FEDERATION'S ATTEMPTED ROLE IN EUROPEAN INTEGRATION

In the context of a newly competitive European industry, the Federation, therefore, has an opportunity to play a key role in producing a genuinely single market in this sector. The Federation has been engaged upon two major projects, which are intended to create a common and integrated infrastructure, to make the exchanges more efficient and to reduce the costs of using the markets. The first is known as the European list, or Eurolist. This is a project to set up a list of the leading equities of the European countries, which would be capable of being listed and traded on every Community exchange. By taking the best securities from each country and displaying them in a market which would have high visibility and transparency, it is intended to make a kind of shop window for the European economy, which would be of particular interest to non-European professional investors. In this way, the separate exchanges can all benefit to the extent that Europe can compete more effectively with the rest of the world. Eurolist will, moreover, have substantial advantages for the listed companies. Many leading companies are already listed at several national bourses. They are required to comply with the requirements of each, in matters of information to be provided, and in various administrative matters, which makes the listings onerous and expensive to maintain. A company which is admitted to Eurolist will need to obtain a listing only on its home exchange. Having satisfied the requirements there, it will be entitled to be listed on any other exchange in the Community.

The concept is simple, but its implementation requires considerable efforts to allow legal, regulatory, and administrative procedures to be met at every exchange. The Federation is only part way through the work involved, but intends to launch Eurolist in the first half of 1993. Its implementation would be facilitated if a number of technical changes to EC directives could be effected. Indeed, a new brief directive may prove necessary and hence the Commission must be mobilized to assist this aspect of European integration. In that sense, there is a mutual dependency between Commission and Federation, although the Commission has so far not established for itself a locus, nor has it the resources, to advance the Federation's more ambitious projects of integration quickly.

As in the other economic fields, the Commission seeks to play an enabling role. It does so by making sure that barriers to the fundamental rights of the Rome Treaty—freedom of establishment, and the right to offer services, throughout the Community—do not impede the development of the single market. This implies legislative measures, via regulations, or, more commonly, directives addressed to the Member States. The Commission can also provide financial assistance for projects in which all the Member States are engaged, but the conditions, as may be expected, are onerous, and the exchanges have so far preferred to finance their own project expenditures.

The Eurolist is essentially a service which will bring benefits to the listed companies. However, exchanges do not thrive merely by admitting companies to listing. Their lifeblood is trading and, as explained earlier, they each wish to protect the trading in their own securities. As the European economies increasingly converge, the securities of companies engaged in particular industries will be compared across national boundaries, and investors will come to look upon Europe as one investment market. So there is a collective need to display the equity markets as a whole. The Federation is considering ways to allow investors to treat the markets as one, to switch from a German chemical company to a British one, or a Spanish telecommunications company to a Danish one, without the costs and delays of currencies and different settlement periods which impede such investments at present. Such a market would have been essentially for professional users and would be characterized as a wholesale, rather than a retail, market. To an extent this is already possible by using the London Market, but a real integration of professional trading would entail a more ambitious project, perhaps no less than the creation of a single form of wholesale, or professional, market organization. So far agreement on such an ambition has been difficult to find.

With efficient trading has to go efficient settlement. All the existing arrangements for settling transactions in securities—that is making payment and delivering title of ownership—operate on a national basis. This makes moving the ownership of securities and money still relatively cumbersome, involving as it does currency transactions (and, even if a wholesale market were to be set up, therefore, currency risks) and cross-border stock movements. As a complement to a pan-European market in leading equities must go a much more fluid method of settling business if a fully integrated market is to develop. This is immensely complex, but once again proposals are being studied within the Federation which would begin to make more of a reality of a Single European Market in securities.

These projects and problems are essentially legal and administrative and have caused difficulties because national interests conflict with a common European interest. However, the exchanges also need a better technical infrastructure to support cross-border trading of securities, and it was for this purpose that the Federation's most ambitious project was undertaken. The member exchanges of the Federation formed a company, Euroquote SA, incorporated in Belgium, to build a network to link the exchanges, and to sell services to market users. The company planned in the first place to create an information service, drawing data from the exchanges about the market and the listed companies, which it would transmit to subscribers, using satellite technology. At a later stage the network would have allowed the markets to be linked so that orders coming from one market could be executed directly in another. And if the wholesale market referred to above were realized, the Euroquote network would allow access to the market from all European countries, and indeed from outside Europe. As a third stage, the Euroquote network would carry settlement instructions, and form the basis for a European-wide settlement system. In the event, and following a good deal of expenditure, the shareholders of Euroquote SA, which were in fact the member stock exchanges of the Federation, could not agree upon the essential objectives of Euroquote, and the project has been abandoned and the company placed in liquidation.

These major developments consume resources and demand strong project disciplines. Their successful completion is vital both to the stock exchange and to the financial infrastructure of Europe. They may not be typical of the activities of European lobbies and pressure groups, but they do conform to some of the predictions suggested by the neo-functionalist theorists cited above, i.e. the principal thrust of these developments is to secure a much more effective system of European integration in the financial sector and the pressure for this is coming from the Euro-group, rather than from national governments, or indeed from the Commission so far. The key to success in overcoming the continuing national rivalries which will inhibit integration will be, therefore, the attitude and role of the Commission and the development of further competition from outside Europe (see Sec. 5).

The original purpose of the Federation was, however, more conventional and in that sense, the Federation's development has followed the path that Haas's analysis would have predicted, i.e. its first task was to ensure that, in so far as power had already begun to shift from national capitals to Brussels in the financial services sector, the common interests of the exchanges had to be represented. It is to this more conventional aspect of the Federation's work that we now turn.

4. CONVENTIONAL LOBBYING

In the 1970s the Community was occupied with a number of directives which sought to harmonize the conditions under which companies operate in the Member States. These had therefore to do with the main pillars of company law, including capital raising and access to capital markets. The Federation did not find it difficult to take up common positions on such directives, and was able to work with the Commission at the level of detail on important technical matters, which made the implementation of the directives more practical. Thus, the Federation accepted one of the main rules of European lobbying—that it is necessary to take a positive attitude to the Commission's proposals and to assist in formulating workable solutions.

For much of the 1980s, the Commission pursued a policy of working together with banks and stock exchanges, so as to create more fluid, open institutions and left aside the pursuit of harmonization through directives. That latter activity was resumed as part of the drive towards the completion of the internal market. A principal plank of official policy has been the Second Banking Coordination Directive, one more or less incidental by-product of which is to allow banks to pursue their business in the securities field in any Community country, using the common passport. Such a measure (even though it may appear to do nothing which is not implied in the Treaty of Rome) would give banks explicit rights in relation to stock market activities which are not ostensibly granted to non-bank securities firms, and the Commission has therefore made parallel proposals, known as the Investment Services Directive and the Capital Adequacy Directive.

These proposals will affect the organization and functioning of the stock exchanges in fairly profound ways. Moreover they have opened up divisions within the Federation which are just as wide

as those created by the competitive forces referred to above. These
divisions of opinion approximate to the differences described earlier between the countries which adopted the Code Napoléon, and
the Northern European countries. They have to do with the place
in the financial system of the national stock exchange. Broadly
speaking, the Mediterranean countries wish to concentrate business
in securities in 'regulated markets', in other words stock exchanges;
whereas the Northern European countries take the view that such
matters cannot be achieved by legislative edict. Business will flow,
they say, to the market offering the greatest liquidity at the lowest
transaction cost. So the exchanges must make themselves more efficient, and thus more attractive. The view taken by the Mediterranean countries (of which Belgium is an honorary member)
smacks of their old centralist habits of mind. The differences
between the exchanges are such that the arguments in Brussels are
carried on by government rather than stock exchange representatives. The Investment Services Directive (which, basically, means
that all dealers in securities would be regulated on a common
basis) has brought to the fore the national differences in the financial services sector. Because of this, national groups are now in a
close alliance with their own governments and rely on their governments to represent them in Brussels. Even where individual
exchanges might adopt a more flexible approach, they cannot in
practice take up positions significantly different from their own
government. The arguments are not yet resolved, and at the time
of writing, October 1991, the positions are so far apart as to place
the Investment Services Directive itself at risk. This would have
adverse consequences for the exchanges. The result of there being
no directive would be that banks would have a 'passport' to carry
on securities business outside their home state which would not be
available to non-bank securities firms. And the very desirable
scheme of regulation contained in the directive, albeit at a basic
level, would be lost. The Commission is even able to use the differences against the exchanges themselves.

Under these circumstances the Federation, at least on these
major questions of structure and role, cannot be an effective lobby.
What it therefore does, once again, is to pay attention to detailed
technical matters—aware always that 'le diable est dans le détail'—
and to work with Commission officials to ensure that directives
come out in a practical and workable form.

It may be asked, if the exchanges themselves are not an effective lobby on such vital matters, then where does the Commission look for guidance and reaction on the 'high politics' issues? The answer to that is that the time is short, the matter is urgent, and the EC authorities—Commission and Council of Ministers—are working to resolve the architecture of the directives and the major differences of policy at official level, through meetings of ministers and government officials. The process of lobbying then goes via the national governments. The large firms look to their own interest and lobby the national regulatory body or bodies of which they are members. Thus in the UK the firms are for the most part members of the Securities and Futures Authority (SFA), which is itself a powerful body. The SFA is in turn overseen by the Securities and Investments Board (SIB), which, being a semi-state body, is permitted to participate directly in Council and Commission working parties. So the individual firms lobby the SIB, the UK Government, and—if they can gain audience—the EC Commission. Similar procedures are followed in other EC countries. In any event, the stock exchanges are not the bodies through which the large firms seek to lobby; and the Commission uses as its own point of reference the national government representatives in the Council of Ministers.

5. CONCLUSION: EUROPEAN INTEGRATION AND THE LOGIC OF COLLECTIVE ACTION

If this account appears to give a picture of a somewhat ineffectual voice in the actual lobbying process, it is because the stage at which the Federation finds itself in the two main directives necessitates negotiation and resolution at the Member State level. Broadly, this corresponds to Hoffmann's distinction between 'high' and 'low' politics (Hoffmann 1966). That does not affect the ability of the exchanges, through the Federation, to use other avenues to fulfil the objectives described earlier. Thus, it seeks to improve the practical and detailed ways in which the exchanges serve their users—issuers and investors—by defining high standards of:

- information for investors, in prospectuses and periodic reports;
- investor protection, through maintaining compensation funds to recompense investors in the event of a failure of a member firm;

- transparency of the markets; and
- publicity about the markets.

In all of these matters the Federation expects to work with the Commission, so that its influence is both constructive and timely. Moreover, in all the activities described here may be seen the elements of something more than simply lobbying for the protection of existing sectional interest, in the traditional manner. These activities appear to reflect a wider conception of the Federation's role in the broader framework of European integration. The very considerable difficulties which have limited this achievement so far, again would be expected from Haas's analysis. Thus he warned that interests would 'not immediately outgrow their separate national ideological experiences and habits. No doubt a much more intense series of stimuli must be injected into the scene before any marked ideological cohesion will develop' (1958: 354).

Four factors may ensure that the process of Europeanization of interests in this sector does continue, via the appropriate stimuli. First, the Commission itself might well be mobilized to be rather more active in identifying and pressing the European interest, as it has in other sectors. Just as the EC's legislative activity in the sector many years ago provoked the formation of the Federation, so could Commission support for some of the integrative ideas floated within the Federation provoke a greater degree of co-operation within the Federation itself. Secondly, there are several reasons why the individual exchanges may be driven to develop more effective co-operation via their Euro-group. The need to defend the common interests of the European time-zone has already been mentioned. Similarly, all of the exchanges face a threat from new entrants as there is a non-exchange market developing—essentially a 'grey' market, outside the exchanges. Threat to the market share of the exchanges is, therefore, perhaps the most powerful factor leading towards co-operation (see Ch. 13). Thirdly, it might be necessary for the other exchanges to pool their resources in order to compete with London. London has a very strong market position and has been holding talks (since discontinued) with the National Association of Securities Dealers in the US, the aim of which could have been a joint venture to create a common technical infrastructure to support the two institution's markets. This might have enabled them to launch the first cross-border equity market to operate across the world's major time zones. A variant of this is that the smaller exchanges may see co-operation as vital if they are to continue to exist when faced with the large exchanges like London and Frankfurt who have shown themselves capable of collaboration within the Federation. Fourthly, the evidence of the 1987 crash suggests that the collective interest can be very powerful when the whole industry is threatened. After the 1987 crash the Group of 30—a private sector organization of leading bankers and industrialists under the Chairmanship of Lord Richardson (former Governor of the Bank of England)—sought to analyse what might have happened if a big securities firm had failed. They realized that something had to be done on a large scale in order to manage national settlements. As a result, the group produced a set of settlement standards that are now being adopted worldwide.

Whether these theoretical benefits of co-operation within a Euro-federation can be translated into practical action remains to be seen. The collapse of Euroquote SA has raised serious doubts concerning the ability of the Federation to develop effective collaborative projects which could lead to a more integrated market in Europe. As it happens the British have presented particular problems—though not for the usual reasons. The British have been uncooperative from a position of strength, rather than weakness. They appear to believe that the Federation is not a suitable body for project development, as they consider that infrastructure projects cannot be sustained by twelve disparate parties. The argument is that partners need to be selected very carefully so as to relate to each other in fairly specific ways. A more cynical view is that the British see no particular need to co-operate because they believe that their market position is such as to lead to eventual dominance in Europe. The decision to discontinue Euroquote SA has caused people to question the Federation's credibility as a lobbying organization because it has provided a public display of disunity.

Yet, there is undoubtedly a continuing collective interest which will need to be represented in the European legislative process. For example, there will always be a regulatory regime within which the securities industry will have to function. That regime can be more or less 'hostile' to the industry depending upon the detailed content of legislation and on the way in which it is actually implemented. Moreover, the conventional stock exchanges provide a usable framework for regulation to be applied in the Member States. So the exchanges may still find common cause in influencing the shape of that legislation.

It would, therefore, be very odd indeed if the European exchanges were to conclude that they had no collective interest to represent and were prepared to abandon the lobbying system, leaving decisions to be reached without any collective voice whatsoever. Other competing 'interests', e.g. the banks, would then exploit the industry's representational weaknesses to their own advantage. This is likely if the climate which currently favours more and more deregulation and competition were to change in favour of reintroducing more stability and predictability into the financial markets, as the costs of deregulation become more apparent.

References

Haas, Ernst B. (1958), *The Uniting of Europe: Political, Social and Economic Forces 1950–57* (Stanford, Calif.: Stanford University Press).

Hoffmann, S. (1966), 'Obstinate or Obsolete: The Fate of the Nation State and the Case of Western Europe', *Daedalus*, 95/3: 862–915.

Jordan, A. G., and Richardson, J. J. (1982), 'The British Policy Style or the Logic of Negotiation?', in J. J. Richardson (ed.), *Policy Styles in Western Europe* (London: Allen & Unwin), 80–110.

Lintner, Valerio, and Mazey, Sonia (1991), *The European Community: Economic and Political Aspects* (Maidenhead: McGraw-Hill).

9

Defending and Promoting a Sectoral Interest within the European Community: The Case of the Textile Polyolefins Industry

JEAN-PIERRE PECKSTADT, SONIA MAZEY,
AND JEREMY RICHARDSON

1. IDENTIFYING AND ORGANIZING AN INTEREST

The origins of the European Association for Textile Polyolefins (EATP) can be traced back to the jute industry. Originally, carpet backings, rope, bags and sacks, etc. were made from jute. When, some twenty years ago, the promotion of polypropylene began, it quickly became apparent that it was an innovation with great potential for the industry. Initially, a specific group, representing the manufacturers of the new product, was set up within the existing trade association. The rate of innovation with polypropylene was such that it soon proved necessary to set up a separate association—namely EATP. Thus, not only does technical innovation lead to the formation of whole new industries—it also leads to the creation of new interests which became politically motivated and with which supranational agencies and national governments have to deal. The result is that innovation and regulation interact with each other in a complex process of change in which regulators try to catch up with the effects of technical innovations and innovators respond to new regulations. Paterson's study of regulation of the chemical industry in Europe has also highlighted this link. The example he cites is the case of VCI (Chemical Industry Association) in Germany which, in dealing with governmental bureaucracy, often stresses 'the threat to innovation imposed by the need to conduct a high proportion of R & D in a defensive mode to conform with bureaucratically imposed tests and regulations' (Paterson 1991: 316).

The early days of EATP were similar to the development of most sectoral associations. The initial group met to discuss problems of common interest, to become acquainted with fellow producers, and to establish statistics for the newly emerging industry. The emergence of common concerns—and hence the potential for a common interest to be represented by an association—was, of course, a pre-condition for any lobbying activities. At this minimal level, even rather mundane selective benefits appeared to be useful—such as holding a yearly 'social event' in some pleasant spot in Europe!

The European Community itself was, as is common, the 'spark' which really enabled EATP to develop into an active representational organization. Basically the EC plays a crucial role in influencing the business environment in which EATP members operate. New and increasingly complex European regulations have been introduced with a range of laws and standards to which EATP members must conform. As Majone has argued, there has been a continuous growth of Community regulation, especially in the field of environmental regulations—a rate of growth which 'appears to have been largely unaffected by the political vicissitudes, budgetary crisis, and recurrent waves of Europeanism of the 1970s and early 1980s'. Thus, he has calculated that, from a single directive on preventing risks by testing in 1969, there were 19 directives/decisions in 1975, 13 in 1980, 20 in 1982, 23 in 1984, 24 in 1985, and 17 in the six months immediately preceding the passage of the Single European Act (Majone 1989: 165). Moreover, he argues that this regulatory dynamic is unlikely to falter, as one essential characteristic of regulation 'is the limited influence of budgetary limitations on activities of regulations'. Increased EC regulation is likely because it both allows the Commission to increase its influence and provides it with the possibility of escaping budgetary constraints by resorting to regulatory policy-making' (ibid. 167). A further complication for industry is that the absence of a central political authority 'implies that regulatory issues are dealt with sector by sector, with little attempt to achieve overall policy coherence'. Thus, the Commission's regulatory ambitions have been the 'motor' for the development of more professional and more complex sectoral representatives associations. EATP is typical in that it exists so that the sector can be aware of what is happening on the European (and world) front; so that it can defend itself against what it sees as unacceptable or excessively complicated regulations, and so that it can seek to persuade the EC to adopt rules which are more favourable to the industry. EATP is, therefore, a classic example of a sectoral interest which has had to become Europeanized simply because the locus of legislative and other rule-making power for this sector has shifted from national capitals to Brussels. Indeed, the Association moved its headquarters from Paris to Brussels in 1991, in order to facilitate its role as a European lobbyist. (It now shares offices with another association in the textile industry—the International Rayon and Synthetic Fibres Committee—which also moved to Brussels.)

EATP currently has sixty members drawn from fifteen European countries (ten EC and five EFTA). The membership is in three categories: (1) Ordinary Members who are involved in the production of polymers for textile polyolefins or the manufacture of polyolefins themselves and whose headquarters and/or production are located in Europe; (2) Associate Members—machinery manufacturers and chemical additive producers who are suppliers to the textile polyolefins industry; and (3) Member Organizations representing the interests of certain categories of members, as follows:

European National Associations
Spain: Apoyfide (Associación Patronal Nacional de Empresarios de la Industria Textil de Poliolefinas y Fibras Duras)
United Kingdom: BPTA (British Polyolefin Textiles Association)
Belgium: Febeltex – Section Polyoléfines (Fédération de l'Industrie Belge)
France: Filcorsac (Syndicat Général des Fabricants de Ficelles, Cordages, Filets, Sacs et Tissus à Usage Industriel)
Italy: Tessilvari (Federazione Italiana dei Tessili vari)

The Association has a central secretariat, headed by a full-time Director-General and three secretaries, with an annual budget of FF 2.2 million. The Secretariat plays a key role in satisfying the needs of members, providing the link between markets and the various European authorities and organizations such as Comitextil (Co-ordination Committee for the Textile Industries of the European Community), CEN (Comité Européen de Normalisation), ISO (International Organisation for Standardisation, a world-wide federation of national standards bodies), several DGs within the EC, and with sister organizations active in Brussels. Thus the network of public bodies and private associations which EATP has links with is unusually broad, reflecting the fact that the polyolefins industry impinges upon, and is itself affected by, a number of issue areas within the European Community and beyond. Moreover, there is a web of quasi-governmental organizations—namely national and international standards bodies—already in existence, complicating the Association's task considerably.

2. PUBLIC REGULATIONS, THE BUSINESS ENVIRONMENT, AND THE ROLE OF EATP

The industry's 'interests' can be grouped under two broad headings of public regulation—standard-setting and ecological problems. In representing the industry in these two fields, EATP's work is underpinned by a recognition of two of the basic tenets of lobbying—the need to develop a reputation for reliable data and information, and the ability to supply technical expertise which policy-makers and fellow policy watchers may not possess themselves.

In accordance with this strategy, the Association has set up a series of Executive Committees, beneath the Managing Committee and Managerial Board (see Fig. 9.1 for organization chart). The EC Standardisation and Legislation Committee is very topical at the moment. It arranges for regular representation and attendance of EATP at the various EC/CEN Technical Committees of interest to the membership. The objectives of this committee are to ensure that the interests of polyolefin textiles are represented in the standardization process. This is a typical example of the vital importance of 'low politics' or technical issues to an industry and of issues which by their very nature are negotiable. The problem for the industry (and indeed for many other industries) is that European standards are genuinely supranational and once adopted will overrule national standards. The 'stuff' of the bargaining process may sound dull to the layperson. For example, standards for sacks used in food transport or for resilient and textile floor-coverings may not seem what European integration ought to be about, but issues such as fire safety in buildings throughout the EC and the nature of sports surfaces are of more obvious relevance to ordinary citizens. All such issues, as suggested in Sargent's chapter in this

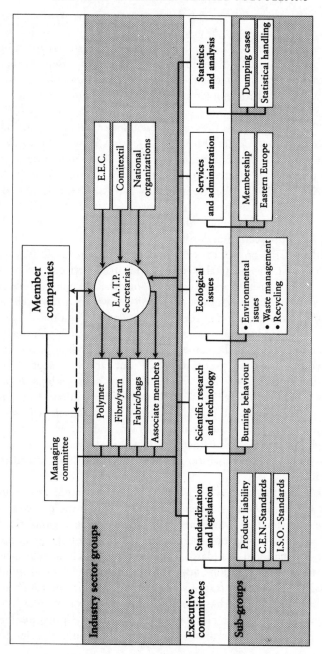

FIG. 9.1.   *Organizational Structure of EATP*

volume, are potentially of crucial importance to the 'bottom line' of individual companies or possibly to their survival. Moreover, there is also a common European interest, as the standard-setting process goes well beyond the jurisdiction of the EC itself. Europe has to ensure that international and global standards take account of its interests and are not dominated by, for example, the USA. Yet, as Sargent also notes, the standard-setting process is not just a threat. For example, as the *EATP Newsletter* pointed out, the announcement that Central European countries were to be invited to participate in the European Committee for Standardisation (CED), provided a strategic opportunity for the industry (*Poly News*, No. 2, 1991). The Commission itself sees the setting of European standards as part of the process of faster technological integration of Europe (see e.g. the CEC Green Paper on the Development of European Standardization, COM (90) 456 – final, approved by CEC on 3 Oct. 1990 and published in *OJ* C20/1, 28 Jan. 1991) and this inevitably brings industrial sectoral interests (and no doubt consumers) more closely into the EC policy process. In reality European integration often boils down to issues such as the establishment of common technical standards. The official standards for such industries as computers, telecoms, and polyolefins constitute key 'rules of the game' for companies trading in the EC and beyond. They are very technical but are not neutral as between nations or firms—as is evident in such areas as high-definition TV where considerable national rivalries have arisen. Companies can lose millions of pounds if the standard developed by a competitor is adopted rather than their own. Indeed, whole industries might go into decline if their products are deemed, hazardous. This possibility is one which no national government can afford to ignore either.

Nevertheless the process by which a trade association can influence the standard-setting process is complex, due to the procedural rules for participation which are laid down. Trade organizations can at best obtain only observer status in CEN. Voting rights are reserved for national standards organizations—such as BSI (the British Standards Institution), IBN (Institut belge de normalisation) or AFNOR (Association française de normalisation). For EATP to be effective, therefore, it has simultaneously to pursue several lobbying strategies. The first task facing the Executive Committee on Standardisation and Legislation is therefore to identify the relevant working groups within CEN in order to ensure that member firms and organizations become directly involved in the work of their national standards organizations. EATP members must try to become a member (within the national standardization organizations) of one of the CEN Technical Committees (TC), each of which specializes in the study of a specific item. For example, CEN/TC 134 'Resilient and Textile Floor-coverings': BSI is responsible for the secretariat of this CEN/TC, but members from each country must try to be active within their own national standards institution on the same TC in order to emphasize EATP's point of view as adopted by the EATP Executive Committee. Observer status may be granted to trade organizations such as EATP, which as such can be represented at CEN meetings by one person only.

In identifying the appropriate lobbying targets, the membership of EATP plays a central role—only the wearer knows where the shoe pinches. Following internal consultations, EATP has identified seven CEN Technical Committees where it is now actively lobbying for observer status and voting rights via the national standards organizations. Observer status had been obtained on four CEN Committees or working groups by 1991. The process of monitoring CEN developments is, however, somewhat complex as it is not always easy for the Association to identify correctly the most relevant of the many CEN activities. As a result, the list of CEN activities in which EATP maintains an interest is fluid as the direct relevance/irrelevance of them to the polyolefins industry becomes more apparent. The task is further complicated by the fact that each TC of CEN covers a broad range of subjects and is therefore divided amongst several working groups made up of experts from the national standards organizations. EATP has recognized that it needs to have its own experts involved in the TCs, and it has been organizing its own internal working groups to support the TC areas for which an observer position has been allowed. Yet another lobbying strategy is EATP's close co-operation with Comitextil and the co-ordination of the activities of EATP members already active in national standards organizations. To this end, EATP is compiling a data base of its own members' participation in national standards organizations.

Closely linked to the work of EATP's Standardisation and Legislation Committee is the work of its Scientific Research and Technology Committee. This is of special importance to keep track of

the latest technical developments, for example, the burning characteristics of materials. Regulation in this field is of crucial importance to the industry and EATP therefore set up its own Technical
Sub-Committee on Burning Behaviour· and commissioned a '
research project at the State University of Ghent. This research
programme is being extended with the objective of obtaining a
robust scientific and experimental base for publication in both
technical journals and at conferences, etc. with the findings being
announced at a press conference in May 1991. The programme is
part of what EATP's Chairman has suggested as one of EATP's
objectives—to be regarded as an authoritative source of information on the polyolefins industry in Europe.

Much of what we have described so far is, of course, highly sectorally based. Another of EATP's executive committees—the Executive Committee on Ecological Issues—has concerns which are
both sectorally based and of concern to other sectoral associations.
The whole of European industry is on the defensive on ecological
issues. Thus, one lobbying strategy adopted by EATP has been to
identify other sectoral industrial associations facing similar problems. In developing EATP's strategy on ecological issues, the committee has made a number of assumptions. Many of these
assumptions emphasize the threat which the politicized nature of
ecological problems poses to EATP's members. For example, it is
assuming that the ecological issue is not just temporary and that,
in effect, the 'halo effect' for anything to do with the environment
(Gregory 1971) will have sufficient longevity for industrial and consumer demand to be long term; that governmental regulations will
force action and will generate constraints (taxes and others) unless
industry acts first; that manufacturers of consumer disposables will
switch material sources or prevent new programmes from starting
unless materials are recycled; that ecobalance questions will
become increasingly important in selection of manufacturing materials; and that long-term and short-term solutions will need to be
developed simultaneously. Of immediate (1991) concern to the
committee is the need to influence the final draft of the EC Directive on the Management of Plastic Waste. In fact it is reported that
the plastics industry 'is likely to face a blizzard of EEC recycling
legislation over the next few years' (ENDS, July 1991: 15). However, because of the dearth of statistical data on both the use of
plastics and the real scope for recycling, industry has considerable

potential to influence policy-making. What has been described as a 'virtual information void' exists, as the Commission found when it began toying with drafting directives on plastic waste. It then 'found itself hampered by a lack of reliable data on plastics consumption, disposal, recovery and recycling'.

[This] expanding legislative agenda has galvanised the plastics industry into action. Accurate information on the consumption and fate of plastics will be essential to provide a baseline against which progress towards any legislative targets can be measured, and to identify potential difficulties and pitfalls with targets before they are enshrined in legislation. (ENDS, July 1991: 16).

The Association of Plastic Manufacturers of Europe (APME) has decided to attempt to provide better data in a new annual publication, the first of which has been compiled by a French consultancy firm Sema-SOFZES. In addition, the European Centre for Plastics in the Environment (PWMI) is the environmental unit of APME. Established in 1990, the Centre is dedicated to the promotion of increased recycling and recovery and comprehensive plastics waste management. The PWMI commissioned a statistical survey of plastics consumption and plastics waste in Western Europe from the Sema Group. EATP's Executive Committee on Ecological Issues is also studying the issue of waste management with particular reference to polypropylene. For this purpose a Technical Sub-Committee has been set up and will probably commission a survey from Sema.

Interestingly, EATP is not confining its lobbying strategy to purely defensive and reactive moves. The Committee is organizing various R & D projects—such as in the recycling of monocomponent carpets, modifications to bitumen compounds, etc. In a sense, the Association is, therefore, intervening in the process of innovation within the industry, as a long-term response to likely changes in the regulatory and business environment. In terms of policy-making styles, EATP, like the Federation of European Stock Exchanges described elsewhere in this volume, is both 'reactive' and 'anticipatory'. In that sense, it both defends the existing industry and may play some role in determining its future configuration.

3. CONCLUSION

Just as the role of the EC is evolving, then so EATP is in the continuous process of change as it responds to the increased relevance of the EC to the industry. In doing so it must demonstrate its current practical relevance to its members in terms of selective benefits, as well as trying to anticipate future threats and opportunities. For example, EATP's Statistics and Analysis Committee has recently demonstrated to EATP members that the collection of statistical material is important, not just for individual members to know how they compare with the rest of the industry, but also to enable the European industry as a whole to lobby effectively at the EC level. The Committee set up a Technical Sub-Committee to introduce a dumping case with the EC against the Peoples' Republic of China in respect of polypropylene and polyethylene woven sacks. In influencing the EC, the quality and reliability of statistics is vital if an anti-dumping case is to be sustained. In the event, EATP's campaign was successful and the Community imposed a duty of 43.4 per cent on such imports. Demonstrating selective benefits must, of course, avoid any kind of restrictive or collusive practices and EATP is careful not to breach any anti-trust restrictions. This is achieved by having a set of Rules of Procedure and Bye-Laws which forbid discussions of prices as such or indeed any matter which could be considered to be in breach of EC competition laws.

EATP has constantly to review its strategy. For this reason the principal Office Bearers regularly re-estimate requirements, threats, and targets facing EATP in order to ensure members are provided with the service they are entitled to expect from the Association.

References

Gregory, Roy (1971), *The Price of Amenity* (London: MacMillan).

Majone, Giandomenico (1989), 'Regulating Europe: Problems and Prospects', in Thomas Ellwein *et al.* (eds.), *Jahrbuch zur Staats- und Verwaltungswissenschaft* (Baden-Baden: Nomos), 159–78.

Paterson, W. E. (1991), 'Regulatory Change and Environmental Protection in the British and German Chemical Industries', *European Journal of Political Science*, 19: 307–26.

10

Lobbying in Europe: The Experience of Voluntary Organizations

BRIAN HARVEY

1. INTRODUCTION: THE VOLUNTARY SECTOR ARRIVES IN EUROPE

Voluntary and community organizations concerned with social policy have now joined the ranks of battalions of lobbyists now entrenched in Brussels, hovering around the European Commission, Parliament, Council of Ministers, and the Economic and Social Committee. Because of their small numbers, they need to make an impact out of proportion to their size if they are to influence social policy and put what has been termed a 'human face' on the single market of 1992.

I will describe the voluntary sector in Brussels, situating it in its historical and political context, and make some assessment of its activities. Then I will examine the objectives and ambitions of voluntary organizations there and make some observations on their lobbying work, discussing the different lobbying options open to the voluntary sector. The role of the Commission and the Parliament are examined.

Associations of voluntary organizations in Brussels use different terminology to describe themselves: some call themselves associations, committees, councils, federations, and unions. The fashionable term 'network' is used here: it now has general currency in covering most of these different categories.

2. THE NATURE OF INTERNATIONAL VOLUNTARY ORGANIZATIONS AND 'NETWORKS' ENGAGED IN LOBBYING

Voluntary organizations engaged in lobbying at international level are neither new nor a phenomenon peculiar to the European Communities. The first international associations of voluntary organizations date to the mid-nineteenth century: the Salvation Army, for example, has operated on an international basis since the 1880s. Others were formed after the First World War—e.g. the Red Cross (1919), the International Council for Social Welfare (1928), and the International Federation of Settlements (1926). There was a dramatic expansion of international federations, associations, and organizations in the period immediately after the Second World War in response to the formation of the United Nations (UN). The UN signalled an early intention of soliciting the views of non-governmental organizations (NGOs) and drew up sometimes elaborate mechanisms so as to hear their opinions: many of these new NGOs located their headquarters in the European seats of the United Nations, neutral Geneva and Vienna. A significant number of these networks were concerned with health and disability.

Responding to the emergence of the Council of Europe in Strasbourg, the second great wave of European networks came in the 1960s. The Council of Europe, which covers twenty-five European countries, drew up what was termed 'consultative status' and encouraged NGOs to apply for such status. The Council outlined nine fields of activity, and NGOs could apply to be consulted under any one or a number of these headings. These include, for example, human rights and fundamental freedoms; social and socio-economic problems; health; and local and regional government. There is an annual conference of all NGOs which liaises throughout the year with the secretariat of the Council of Europe. As a result, many of the NGOs in this second expansion are based in Strasbourg or in nearby Luxembourg. The majority of international networks of voluntary organizations still transact their business with the Council of Europe and the United Nations, rather than with the European Communities. An even small number, a mere six, have taken up consultative status with the Organization for Economic Cooperation and Development (OECD).

Evidence of a shift in focus towards the European Communities came in the late 1970s when some of these networks, like the Red Cross and Rehabilitation International, set up liaison offices or EC sections or units in or close to Brussels, principally to lobby the Commission. One international network, the association of radical community groups, ATD Quart Monde, set up an all-party liaison group with members of the European Parliament in Strasbourg, one of the early intergroups of MEPs. One hundred and fifty MEPs joined the intergroup, the first of several concerned with social affairs. The ATD Quart Monde intergroup—consisting of MEPs and ATD staff, liaison officers, and members—began to meet before and after parliamentary sessions to review issues and see how social concerns could best be raised and progressed.

It is interesting that networks concerned with social policy were virtually absent from Brussels in the mid-1970s when several key instruments of EC social policy evolved through their formative stages. The social action programme, the anti-poverty projects, and the action programme for women's equality were all formulated in the absence of pressure from lobbyists from the social sector. One can only speculate if these programmes would have had a different focus or cutting edge had they been present.

In the late 1980s the Commission of the European Communities deepened its interest in international networks of non-governmental organizations in the social field. The Commission took the decision to fund six specialized anti-poverty networks, all of which arose from groupings of projects which participated in its Second Programme against Poverty (1986–9). These networks were concerned with:

- women in poverty;
- elderly people (Eurolink Age);
- the homeless (FEANTSA, the European Federation of National Organizations Working with the Homeless);
- one-parent families (Network for One-Parent Families);
- rural development (TERN, the Trans-European Rural Network);
- ATD Quart Monde.

The Commission also took the decision to fund a generic Anti-Poverty Network, which was launched in 1990 (Harvey and Kiernan 1991). An early problem faced by the Commission-funded networks was that their donor could take away as speedily as it could give. At one stage (in August 1991), the Commission decided that specialized networks would be integrated into the generic anti-poverty network. The official reasons given were budgetary and to prevent the duplication of effort in the field. The networks themselves were unconvinced by such explanations, fearing that their forward political role had made enemies within the Commission. The decision was eventually rescinded in the case of some of the specialized networks.

These are not the only lobbying networks being funded by the European Commission. Whereas the core costs of running these networks (secretariat and staff) are met by the Commission, projects and seminars run by other networks are met on a case-by-case, but none the less regular basis. Examples of these networks of voluntary organizations are Europil, a French-based group concerned with housing resettlement, and the European section of the International Federation of Social Workers: their annual conference costs are met by the Commission, in exchange for a comprehensive report on the issues facing the organization and its clients at the time. It is not unusual for several of the Brussels networks of voluntary organizations to receive Commission funding averaging about 40 per cent of their income.

The Commission's precise reasons for funding these networks and associations have never been clarified, beyond generalized statements about 'seeking convergence in social policies': one may speculate that it is simpler for the Commission to deal with a single source of international opinion on a particular social issue or sector than twelve national organizations at a time. Voluntary organizations may also be in a position to provide the Commission with information and research on social developments that are a valuable complement—or even a counter—to that provided by national governments. This information may in turn fuel the ambitious social agendas of individual sections of the Commission, or its President.

For their part, hardened members of some of the networks suspect that funding network activity is, in the overall scheme of things, an inexpensive method of expressing social concern and 'putting a human face' on '1992'; a subtle means, too, of capturing networks and inhibiting their role. The funding of networks has been cited by commissioners in the Parliament as evidence of a Commission response to an articulated social concern. At the same time, for all the many reports produced in the course of Commission-funded projects, there is no ready evidence of attempts by the Commission to steer networks towards, or for that matter away from, particular policy positions.

Not only would the Commission disclaim any such interest in navigating the networks in a particular direction, it would insist that the disinterested funding of networks was part of the processes of political pluralism which guide the European Communities in their decision-making. The presence of the networks, it would argue, adds to the richness of the social-policy debate, and to what is sometimes referred to as the policy of transparency. This elusive concept has yet to be formally defined but has nevertheless featured obliquely in discussions on how greater propriety can be brought to political lobbying around the Commission. Transparency is understood to mean four things: the accessibility of the Commission to interested parties; open dealings with interested parties (lobbies are entitled to know which other lobbies are consulted); the forewarning of policy initiatives (decisions should not be sprung on people and rushed through before they have time to react); and decisions, announcements, programmes, and legislation are what they say they are, and for the purpose for which they are stated, without ulterior motive.

It is interesting to note that although being forthcoming in funding non-governmental organizations and soliciting their concerns, the Commission has not established mechanisms of consultation comparable to the consultative status of the Council of Europe. There are three exceptions: one is the liaison committee of voluntary organizations concerned with development aid issues: it has a formal structure for meeting with the Commission every year, to which parliamentarians also contribute. Others are the Consumers Consultative Council (CCC) and the liaison group concerned with disability.

About twenty sectors of voluntary organizations are now represented in Europe, mainly through international networks. Over a hundred such networks have now been identified (Harvey 1992). These include diverse sectors such as social services, youth, family bodies, migrants and refugees, conservation and environmental action, disabled people, regional and rural concerns, community development, and unemployed people. There is even a set of groupings dedicated to improving the consultative position of the overall voluntary sector itself.

In the course of time, the late 1980s and early 1990s may come to be seen as a period of explosive growth in the international voluntary sector. The formation of a new international network of voluntary organizations is announced approximately every four to six weeks. For example, April 1991 alone saw the emergence of the European Communities Child Welfare Group, and another network dedicated to rural development, called VIRGILE. Most of the international networks around the European Communities are led by (led in the sense of inspired by or comprised of people in senior staff or officer positions) three countries: Britain, France, and Ireland. Few networks owe their existence or persistence to voluntary organizations from the southern countries. Why this should be so is unclear: European networking may for the British, the French, and the Irish be a logical extension of their national experiences in coalition-building. By contrast, the voluntary sector in the southern countries is still parochial, local and regional, rather than national, though this may change rapidly.

3. NATIONAL VOLUNTARY ORGANIZATIONS IN BRUSSELS

Few national voluntary organizations have the resources to set up lobbying facilities in Brussels or Strasbourg themselves. Some of the large German ones have been able to do so. The representative body of the six main German welfare organizations, the Bundesarbeitsgemeinschaft der freien Wohlfahrtspflege (BAGFW), has a Brussels office which it shares with another large German charity, Caritas (Deutsches Caritasverband). The lobbyist of the small German welfare organizations, the Paritätscher Wohlfahrtsverband, has already taken up appointment in the Belgian capital, and two other leading German NGO groupings (Arbeiterwohlfahrt and the Evangelical Church (Diakonie) are not far behind. National voluntary organizations in other countries do not have comparable resources, and for this reason have pooled their efforts. For example, the National Council for Voluntary Organizations in Britain, and the Fondation de France, have together with other, similar large national umbrella voluntary organizations, established the European Social Action Network (ESAN), to ensure that the social concerns of the national voluntary sector do not go by default in Brussels.

4. A PROFESSIONAL LOBBYING AGENCY FOR THE VOLUNTARY SECTOR?

For others, the idea of a specialized lobbying force dedicated to the voluntary sector promises a number of attractions. The European

Citizen Action Service (ECAS) is a professional lobbying, information, and advice service in Brussels specifically designed to help the voluntary and community sector. Formally launched in May 1990 after a market survey found that over 400 voluntary organizations in Europe would support some kind of citizen's lobby in the European Communities, ECAS describes its aims as

to advise, inform, and strengthen the position of the voluntary, non-governmental organizations (NGOs) in relation to the European institutions. It hopes to be a focal point for many NGOs in their dealings with the EC, and, by doing so, correct the imbalance between lobbying on behalf of business and lobbying on behalf of the public interest.

Two individuals were guiding forces in the evolution of ECAS— Tony Venables, former director of the European Consumers Bureau (BEUC), and Marie Spaak, formerly of the office of the United Nations High Commissioner for Refugees. The executive council of ECAS includes Godfrey Bradman, one of the founder members of the Campaign for Lead-Free Air (CLEAR).

ECAS has 200 members, of whom 60 per cent come from the UK. Most of the others are from the northern countries, and southern members are joining slowly. ECAS has a mailing list of up to 7,000 names and voluntary organizations across Europe. Membership of ECAS falls into four main categories: citizen's rights, health, social affairs, and culture.

Membership costs of ECAS are on three scales: corresponding membership costs 150 ECU (£110); associate membership 1,200 ECU (£875), and full membership 4,300 ECU (£3,135). Corresponding members receive the publications of ECAS and general information on the development of EC programmes and legislation. Associate members are entitled to advice about how to approach EC institutions, receive reports of particular interest to their sector, and may use office space in Brussels. Full members receive a personalized service, a watching brief on specific issues and decisions as specified, and legal advice. Although the membership rates have struck many in the voluntary and community sector as expensive, ECAS stated from the start that it did not want to cut corners by providing an underrate service.

Some people who work in the voluntary sector have been nervous about professional lobbying services for the voluntary sector, feeling that it runs contrary to the ethos of the voluntary sector.

The European Anti-Poverty Network (EAPN) and the European Women's Lobby both devoted resources and time towards ensuring that their networks were rooted in consultative, democratic fora of activists in the Member States, elaborate electoral colleges being devised to ensure a broad-based representation of all those concerned. The specialized networks, described above, eschewed the idea of professional lobbyists for more pragmatic reasons, preferring to keep these skills in-house and learn them directly themselves.

5. AIMS AND OBJECTIVES OF THE VOLUNTARY SECTOR

It is difficult to make an assessment of which, if any, networks and lobbies are successful in advancing their aims and objectives. Few networks commit themselves, at least publicly, to precise short- and medium-term political objectives, such as specific legislation, action plans, parliamentary resolutions, or specialized programmes, or comment on their own progress in achieving these objectives. As a result, it is difficult for outsiders to measure what progress they are making. Several networks declare their objectives in very general terms, like 'representing the interests of our clients or our members': this may well be true, but these generalized aims are not a useful yardstick by which to measure their effectiveness.

If challenged about the reasons for their involvement in Europe, organizations respond by voicing a diffuse concern about decisions being taken there which may be of concern to them. Others express an interest in ensuring their member organizations in the national states are able to benefit from the structural funds or other financial opportunities. Few present an interest in large-scale political objectives. Few organizations associated with the voluntary sector have made a contribution on the EC's future social objectives by forwarding submissions to the intergovernmental conference which met over 1990–1 and which matured as the Treaty of Maastricht. Those that did so were ECAS, which prepared a memorandum *Citizen's Europe and the Revision of the EC Treaties*; the European Women's Lobby; the Churches' Committee on Migrants in Europe (CCME); and the Free Legal Advice Centres (Ireland). The views expressed in the ECAS document were based on the concerns voiced by its various members. In the memorandum, ECAS argued for a ten-point plan for the improvement of the European Treaties to include an expansion of the competence of the European Communities, and a common European statute for voluntary organizations.

The presence in Brussels of leading German welfare organizations seems to be entirely defensive in nature. The conferences which led to them being established there referred to the 'dangers' of '1992': dangers that other welfare organizations will be able to compete with them by bidding for contracts for the provision of social services in Germany, and that their secure (critics might say cosy and privileged) position as providers of services might be outlawed under new competition laws.

6. ASSESSING THE EFFECTIVENESS OF LOBBIES IN THE VOLUNTARY SECTOR

Few lobbies in the voluntary sector seem to have attempted to assess their own ability to achieve specific results. One exception (there are others, like the consumer groups) is the lobby for elderly people, Eurolink Age. Conceived initially as a European wing to the lobbying effects of Age Concern in Britain, and still deriving substantial funding from Age Concern, Eurolink Age has specific objectives in the fields of anti-discrimination legislation, anti-poverty projects for elderly people, a seniors' pass in Europe, and a rolling action plan for the elderly incorporating a number of short-term, medium-term, and long-term elements. In pursuit of these objectives, it has set up a Brussels office; in Strasbourg it services an intergroup of MEPs which has eighty nominal members (fifteen to twenty-five regulars) which meets four times a year. It is one of about forty-eight intergroups in the Parliament, of which a small number are interested in social affairs.

The European Commission seems to be the focus of the work of most of the networks of voluntary organizations. Almost all of the networks engaged in lobbying have Brussels offices; most concentrate all their staff there. The Commission's actions, proposals, and rumoured intentions seem to dominate thinking, planning, and strategies within networks, but this may have more to do with the Commission's ability to dominate the information environment than anything else. Networks, when challenged on this point, take the view that since the Commission is the initiator of proposals and the principal influence on funding priorities, limited resources should be concentrated there. The Parliament, most networks say, has so little power as to be worthy of little lobbying attention.

But could this view represent a faulty appreciation of the role and influence of the European Parliament? Some networks have used the European Parliament to fortify their position. The six directly funded networks, for example, have several times persuaded MEPs to add budget lines, not only for a continuation of their own funding, but for funding special projects and activities which they have promoted. In 1990 the European Secretariat of the World Deaf Federation managed to persuade the Parliament to add 1.26 mECU to the Commission's proposed 5.5 mECU budget for disabled people. The ability of the networks to flex their muscles in the Parliament has, one suspects, been part of the process of persuading the Commission of their seriousness and professionalism.

Eurolink Age employs a European Parliament Liaison Officer half-time on retainer in Strasbourg, in addition to its Brussels staff. It is one of few networks to have such explicit links with the Parliament. Several MEPs have spoken of the animal-welfare lobby as a model for others. Its three staff are deployed as follows: one liaises with MEPs, a second travels throughout the European Communities building up support for its issues of concern, and a third runs the lobby's office. One MEP reported that 'they seem to have a staff member permanently parked outside the entrance to the Parliament building'. The intergroup on animal-welfare lobby is very conscious of the level at which it pitches its proposals, being careful to be reasonable, and distance itself from the extreme wing of some animal-welfare organizations. Its intergroup is always well attended (about thirty to forty MEPs attending as a rule). A vet, who is attached to the group, gives MEPs briefings of a technical nature when required. The animal-welfare lobby appears to have achieved some success in restricting the transport of live animals, reducing animal experimentation, banning the trade in skins of endangered species, and controlling the fur trade, yet most of this appears to have been accomplished through the Parliament more than the other institutions. The lobby is strongly rooted in the constituencies of MEPs, whose voting behaviour on animal-welfare issues is closely scrutinized and reported. MEPs voting favourably are courteously thanked by branches based in their constituencies;

those who vote unfavourably are quickly confronted. Commission proposals in the field may well have come in response to parliamentary concern.

The Parliament and the Economic and Social Committee provide fora where issues can be raised, debated, and promoted. But while Parliament can adopt resolutions, set the tone for the discussion of issues within the European institutions, and provoke a Commission response, it has little power to ensure effective implementation in the Member States. For this reason, the quality of the follow-up work by the networks has proved all-important. This includes ensuring that the relevant parliamentary debates are well publicized in the Member State concerned, and making sure that the text adopted is used as the bench-mark for effective lobbying at home.

A successful campaign of this sort followed the adoption by the European Parliament of a hard-hitting report on homelessness in 1987. Part of the report condemned the manner in which two states used vagrancy laws to lock up people for being homeless. Voluntary organizations in the two countries concerned (Belgium and Ireland) used the report to shame their national governments into suspending or repealing these laws. Another section of the report, prohibiting hospitals from discharging homeless people on to the streets without aftercare services, was quoted against Irish health boards which continued these practices. In other words, lobbying through networks at the European level has proved as effectual as the campaigning capacity of the members of the network in their home countries. The European institutions are persuaded to adopt policies more favourable than what is possible for the lobbyist to achieve in the home state; this *position prise* is then used to embarrass the home country for being out of line with what the lobbyist presents as 'mainstream European opinion'. Some countries, and some governments are, as one might imagine, more amenable to this form of pressure than others.

7. SOME OBSERVATIONS

At this stage, the picture of voluntary organizations in Europe is one of considerable activity. To the mesh of organizations around the UN and the Council of Europe is now joined a third web: the

European Communities. International networks of voluntary organizations are now undergoing a period of unusual growth.

Insufficient information is available to explain this process of growth. Few of the organizations have for their part been explicit about how they see the European process helping resolve the policy problems faced by their constituents. We await an evaluation that will shed light on whether voluntary organizations locating in Europe, and international networks already there, have found participation in the European process fruitful. The opinions of their constituents as to whether involvement in Europe has proved worthwhile for them are also awaited with interest. It would be instructive to learn more about how these networks and voluntary organizations approach their interfaces with the EC institutions, the strategies that they lay down, and the skills they see as essential to make these relationships profitable.

There is some evidence that the presence of European networks in the social field has widened the scope and horizons of the EC's social policies: EC competence in social, environmental, and consumer affairs has expanded commensurately with the presence in Brussels of lobbies related to these fields of activity. It is possible that the main effect of the presence of the networks in Brussels has been to broaden the field of political and social debate; there is less evidence of the ability of the networks to see ideas and proposals through to legislation, programmes, or changes in funding priorities.

So far, there has been little use of the European Court of Justice as a means of advancing social policy objectives. The taking of test cases to the Court has rarely featured in strategy documents drawn up by voluntary organizations, even though the use of the Court appears to offer possibilities for networks promoting women's equality, the rights of pensioners, and the position of migrant workers. It is possible that networks of voluntary organizations either lack the legal expertise to take such cases through, or are intimidated by the complexity and slowness of the proceedings involved. Exceptions are the Child Poverty Action Group, which monitors and publicizes ECJ cases; and the Free Legal Advice Centres which successfully brought the Irish Government to book for discriminating against women in their social security entitlements (FLAC 1991). This may be an area of future development.

References

Harvey, B. (1992), *Networking in Europe: A Guide to European Voluntary Organizations* (London: Bedford Square Press).

——and Kiernan, Judith (eds.) (1991), *Poverty—A Challenge to us all: The Foundation of the European Anti-Poverty Network from Working Group to Launch* (Dublin: European Provisional Working Group against Poverty). Available from Northern Ireland Council for Voluntary Action, 127 Ormeau Rd, Belfast 7.

FLAC (1991), 'Women win Equality Case—Government faces £200m Pay-out', *FLAC News* (Dublin), 1/3.

11

The Confederation of British Industry and Policy-Making in the European Community

RICHARD EBERLIE

1. INTRODUCTION

I start from the premiss that British industry's interests are not being taken as fully into account by the European Community institutions as they should be. I first report how the Brussels office of the Confederation of British Industry (CBI) is organized and what we are doing at the moment, and how we relate to UNICE, our European confederation.

Secondly, I go on to explain how we have recently developed our operations in concert with some member trade associations. We have a very long way to go in attaining the same degree of influence over the Brussels legislators as we presently have over those in Whitehall and Westminster.

As one of our aims is to encourage more trade associations to join the EC lobbying process, I then outline the kind of advice which the CBI gives to trade associations whenever they are prepared to listen. In my conclusion, I explain and explore my Brussels 'bafflement' at the failure of our lobbying on some key issues, for example the GATT talks, and pose one or two key questions for the future.

2. THE CBI AND LOBBYING IN BRUSSELS: FOUR MAIN TASKS

The CBI set up an office in Brussels in 1971 with two people, some time before the UK's accession to the Community. We did this for three main reasons: to demonstrate our conviction that British business' future lay in the Common Market; to begin to find out what was going on there and set up an early warning system; and to give direct and firm support to UNICE (see Ch. 12). In practice, four main tasks were identified at that time, which remain crucial to the work of our Brussels office.

2.1 Developing Long-Term Relationships with EC Policy-Makers

We keep channels open with the Commission, the European Parliament, the Economic and Social Committee, the UK Permanent Representation, UNICE, and all its member federations. We are 'gardeners', with the role of nurturing the grapevine that our forebears planted (watering, fertilizing, and weeding it) so that in the fullness of time our own experts from the CBI in London and from companies in British industry may pluck the fruit—and through our contacts secure the opportunity to influence the decision-making process.

Staff in the Brussels office also have the duty of directly representing the CBI on some specific issues—perhaps 20 per cent of all that come up. We do so for a variety of reasons:

- we are on the spot;
- no expert can come out from London in time;
- we happen to know as much as anyone in London about the subject in question;
- our own specialization is the working of the EC machinery.

For example, I have spoken for the CBI on subjects which I, personally, know quite well, such as environmental legislation, health and safety law; on subjects of which I know little, like accountancy standards, UK trading relations with Japan, and petro-chemicals in the Gulf; and, on subjects in which I specialize, like institutional reform.

The remaining 80 per cent of CBI representations in the EC are done by professional lawyers, environmentalists, industrial-relations experts, and so on from the CBI London headquarters and by member companies. On these occasions, our function is merely to accompany these professionals and perhaps use our contacts to get them out of difficulties or help resolve a particular problem.

2.2 Monitoring EC Developments

Our second job is to monitor developments in the Community and
to contribute to the CBI's policy work in London and in our
Regional Councils by providing early warning and background
information. We cover the whole range of issues of interest to
trade and industry in Britain: from DG I (External Relations) to
DG XXIII (Enterprise Policy, Distributive Trades, Tourism, and
Social Economy); from the GATT talks to the harmonization of
intellectual property rights; from the directives on professional
qualifications to those on energy supply. We are duty-bound to
concern ourselves with anything in Brussels and Strasbourg that
happens to be of interest to any of our members. We carefully
avoid involving ourselves in those matters that are the responsibility of industrial and trade sector bodies which are directly represented in Brussels, e.g. the National Farmers' Union.

Perhaps one-quarter of our time is spent collecting and reading
'hot' press reports and numerous other documents obtained from
friends in the Commission, UKREP, sister federations, and UNICE.
Nothing stays with us, however. We can do nothing with the information we collect because British industry's views are framed not
by us, but by committees of businessmen under the CBI umbrella
back in the UK. The most crucial and interesting part of our work
is the collection and transmission of information to headquarters
so that the CBI can then develop its policy position on EC proposals and begin the task of lobbying. For this purpose we need to
meet as many people as we can and chat to them, not so much
about specific proposals, but about the 'whys and wherefores',
'hows and whens'. Essentially, our task is to identify Commission
policy change early and to understand the reasoning behind it, so
that British business can frame its responses realistically and in sufficient time for subsequent lobbying to be effective.

2.3 Maintaining Links with UNICE

Our third function is to keep in permanent and close touch with
UNICE. As this body is European industry's principal spokesman
to the Commission and Parliament, we have always believed we
must put out weight behind it. We played a major part in its
reorganization in 1984–5 and see ourselves as having given solid

backing to the new Secretary-General, Zygmunt Tyszkiewicz. My formal position is that of CBI's Permanent Delegate to UNICE, and I sit with thirty colleagues on a committee which meets at UNICE fortnightly. We compare notes, look at the future work of the Commission, Council, and Parliament, plan UNICE's programme, and exchange titbits of useful information.

It is worth stressing that we see UNICE as our lobby and no more than our lobby. Three years ago we stretched a point and agreed that it should become a social partner, i.e. that it should meet in joint session with the European TUC, under Commission chairmanship and should develop the social dialogue (popularly known as the 'Val Duchesse' agreement). This arrangement was formally recognized in the Single European Act in Article 118b which states that

The Commission shall endeavour to develop the dialogue between management and labour at European level which could, if the two sides consider it desirable, lead to relations based on agreement.

Within this framework we have agreed that UNICE and ETUC should draw up joint opinions on issues of current interest to the representatives of employers and workers, such as access to vocational training and information and consultation with workers on new technology. However, we are now being asked by Mme Papandreou (EC Commissioner for Social Affairs) to allow UNICE to negotiate with the ETUC collective agreements at the European level.

Indeed, a wide-ranging discussion started in the Intergovernmental Conference on European Political Union on the possibility of employers and trade unions (represented by UNICE and the ETUC) being empowered to conclude framework agreements on working conditions through negotiation at the European level. It was also suggested that such agreements should be made binding on the parties and take the place of Community legislative instruments. My own view is that there is some benefit in the idea that UNICE and the ETUC should prepare the first drafts of prospective legislation in areas of common interest, provided that neither party is put under pressure to conclude agreements on any particular subject or within any particular time-scale.

The trend is towards a decentralization of labour-market questions in nearly all European countries: the Swedish employers and central unions, for instance, have recently broken off their long-standing national pact. The CBI believes that the Commission would do better to recognize cultural and social differences and push collective bargaining down to plant and workplace levels where issues can be most effectively resolved by means of local negotiations. European employers are unlikely, therefore, to encourage the extension of Community competence on social mat-ters, few of which are, in our view, the proper responsibility of the Community. In short, the CBI sees no grounds for the extension of collective bargaining to the European level, nor does it see UNICE as a body able to negotiate on its behalf in Brussels.

2.4 Advice to CBI Members

Our fourth role is to help and advise our own members in their dealings with the Community. We do this in three ways. First, by means of regular reports in the CBI News, and other publications on specialist topics, especially in our bi-monthly looseleaf briefing called Europe sans frontières. Secondly, we are available to speak to all and any of our members, severally and jointly, in our office, at seminars and meetings wherever we are invited. Thirdly, we are ready to provide them with briefs to the extent of our knowledge on matters of special interest to them.

We receive a steady stream of visits from CBI members. This increased to a flood in 1987 and 1988 as members came to us with the question 'What is this thing called "1992"?' There are fewer visits from our members now, but we nevertheless do a good deal of consultation by fax and telephone in order to advise on the latest developments, representational strategy, contacts in the Commission, and links with UKREP. We also help make appointments and arrange visits for groups of members with relevant EC personnel. This 'facilitator' role is an aspect of lobbying of considerable value both to our London specialist staff and to our members.

3. A CBI RESPONSE TO '1992'

One of the CBI's responses to the '1992' pressures has been to send out to Brussels people with more specialist knowledge of particular policy sectors. In addition, in January 1991 we appointed a third experienced person in Brussels to serve the interests of UK industrial and commercial sectors. The extra costs are being shared by supporting federations, eight of which have so far contributed. They are in the following industries: clothing, plastics, engineering, machine tools, printing, the manufacture of sports equipment, contract diving, and technical qualifications. We were thus able to create, under our umbrella, a British Business Bureau. The Bureau will perform four tasks for its client federations in parallel to what the Brussels office does for the CBI as a whole. They are as follows.

First, to help the sectoral organizations make the best use of their EC-level branch bodies. Those that are any good (perhaps only 50 out of the 400 believed to exist) have traditionally dealt with sector-specific proposals. These sectoral organizations are increasingly being drawn into more general questions, such as the environment, social legislation, competition policy, and standards policy (see Ch. 9). However, far from rendering independent representation redundant, we see the existence of European-level representative bodies as making it more important for a UK sector to have someone on the spot in order to participate throughout the decision-making process and not just at the final stage.

The Bureau's second job is to make effective contacts, particularly with all those in the various EC institutions working in areas of specific interest to its client sectors. Its aim is to create long-term relationships that facilitate early (and hence effective) lobbying.

The third job is to gather information for the Bureau's clients. This is done in two ways; by sitting in the CBI Brussels office monitoring our regular flow of intelligence; and by getting out and making day to day contacts around the Brussels circuit, in close relationship with UNICE and UKREP. This information provides the basis of a quarterly newsletter which is circulated widely among members of the client associations.

Fourthly, the Bureau, like the CBI Brussels office, is door-opener and bag-carrier! The task is that of facilitator, making sure that visitors from the UK see the right people in Brussels and receive appropriate attention. More and more UK bodies are finding that this function simply cannot be performed effectively from London.

In London there is a management committee of the eight sectoral associations. The Bureau Director reports to it each quarter, both to keep it up-to-date with developments and to enable members to check that their resource is providing value for money. It is worth adding that while we are still in the experimental phase, other national confederations had the same idea some time before us. For example, the French CNPF formed *La Maison des Professions et des Entreprises* in Brussels, thereby increasing its numbers in Brussels from two to five people. West German industry took a similar step in 1990. All the Scandinavian federations increased their staff then too; the Irish have for three or four years employed three people; and in 1990, the Dutch appointed a resident director in Brussels.

In forming the British Business Bureau, the CBI believes it has identified a need among a number of its members. They seem to have readily accepted the fact that normal CBI subscriptions did not permit any increase in the size of our Brussels office, and that, whilst it is prohibitive for any single association to set up its own office, a fairly small additional contribution to CBI would permit a small group to club together to secure the desired level of representation. The scheme provides clients, in effect, with their own person in Brussels. Thus, they acquire a presence, advance intelligence, and a voice that would otherwise be beyond our existing resources.

In forming the British Business Bureau, the CBI sees itself as directly answering, if not anticipating the DTI complaint that 'clearly trade associations . . . have still much to do to improve their services, raise their credibility and be used more efficiently by firms' (DTI 1991). We agree with the DTI and consider that we have precisely directed our efforts at solving at least part of this problem. We have sought in a practical and cost-effective way both to increase the trade associations' effectiveness in Brussels and to raise their standing there. This approach can be easily extended: if more trade associations want to become our clients, there would be few problems in increasing the number of staff.

4. THE CBI AND UK TRADE ASSOCIATIONS

We are seeking to stimulate this demand, as we are confident it is very much in the interests of the trade associations themselves. It is no longer safe for any sectoral trade association to rely on lobbying the UK Government and on persuading the UK civil service to accept its views. If ever that were enough, the Single European Act put an end to reliance on national lobbying. The introduction of qualified majority voting and the co-operation procedure revolutionized the lobbying rules: first because thenceforward no one minister could stop a proposal subject to these rules by threatening to use the veto: secondly, because the European Parliament was then granted real power in certain key areas and was given the opportunity to develop a position of greater authority in the system. The weight of national governments in the European policy process could be further eroded by the 1991 Maastricht Treaty which would extend majority voting to new sectors and further strengthen the legislative powers of the European Parliament.

In any event, on most issues, it became necessary with the SEA to switch the lobbying effort from London to Brussels and Strasbourg. Alliances had to be formed by both governments and MEPs in their different fora whenever they wished to change a proposal. Business has had to try to identify these alliances and seek to influence their composition. It sounds simple, but it is immensely difficult to do effectively: there must be international action; there must be one message; and there must be co-ordination at the European level.

In this predicament, the CBI is urging Britain's business organizations to redouble their efforts to do four things.

4.1 Present the Positive Side

In Britain we have a different form of law and nothing like as much of it as our Continental partners. We have a statute law that is confined to controlling specific abuses, and we lack the comprehensive blanket of a Code Napoléon that regulates and restricts even the most basic human activity. We see no reason for drastic change to the system. So it falls to the British business community to demonstrate what it believes are the excellent high standards achieved, for example, in the fields of tobacco advertising and merger control by our national regulatory practices, based for the most part upon social pressure, voluntary co-operation, and self-regulation.

We urge a constant effort on the part of British trade associations to show that British industry can operate in the public good under a reasonably light legal and regulatory framework. We must go on the offensive to market the British approach of self-regulation and of minimal legislation, to promote those desirable elements in our European partners, as well as ourselves. As part of this campaign, the CBI has published, *The Europe of Opportunity for all*, *Environmental Action Programme*, *Developing a Safety Culture*, and a series of other similar books. In May 1991 we produced a looseleaf binder entitled *Improving Business Success through Employee Involvement*. A number of sectoral bodies in the UK act in a similar way—for example, the Chemistry Association's *Responsible Care* campaign.

4.2 Work with Sister Federations in the European Bodies

Commission officials and MEPs do not want to hear the views of one country alone. They do not have time to listen to twelve different sets of representations and they want the concerted and consensus position. Moreover, it is obviously to our own advantage to present the combined strength of all European business to the decision-makers and opinion-formers. An agreed European view, from business, is likely to carry weight with decision-makers, whereas a divided view will not. Most importantly, talking to our sister federations from other countries is by far the best way of stimulating parallel representations from business interests in other individual Community countries. If several European governments are under the same pressures at home, the chances of success for us in Brussels are that much greater.

4.3 We must never say 'No, because . . .', but always say 'Yes, but . . .'

This was the burden of a speech made by Sir Leon Brittan to the CBI's National Conference in November 1989. He said that we will not be heard if we say 'No'. We have to accept the aims of the legislators, even if we object to the means they prescribe. We have got to work with the grain, to show a commitment to the Community's broad approach and principles; to agree to the maintenance of high standards and good practice in business dealings. Unless we do these things we shall be marginalized and ignored as lobbyists.

We do not advise our friends that they should turn a blind eye to differences of view between various parts of the Commission and Parliament. To exploit these divisions seems to us as a legitimate part of lobbying. But we urge our members, however they approach the issues, to show themselves constructive and offer possible alternatives in order to achieve the desired ends. It is a poor lobbying tactic merely to complain and protest about a proposal from the Commission.

4.5 Stay in There

Finally, we tell our associations to stay plugged into the Brussels network from the initial stirring of interest to the bitter end. They have to be able to react promptly as the matter comes up, watching the debate at each stage round the institutional circuit, knowing that it is sometimes only at three in the morning of the last Council debate that brinkmanship wins the final point, or loses it! We tell them to fight with every means at their disposal to get the changes made that they see to be necessary; they have to do so at every stage, and every level, and in every influential body. They may have to do it three times over if they are to win public and political opinion to their side and finally to win the decision they want.

5. THE BRUSSELS ENIGMA

At the end of the day, it has to be admitted we are not winning the issues that really matter. The GATT negotiations are a case in point. The CBI and UNICE have been totally committed to the success of the Uruguay Round, from its beginnings and through to its relaunch in January 1991. At each stage, the CBI and UNICE have made high-level representations and public statements—not only in European capitals but also in the United States and Japan, sometimes jointly with the industrial spokesmen from those countries. However, there seems very little chance that the Round will be completed satisfactorily. Somehow and somewhere European industry's case has been lost, despite the intense and desperate need of the whole world for freer and fairer trade through the GATT machinery.

Similar problems have arisen with the proposed European Economic Area. Here again we believe that an overwhelming case exists that the barriers put up by EFTA Governments and by the Community around themselves should be removed in the interests of all the people of Western Europe. The Community's four freedoms are just as valid outside it as within; the same environmental and safety standards can be set reasonably objectively. Yet, here too, something has gone wrong in the negotiations by governments with this extension of the single market.

Even the Single European Market is presenting problems. In November 1990 the CBI published *The Business Agenda for Europe in the 1990s* because we felt that the politicians were taking their eye off the ball. The overriding business priority was the successful completion of the single market on schedule by the end of 1992. We want to see the gaps filled in the original Cockfield plan and continued progress towards the goal of economic and monetary union. These policies alone can provide a sure foundation for real growth and for the Community's continuing development. Only a truly single market and a single currency of the sort which exists in the US will permit the improved business performance that will, in turn, enable living and working conditions to rise. Yet, we constantly find it necessary to remind governments and the Commission to respond more vigorously to this unique and immense opportunity.

Agreement of some of the key Common Market issues is not yet in sight. Too little of the agreed programme has as yet been enacted into national law; too little attention is being paid to the fair application of new domestic laws; and too little effort is being made to go beyond the Cockfield plan even though it has always been acknowledged that it had important gaps.

Meanwhile, the Commission presses ahead with a Social Action Programme, in the face of objections from all of European business to some of the Commission's specific proposals. Too much remains to be done to improve the performance of the Community's economy to risk diverting attention and resources to the field of social legislation where—in our view—the need has not been demonstrated. This is an urgent and compelling message.

If I were asked to explain why this message is not being heeded in Brussels and Strasbourg at present I could perhaps suggest three reasons. First, the business lobby is obviously just one among hundreds to which the Commission and the European Parliament listen. The farmers' lobby, for example, is in some parts of the Commission extremely influential; in other parts, environmentalists have the ear of officials. In some places, the consumer voice is loudest, whilst in others trade unions have the greatest influence.

Secondly, many decisions are taken not in Brussels, but in caucuses in the politicians' home base where the business lobby may have little influence. So much policy seems to be determined according to doctrine and dogma that cannot be easily modified subsequently in the Brussels arena. The consensual philosophy of Christian and Social Democratic Parties in Continental Europe goes back a long way and is firmly set. The mainstream of European centrist politics is in many respects friendly to small businesses, but in our view seems determined to tie down big manufacturers and employers within a rigid framework of regulation.

Thirdly, the British business lobby has a particular problem. Britain has quite different regulatory and judicial systems to those of mainland Europe, just as it has different social and cultural attitudes. Inevitably, therefore, British employers are in a minority within UNICE on many issues and must expect, at times, to be on their own. This does not mean that they should not seek compromise, consensus, and allies—whether in UNICE, the Parliament, or the Council of Ministers—but they should certainly not be surprised to find themselves holding a different view to their Continental counterparts. Nevertheless, British business should also recognize that it has the great advantage of a close working relationship with UK civil servants and politicians of all parties. This is a special asset in the EC lobbying game and one not enjoyed by all our Continental partners.

References

DTI (1991), *Usefulness of Representative Organisations on Single Market Matters*, Feb. 1991.

12

Business Lobbying in the European Community: The Union of Industrial and Employers' Confederations of Europe

LYNN COLLIE

1. THE ORIGINS AND DEVELOPMENT OF UNICE

The Union of Industrial and Employers' Associations (UNICE) was set up in 1958 by the industrial federations of the six founder Member States of the European Community. It was an early recognition that the European Community was going to be important for business and that business therefore needed to develop a European-level association to represent its common interests. Not surprisingly, the evolution of UNICE has in many respects mirrored that of the European Community in its move from the 'Euro-Sclerosis' of the late 1970s and early 1980s to 'Euro-Acceleration' in the mid-1980s. As the European dimension increased in importance, member federations became dissatisfied with UNICE. It was considered to be lack-lustre, under-resourced, and hide-bound in its method of operation and ineffective in representing the interests of business. A major internal review was undertaken in 1984 by a committee under the chairmanship of Mr Schade Poulsen, then Director-General of the Danish Employers' Federation. Its recommendations form the basis of the present UNICE structure.

As UNICE embarked upon the process of internal reform, the creation of the internal market emerged as an issue around which European business interests began to rally. Just before the first Delors Commission took office in 1985, UNICE presented it with a memorandum, which stated that 'top priority must be given by the Community institutions to the creation of a genuine internal market' (UNICE 1984). UNICE subsequently gave its enthusiastic support to the Cockfield White Paper which set out in concrete terms those measures which would need to be implemented in order to bring about an internal market and the setting of a binding timetable for its completion.

As a result of its internal reforms, UNICE has become better equipped to deal with the challenge of the rapidly changing institutional context in which it operates. A dynamic and highly articulate Secretary-General, Zygmunt Tyszkiewicz (formerly of Shell) was appointed in 1985. Under his leadership, it was agreed in 1989 that in order to defend the interests of European business and industry, UNICE should, by spring 1992, develop into an organization with a permanent Secretariat of thirty-six, including seventeen executive staff. This would be funded by a change in the basis of UNICE's subscription rates, intended to make membership costs more equitable and realistic. A UNICE Advisory and Support Group (UASG) was also to be created, membership of which was to be open to individual companies (see Sect. 3 below). This would enable UNICE to draw upon the additional expertise (and finance) of individual companies, as full membership of UNICE itself is open only to federations. As other chapters in this volume argue, technical expertise is perhaps the key factor in successful lobbying: UNICE recognized this fact in making this particular change in its organizational rules. As an interest group, it has therefore developed an organizational reform dynamic which reflects changes in the EC itself.

2. PRESENT STRUCTURE OF UNICE

UNICE now brings together thirty-two federations of industry and employers from twenty-two countries—the EC, EFTA, plus Turkey, Cyprus, Malta, and San Marino. No distinction is made between members from EC and non-EC federations—the notion of Associate Membership having been abolished post-Schade Poulson reforms. Its supreme decision-making body is the Council of Presidents, which comprises the Presidents of member federations. Since 1990 its twice yearly meetings have been held in the country of the EC Presidency, usually just prior to the European Council. The Executive Committee, which consists of the Directors-General of the member federations and which meets in Brussels, is responsible for the overall management of UNICE and general advice on the policy direction. It is assisted by a Finance Committee and a Committee of Permanent Delegates (Comité des délégués permanents).

The Committee of Permanent Delegates is UNICE's COREPER. It is made up of the Permanent Delegates of member federations, the majority of which are based in Brussels. Delegates also act as 'ambassadors' for their national federations in relations with the EC institutions on the one hand and with their respective Permanent Representations on the other. The committee meets fortnightly to ensure the day-to-day co-ordination between UNICE and its member federations, to exchange information on developments in the EC, and to organize concerted lobbying action at the level of national federations. It is also a very important link between the EC and non-EC federations. In short, it has a crucial information exchange and co-ordinating role to play. As Zygmunt Tyszkiewicz suggests, 'This committee, unique to UNICE, is one of the strengths of the organization. Without it the reconciliation of differing national views and the elaboration of genuine European policies would be far more difficult' (Tyszkiewicz 1990: 5).

Advance intelligence is power in Brussels as in all lobbying circles. As 'each Permanent Delegate has created a network of contacts through which a great deal of information is communicated and received', (Tyszkiewicz 1990: 5), this is a very important resource to the organization itself and to each of its members. The common pooling of this policy intelligence represents enormous 'added value' to all participants, even when they have different perspectives and sometimes competing interests.

The increasing specialization of UNICE's work is reflected in its five main Policy Committees, as follows:

• External Relations
• Economic and Monetary Affairs
• Social Affairs
• Industrial Affairs (Energy, environment, transport, telecommunications, public procurement, SMEs)
• Company Affairs (Legal affairs, technical harmonization, intellectual property rights, competition policy, consumer policy)

The Committee Chairpersons and Vice-Chairpersons are appointed by the UNICE President after consultation with member federations. Their term of office is two years with a possible extension for a further term. The committee system further extends the pool of expertise upon which UNICE is able to draw, since in many cases members are senior managers and experts from operating companies, rather than federation representatives (Tyszkiewicz 1990: 6).

These Policy Committees have in turn spawned some fifty specialized working groups and several *ad hoc* groups (see Appendix 1). It is at this technical level—again, the committees are made up of experts from the member federations and companies—that UNICE's main product, namely its position papers, are drafted before being passed to the Policy Committees for approval and thence to the Council of Presidents for its final approval. In practice this approval is often secured by written procedure, rather than via meetings. Given the increasing volume and scope of EC Community legislation of direct concern to industry and the need to reconcile the views of so many different federations from so many different countries, it is—as Tyszkiewicz has commented—a 'miracle' that position papers are written at all. But written they are, with a few notable exceptions, for example, where a conflict of interests has proved impossible to resolve. However, in cases of conflict of interest, UNICE is obliged to favour the users of a service over its providers.

3. THE EXERCISE OF INFLUENCE

Significantly, UNICE's present Statutes (Article 7.1–7.7) do not require unanimity when voting takes place on policy matters. Such a requirement can condemn a European federation to inertia and even collapse. The failure of the Common Market Automobile Constructors (CCMC) to agree upon its response to EC legislative proposals affecting the industry during the 1980s is a case in point (see Ch. 7). Indeed voting is only resorted to when no consensus can be found and when all reasonable attempts to reach common agreement have failed. Each member federation with voting rights has twelve votes and a proposal may be blocked if thirty-six votes are cast against it. Thus a minimum of three out of the thirty-two federations can block a proposal. It is also possible for Federations to add a footnote to the official UNICE opinion, which must be mentioned every time the association's position is put forward.

In practice, in only a few notable cases has a conflict of interests within UNICE proved impossible to resolve. This was the case for instance with the UNICE opinion on the insurance market. In most cases however, position papers are adopted with unanimity and they then become official UNICE policy which each member federation is expected to promote and defend (Tyszkiewicz 1990: 6). Position papers are UNICE's formal means of influencing EC policy-making. However, it is important not to ignore the importance of the whole gamut of daily contacts with the EC legislator: the unattributable briefings, high-level missions, and expert visits to the Commission and elsewhere that characterize UNICE's lobbying activities.

If UNICE's *raison d'être* is to influence the EC policy process by presenting in good time the clearly defined views of European business and industry, how effective is it as a lobbying organization? In judging its effectiveness it is useful to ask five key questions, all addressing the relationships between UNICE and other actors in the policy process:

  (i) How readily is it consulted by EC legislators, i.e. by the Commission, Parliament, Economic and Social Committee?
 (ii) How does it relate to other European business lobbies?
(iii) What is its relationship with the European Trade Union Congress (ETUC)?
 (iv) What is the nature of its relations with national member federations?
  (v) How is it used by its 'member' companies?

3.1 UNICE's Relationship with Legislators

As the initiator of legislation, the Commission is of course, the main target of UNICE's lobbying activities. It is consulted on a regular basis by the Commission services in three ways: officially in the Advisory Committee on Health and Safety; semi-officially in the context of the Social Action Programme Proposals; unofficially, on a day-to-day basis UNICE representatives maintain informal contact with Commission officials.

Whatever might be said about UNICE's actual influence over policy, it is not unhappy with the level and degree of consultation. If it had more resources, no doubt it would be able to make better use of the opportunities presented to it in the various consultation processes which take place. However, access and recognition—essential to any successful lobbyists—are certainly not problems for UNICE. It can virtually guarantee access on any issue of relevance to European industry.

But does such consultation actually change anything? In general, draft EC directives do change and UNICE is able to make many of the more 'difficult' legislative proposals less unpalatable to European industry. For example, since 1978 UNICE has been instrumental in blocking the Vredeling Directive on worker representation. Countless other directives have been modified in some way following UNICE's efforts to remove provisions perceived to be harmful to business interests. Examples include the Financial Participation (Promotion of Employees Participation in Profits and Enterprise Results) proposal. UNICE lobbied successfully in its meetings with the EC Commission that this should not be a legally binding instrument. The Commission finally proposed a Recommendation (i.e. not legally binding) rather than a directive on the issue. UNICE was also able to influence heavily the formation of the Merger Regulation, helping the Commission to produce a workable policy. Once this was done, UNICE also helped to get the regulation through the Council. The three main ideas which had been proposed by UNICE were, in fact, all retained in the final regulation—namely that it should be 'a one-stop shop'; that the procedure should be short with a provisional decision to be given within one month and a final answer within a few months; and that the competition criteria should be 'forward looking'. Nevertheless, even though UNICE is willingly consulted by the EC Commission, the federation does encounter some difficulties. Due to time constraints and the pressure of the EC legislative timetable, there is often insufficient time and too little information provided to ensure that UNICE's contribution to the consultation process is as relevant and pertinent as it might be. In order to ensure the best possible input of business expertise into the EC policy-making process, UNICE would like to see increased use of Green Papers (i.e. consultation documents) such as those produced on telecommunications policy and standardization. This would in turn lessen the lobbying pressure on the Commission at the later stages preceding the adoption of a proposal by the College of Commissioners and would permit a more focused lobbying input.

Since the Single European Act granted the European Parliament more power in the EC decision-making process, it has become an increasingly important target of lobbying. Business interests now need to devote to it far more time and resources than previously; a tendency that must surely increase following the proposed Treaty changes agreed at Maastricht in December 1991 which will further extend the legislative role of the European Parliament. This message has certainly been understood by all lobbyists, as is witnessed by the lobbying explosion experienced by the European Parliament. Indeed, the pressure under which MEPs now have to operate, combined with the antics of certain unscrupulous lobbyists, has led the European Parliament to begin drawing up a lobbying code and register.

Given the growth in lobbying directed at the European Parliament, it is important that UNICE be able to speak with one authoritative voice on behalf of European business if it is to make its voice heard above the babble of other competing interests, some of whom see the Parliament as a more receptive organ than either national governments or the Commission itself. The increased use of Parliamentary Hearings organized by Parliamentary Committees and political groups renders the policy process more visible. For UNICE these Hearings represent an important forum for the expression of business views. This is doubly important in the field of social policy where there is a wide gap of opinion between business and Parliament (Tyszkiewicz 1990: 24). Influencing the European Parliament can come about only through the painstaking process of building up personal contacts and trust with Committee Chairman and Rapporteurs in order that parliamentary amendments reflecting UNICE's views can be incorporated in Resolutions. UNICE has its own parliamentary consultant to help it in this process. In reality, the European Parliament is a more problematic institution for business interests than the European Commission. Whereas the policy process within the latter emphasizes technical expertise as a condition of effective participation (see Ch. 1), parliamentary debate tends to revolve around party political and ideological cleavages. Given the current Socialist/Christian Democratic majority within the Parliament, UNICE has to work hard to win support for its views among MEPs.

The Economic and Social Committee (ESC) is a third (though generally weak) legislative arena. It is made up of three groups: Group I represents employers, Group II represents Trade Unions, and Group III represents various interests (including consumers and farmers). The 189 members are appointed for a four-year term. It would seem natural that the positions of UNICE and of Group I should coincide. However 'for various complex reasons this group sometimes adopts positions that are at variance with those of UNICE. This can enable the EC Commission, Parliament or the Council to claim they have Employers' full support for a measure, even when UNICE has opposed it' (Tyszkiewicz 1990: 7). This situation can arise for two principal reasons: the selection process for the ESC and the resources devoted to lobbying it by UNICE and its member federations. The selection process for ESC Counsellors differs greatly from one Member State to another. Nominations are put forward by organizations to the national governments. In the case of nominations to Group I, in some countries it amounts to a *de facto* appointment by the employers' organization. In other countries, notably the UK, employers organizations merely have the right to nominate candidates and this advice is either accepted or rejected by the government. This results in varying degrees of loyalty and attachment felt by the Group I Counsellors to the national employers' organizations. Of course, all counsellors are nominated on a personal basis and are in theory at least, expected to remain independent. However, in practice, they are inevitably influenced by their national and professional background. There seems to be no obvious systematic criteria for the selection of Group III members and in practice this often leads to informal alliance-building between Groups II and III, which then out-vote the employers. The employers' voice in the ESC is thus further weakened.

For UNICE to be more effective within the ESC, more time and resources need to be devoted to maintaining contact with and briefing members of the ESC. UNICE staff do serve as experts on ESC Study Groups and many member federation representatives serve as alternates on Group I. But this is not always effective. National member federations will have to devote more resources to the briefing of their nationals on the Committee if they are to influence outcomes. When resources are deployed in this direction, lobbying success within the ESC is achieved—e.g. as with the Minority Declaration adopted by Group I of the ESC on 21 March 1991 on the Commission's Proposal on European Works Councils.

The Council of Ministers is, of course, a key decision-making arena, although perversely UNICE's European-level focus carries less weight in the Council, where national interests predominate. UNICE does send its position papers to the Permanent Representations of each Member State and there is evidence that these are used during negotiations. UNICE's influence in this arena could be very great if it were able to better co-ordinate and orchestrate nationally-based lobbying campaigns directed at national governments by member federations. Harnessing the usually privileged access which each member federation has to its own government, in order to press an agreed UNICE policy could, in principle, lead to the Council of Ministers facing a fairly co-ordinated lobbying effort via the individual national governments. As yet however, this potentially powerful lobbying resource seems largely unexploited by the business community in Europe.

There is also another aspect of the role of business in the EC lobbying process. It is often supposed that lobbying is a one-way process with business trying to influence governments. Increasingly, however, governments also lobby business organizations as part of their own attempts to influence EC policy outcomes. This is especially true on issues related to EC Social Policy where employers and unions often have more privileged access to EC decision-makers than governments.

3.2 Relationships with other EC-Level Business Organizations

UNICE is of course not the only European-level organization representing business interests in Brussels. There are a number of such organizations, e.g. the European Round Table, Eurochambres, and even the American Chamber of Commerce. This increases the likelihood of the employers' message becoming diluted and even contradictory. In order to be effective, UNICE will have to strengthen its existing links with these organizations so that where possible it can make common cause, and where this is impossible it can at least ensure that each body knows the reasons behind any divergence. Although at present the spirit within UNICE is willing to do this, its resources and time are limited.

Febies (Federations des industries par branches d'industries or Sectoral Organizations) UNICE deals with cross-sectoral issues of interest to business and industry as a whole. This cannot, however, be a rigid division. UNICE does deal with a sectoral issue 'when no relevant sectoral organization exists or when the issue is of exceptional importance', or when it threatens to have implications for the whole of industry (Tyszkiewicz 1990: 3). Examples of this include UNICE's role in the patentability of software programmes, the intellectual property rights on biotechnology inventions, and the issue of packaging and the environment. UNICE also supported the pharmaceutical lobby in its protest against the use of a 'fourth hurdle' of 'social acceptability' in the marketing and use of its products. In these instances, staff from sectoral organizations are typically co-opted on to UNICE working groups where they provide invaluable technical expertise.

In some instances, UNICE provides the means for the creation of *ad hoc* umbrella organizations on specific and technically complex issues. An example of this was the creation in December 1990, of the UNICE Packaging Communication Network (PCN). This is a grouping of representatives from some twenty-two sectoral organizations as well as federation representatives (see Appendix 2). Its task is to examine the implications for the industry of the Commission's proposition on packaging and to represent these views directly to the Commission. UNICE also brings together Febies to exchange information on developments in Social Affairs. This is becoming ever more important given the proliferation of the social dialogue at sectoral level. Despite this co-operation, we need to underline the real challenge presented to UNICE by the need for closer co-operation with such bodies. Febies have their own deep-rooted traditions and there is often rivalry both within Febies and between them. Creating workable and stable lobbying coalitions for this diverse set of interests is exceedingly difficult and complex.

ETUC UNICE is in close touch with the European Trades Union Conference or ETUC. It has frequent formal and informal contact with the latter through the social dialogue, the production of joint opinions, pre-consultation meetings on the Social Action Programme proposals, and in the current (1991/2) talks which are taking place on the future role of the social partners.

In one sense, UNICE is, however, at a disadvantage compared to the ETUC. This is the result of a common misconception by those outside UNICE. UNICE, as an organization representing business and industry, is perceived as a rich body with the unlimited resources of business at its disposal. This is however not the case. In reality, UNICE is run on a very tight budget, and like its member federations which provide much of its financing, must operate on tightly-managed resources (see Ch. 13). Indeed, given the tasks which business expects it to perform, UNICE is severely under-resourced. Its budget in 1991 was just BF 130 million. It has a staff of thirty-one, twelve of whom are of executive rank, plus two executives on secondment from companies, free of charge. It has no proper research capability, a factor which will increasingly handicap it in its relations with the Commission and Parliament.

UNICE does not receive funding from EC institutions. This seems to be due in part to the assumption by the EC institutions that business groups are always well-funded. Lack of EC funding may also be explained by a fear expressed by UNICE in the past that its independence might be compromised by accepting funding from the EC institutions. There is evidence, however, that the desire for UNICE to remain 'poor but pure' no longer receives the unanimous support of all UNICE federations. A debate on this issue is currently taking place within UNICE. ETUC on the other hand receives a great deal of its funding from the EC. This includes the provision of a European Commission financed Trade Union Research Institute and a special secretariat dealing with health and safety matters. New developments include the proposed creation of an EC-funded Trade Union Academy. Not only does ETUC receive financial help, it also benefits from less tangible support and aid from EC institutions. (For example there is a special unit within DG X dedicated solely to the diffusion of information to trade unions.) Also, in its dealings with the European Parliament, ETUC enjoys a close relationship with the Social Affairs Committee, which shares its objectives. For instance, the Committee often adopts by a large majority, Resolutions favourable to ETUC's position (Tyszkiewicz 1990: 13).

Given that the Commission is putting UNICE under a great deal of pressure to draw up EC-level collective (some might say corporatist) agreements with the ETUC, the issue of resources will have to be seriously tackled if UNICE is to participate in this process as an equal partner. The creation of UASG has increased UNICE's resourcing considerably, but it is still under-resourced as an association for European business. In an attempt to develop further its expertise, UNICE is currently investigating how it might fund research projects to be undertaken by an independent research body. In addition to redressing the financial imbalance UNICE also has to try and counter public perceptions of its activities which are often viewed in a much less favourable light to those of the ETUC.

National Federations   The representation of national federations in Brussels is growing—both in terms of established federations increasing their staff in Brussels, and federations not previously represented in Brussels, opening new offices. UNICE has demonstrated that it can unite its member federations to provide position papers. Can it then go one step further and build transnational lobbying coalitions whose operation at the national level is becoming vital for effective lobbying? It is in the field of Social Affairs that the greatest increase of this type of action by employers has taken place.

The increased use of qualified majority voting in the Council, the increased legislative powers of the European Parliament, and the inclusion of more policy areas within the EC's remit prompted a review of UNICE's operation by the UNICE Council of Presidents on 3 December 1991. The possibility that UNICE will be drawing up collective agreements and the continued development of the social dialogue all point to increased incentives for greater co-ordination of lobbying by industry and commerce. At the above meeting, held at Scheveningen in the Hague, it was agreed that the existing target for the growth of UNICE should be met with provision for a modest increase in resources to meet any future needs. This would allow for a gradual expansion in staff numbers. In particular, it was thought desirable to employ someone to co-ordinate the research work currently being carried out by UNICE member federations and to supervise involvement by senior businessmen. Further staff secondments from member federations and member companies were also to be encouraged. Opinions differed on the issue of the desirability of accepting funding from the EC institutions. A small drafting committee is to be formed to draw up a paper on the future organization of UNICE, based on the Scheveningen conclusions. This paper was submitted to the spring meeting of UNICE's Executive Committee (2 April) and, for final decision, to its Council of Presidents, meeting in Lisbon on 11–12 June 1992.

Member Companies A considerable resource is provided to UNICE by the involvement in UNICE committee work of company representatives from member federations. The contribution of such personnel is impossible to quantify, but is invaluable to UNICE. Indirectly then, UNICE is benefiting from those national federations who have direct company membership. Such direct, specialist, industrial and commercial experience is vitally important in the drawing up of realistic position papers and in building UNICE's credibility with policy-makers who demand, above all, expertise.

UNICE had for some time been considering ways of increasing the involvement of companies in an advisory capacity. As indicated earlier, in June 1990 it created the UNICE Advisory and Support Group or UASG. According to its founding Regulation: 'It is an Advisory but not a decision making body.' It's financial contribution to UNICE is restricted to 25 per cent of UNICE's total budget thus 'ensuring that member federations remain clearly in a position of authority'. In order to become members of the UASG, companies must be 'a member directly or indirectly through a sectoral association of its national federation which must be a member of UNICE'. The advantage to UNICE is that it will provide the organization with 'closer links with the economic operators on whose behalf it speaks', and will enable it 'to compare its own priorities with those of the UASG member companies and adjust its actions if necessary' (Tyszkiewicz 1990: 8). The advantage to the companies is that it will provide them with regular opportunities of review and comment on UNICE's work, priorities, and overall strategy. It will also provide a regular flow of timely information of European issues of interest to business.

4. CONCLUSION

UNICE has undoubtedly achieved much to date. It is invariably consulted by the Commission, almost as a matter of right. With regard to official consultative committees and advisory bodies, UNICE is in many cases responsible for nominating all employer members (e.g. training, health and safety, customs, consumer policy). It has begun to address its resourcing problem and has developed a decision-making style which does produce agreement. And it has learnt to move faster in response to the increased rhythm of EC legislation and is ever conscious of the 1992 deadline.

Nevertheless, it is evident that companies, especially large multinationals, will not use UNICE as their sole lobbying channel. Their participation in UNICE will be merely one part of a multi-faceted strategy which will include direct representations, lobbying through their national employers' organization their national and European-level trade associations, and lobbying through *ad hoc* organizations (see Ch. 13). They may also be members of the European Round Table and/or of the informal grouping of European multinationals known as the European Enterprise Group (EEG). If lobbying is compared to duck shooting, then companies hunting ducks are going to load their guns with more than one bullet. This in itself presents a particular challenge to bodies like UNICE.

UNICE faces many more challenges in the future. Leaving aside the potential problems of internal disunity—a problem encountered by most, if not all, European federations—UNICE will have to respond to a rapidly changing external environment. The recent extension of the Community's legal competence to such sectors as the environment, social and regional policy, will have far-reaching implications for UNICE members. Meanwhile, EC institutional reforms introduced by the SEA and, more recently, by the Maastricht Treaty, significantly changed the EC policy-making environment. In order to be effective, UNICE must now develop new lobbying strategies which take account both of the increasing importance of the European Parliament and the need to build horizontal coalitions with their European counterparts at the national level. More generally, recent developments in Eastern and Central Europe will bring new opportunities and problems for UNICE.

Appendix 1

UNICE Sub-Committees and Working Groups

Economic and Financial Affairs Committee Working Groups

Economic Policy Group
Fiscal Affairs Group
Financial Group
Community Statistics Group
Regional Policy Group

External Affairs Committee Working Groups

Japan Group
Customs Legislation Group
United States Group
New Multilateral Trade Negotiations Group (GATT)
EEC/Eastern European Countries Group
Export Credit Insurance Group
Export Controls on Dual Use Products
Ad Hoc Group

Social Affairs Committee Working Groups

Education/Training
Health and Safety
Industrial relations
Employment
Social Security

Company Affairs Committee Working Groups

Competition Group
Company Law Group
Technical Barriers Group
Employee Information and Consultation (Jointly with Social Affairs Committee)
Consumer/Marketing Groups
Expert Group on Unfair Contract Terms
Intellectual Property Sub-Groups:

• Patents
• Expert Group on Biotechnological Inventions

- Trademarks
- Licences
- Copyright
- Industrial Designs
- GATT and Intellectual Property

Insurance Ad Hoc Group
Liability of Businesses Ad Hoc Group
Liability and Environment Ad Hoc Group
Accounting Standards Ad Hoc Group
Data Protection Ad Hoc Groups

Industrial Affairs Committee Working Groups

Environment Group
Water Pollution Group
Waste Group
Air Pollution Group
Ad Hoc Group Environmental Audit
Ad Hoc Group Greenhouse Effect/EC Policy on CO_2
Small and Medium-Sized Enterprise Groups
Transport Group
Energy Group
Telecommunications Group
Research and Technological Development Group
Public Procurement Group
Services Task Force

Appendix 2

UNICE Packaging Communication Network (as on 22 Jan. 1991)

Confédération Européenne de l'Industrie des Pâtes, Papiers et Carton (CEPAC)
Association of Plastics Manufacturers in Europe (APME)
Confédération Internationale des Transformateurs de Papier et Carton de la Communauté Européenne (CITPA)
Association Professionnelle des Producteurs Européens d'Aciers pour Emballage (APEAL)
Association Européenne des Métaux (EUROMETAUX)
The Alliance for Beverage Cartons and the Environment (ACE)
Ad hoc Packaging Legislation Group (Multi-FEBI Group)

Association Européenne des Industries de Produits de Marque (AIM)
Organisme de Liaison des Industries Métaliques Européennes (ORGALIME)
Conseil Européen des Fédérations de l'Industrie Chimique (CEFIC)
European Organisation for Packaging and the Environment (EUROPEN)
Fédération Européenne du Verre d'Emballage (FEVE)
European Recovery and Recycling Association (ERRA)
Fédération Européenne des Activités du Déchet (FEAD)
Confédération Européenne du Commerce de détail/Federation of European Wholesale and International Trade Associations/ Groupement Européen des Entreprises de Distribution intégrée (CECD/FEWITA/GEDIS)
European Plastic Converters (EPC)
Fédération de la Sidérurgie Européenne (EUROFER)
Confédération des Industries Agro-Alimentaires (CIAA)
Comité Permanent des Industries du Verre de la CEE
Association Internationale de la Savonnerie et de la Détergence (AIS)
Federation of European Aerosol Associations (FEA)
Fédération Internationale des Associations de Fabricants de Produits d'Entretien (FIFE)

References

Tyszkiewicz, Z. J. A. (1990), 'UNICE: The Voice of European Business and Industry in Brussels', paper presented to the IREC conference, Trier, 28–30 Sept. 1990.
UNICE (1984), *Memorandum to the New Commission* (Brussels).

13

The Corporate Benefits of Lobbying: The British Case and its Relevance to the European Community

JANE A. SARGENT

1. INTRODUCTION

I would like to discuss lobbying in the European Community from the perspective of business pressure groups' members—namely the companies they exist to represent. We cannot reach a meaningful understanding of the role of interest organizations in the European Community until we understand the pressures exerted on them by their members. We all know that pressure groups do not exist in isolation from their members and that they are not their members' only channel of representation in EC matters. But what does this mean in practice? What does it mean, for instance, for a trade association official hoping to influence EC policy-making? Conventional wisdom states that in relation to policy-making, trade bodies can deliver only collective goods—benefits which apply equally to their members and non-members—to those who have championed a cause as well as to those who have not. For this reason, trade associations try to attract members by promising additional selected benefits which are available only to members, for instance preferential insurance policies, legal advice, etc. (see Ch. 7). What is less well documented is exactly what an individual company expects a trade association to provide in relation to EC policy and how this expectation affects the trade association's capacity to influence such a policy. To help develop our understanding of this issue I propose to address two questions. First, what benefits do companies expect from taking an active interest in EC policy? Secondly, what assistance do companies expect pressure groups to provide when seeking to achieve these objectives? The following observations are based on my experiences as both a trade association official and an independent government-relations consultant.

2. WHAT DO COMPANIES EXPECT FROM EC INVOLVEMENT?

The circumstances in which companies first take an active interest in EC policy is a useful pointer to the answer to the first question. In every case, of course, they first become interested the moment they realize that EC policy affects their daily lives. In some cases this has been the day they were caught out by an EC policy! In one case, some years ago, DG IV officials knocked on a company's door in a swoop against a suspected cartel (in much the same style of the January 1991 raids on British Steel). The company's management had no idea that Commission officials had such powers of intervention. In another case, an active interest in EC policy-making began when the company in question found that it had goods on order which were about to become illegal (and therefore unsaleable) under new EC laws. As companies have become more aware of the importance of the EC, such cases are now less common. Other companies, however, have been better prepared. They are aware well in advance of potential problems arising from EC membership and latterly from completion of the Single European Market. They have also been helped by awareness-building campaigns by government departments, such as the DTI's '1992' initiative, and by pressure groups such as the CBI. Yet, whatever the catalyst, the basic motivator is usually the same—the implications of EC policy for the company's 'bottom line'—both negative and positive. The return companies seek from their involvement in EC policy can be broadly categorized under five headings: timely compliance, damage limitation, safeguarding trading environments, business opportunities and ideas, and 'insurance' policies.

I have already referred to the most obvious objective, namely timely compliance with EC-inspired legislation. Being caught off-guard in this respect can involve substantial costs, if not in terms of fines and legal costs, then in the form of unsaleable merchandise. Also, inappropriate planning and investment decisions might be taken, resulting in a firm having to spend even more money to modify relatively new plant, machinery, or vehicles. An individual's future as a director could also be jeopardized if a criminal offence is involved. And, not least among a company's concerns, failure to keep up with EC developments and react accordingly may damage its reputation among employees, customers, or shareholders, possibly to the extent of undermining years of work invested in the cultivation of a favourable image. For instance, a number of British companies which projected themselves as 'good employers' in the past, are now struggling to maintain that image given their opposition to Commission proposals for pro rata rights and benefits for 'atypical' and full-time and permanent employees. What was previously regarded as generous on the companies' part is now considered somewhat less generous in comparison with what is on offer in some other Member States and with the EC Commission's proposals.

A second priority for companies taking an active interest in EC policy-making is the opportunity to limit the damage anticipated from potentially costly proposals. Such action can range from seeking an exemption for a particular range of goods or companies, to deferring the implementation date for the industry as a whole. When damage limitation exercises are successful they can more than compensate a company for the investment required in terms of funding and management time devoted to lobbying or to supporting the lobbying efforts of a trade body.

EC policy also presents companies with opportunities to improve their general trading environments. This can involve opening up new markets, pressing for more stringent standards in order to outlaw so-called 'cowboys' within an industry, or campaigning for specific national laws which act as barriers to trade within the EC to be overruled. However, those companies which allocate sizeable budgets to EC-related activities, give highest priority to the new business opportunities and ideas, exclusive to the company, presented by EC policy. These companies have realized that EC policy can be a useful source of ideas for new products and new marketing initiatives, as well as for uniform standards and procedures.

The fifth main reason why a company will take an active interest in EC policy-making is to provide itself with a valuable insurance policy to be redeemed in times of crisis, e.g. in the event of an unwelcome takeover bid from a foreign-owned company. Rowntree, for instance, regretted having neglected this function when it tried to persuade European MPs to back its case against Nestlé.

The reaction of many of the MEPs who turned up to listen to members of the Rowntree's Board present their case in Strasbourg, was 'why have you not been to see us before? Because we don't know you, what do you expect us to say when you tell us you are a "good employer" etc., other than that "you would say that wouldn't you"?'

In reality, not all companies are quite as aware of the significance of the EC as my list suggests. Most British companies are still predominantly passive and reactive in their approach to the EC, focusing more upon timely compliance, damage limitation, and building up political contacts than on the promotion of company-specific business opportunities. Some companies still pursue political contacts more for their own sake than with a long-term insurance policy in mind. But those companies which do allocate a sizeable budget to active EC involvement—and the number is increasing—are looking for a significant return on their investment. What part do they expect pressure groups to play in helping them realize that return? To answer this question, we need to consider how and when companies use pressure groups in order to achieve each of their five broad commercial objectives.

3. WHERE DO PRESSURE GROUPS FIT IN?

3.1 Timely Compliance

The role of established trade associations is understandably circumscribed in helping companies meet their objective of timely compliance with EC-derived legislation. Here, of course, the main requirement of the trade association will be information rather than influence. But this is the forte of such groups, which are often able to provide an unrivalled service. The information provided by trade associations constitutes a selective benefit which is available to members for a relatively modest fee.

3.2 Damage Limitation

Established trade associations also have a significant role to play in the context of corporate damage-limitation objectives. In general, companies are content to rely on trade associations to protect their interests in two contexts where the cost implications are broadly similar for all members of the industry concerned; and in connection with essentially technical proposals of relatively low priority for the companies. Fortunately for the trade associations, the majority of EC policy falls within these categories. The work required is essentially that of advocate rather than campaigner and the personnel appointed to staff such organizations often reflects this requirement. So too do the trade associations' budgets.

The question of budgets is an important one. It highlights a significant constraint under which trade associations operate when seeking to influence EC policy, even when they have the full backing of their members. This constraint is the requirement to provide value for money. There are very few issues which justify a win at any price. Those which do typically involve specific benefits to the affected companies which, for this reason, are usually prepared to provide the necessary funding. However, when the stakes are this high the companies in question generally prefer to take independent action or launch a new campaign group to achieve their objectives, rather than rely upon their trade association.

A typical example of such a group was the 'Hands Off Reading (VAT)' campaign. This was sponsored mainly by leading newspaper publishers, with moral support from hundreds of individuals and groups interested in the printed word—local authorities, librarians, book and periodical publishers, educational bodies, and retailers. Significantly, the Newspaper Publishers' Association was not considered by the publishers in question to be an appropriate body through which to present this case, partly because it would have looked like blatant special pleading. By establishing a campaign group, publishers were able to attract the support of influential non-producer groups. There was also some scepticism about the NPA's ability to manage such a campaign effectively alongside its other duties.

Even in the case of the relatively low priority technical issues which constitute the bulk of trade associations' day-to-day activities, company members are sometimes prepared to see their association lose its case due to lack of adequate funding or back-up. This is illustrated time and again by the inadequate state of UK trade associations' data bases about the sectors they represent. The retail trade associations are a typical example. Despite the technical resources available to the Consumers' Association (and thereby the

Consumers in the European Community Group), British retailers have consistently refused to provide the necessary funding for their own trade associations to undertake in-depth research on the cost, employment, and administrative implications of EC proposals. All too often in the past, comments from the relevant retail associations have been restricted to detailed recommendations on how proposals should be amended. These have been supported by only general observations indicating that a specific proposal would be costly or administratively burdensome, or result in job losses. Rarely has there been any attempt to quantify precisely the impact. This shortcoming limits the persuasiveness, in its turn, of the retailers' European trade associations.

Nevertheless, companies still turn to their national and European trade associations when seeking favourable amendment of EC legislative proposals, and damage-limitation exercises are probably the trade associations' speciality. Damage-limitation activities may involve attempts to limit the scope of a particular piece of legislation, to exempt a category of companies altogether, or to remove from the scope of the proposal some of a company's most sensitive products. In a number of EC states, including the UK, temporary employment agencies for instance, are actively seeking exemption for their operations from the Commission's draft directives on atypical workers and the relevant national and European trade associations are playing a key role in this process. Similarly, UK manufacturers pressed long and hard through the CBI to have the provisions of the draft product-safety directive restricted to consumer goods. At other times, attention focuses on taking action to achieve as late an implementation date as possible, in order to avoid the consequences of being unable to meet the requirements by the original deadline. Mail-order traders, for instance, are adept at campaigning for deferred implementation dates in relation to their catalogues. The UK Mail Order Traders' Association and its European body have built up a significant reputation in this respect among UK and EC policy-makers.

Sometimes, however, independent lobbying by members can undermine the work of the trade association. For instance, in response to by-election defeats and the government's poor ratings in opinion polls in 1990–1, a number of British companies began, 'off the record', to talk of accepting a negotiated agreement on the most contentious aspects of the Social Action Programme. The possibility of a Labour Government being elected, pledged to implement the EC Commission's original proposals, persuaded these companies of the need to negotiate an earlier compromise more favourable to their interests. By acting in this way, these companies risked compromising the positions of established trade associations such as the CBI, which, hitherto, had backed the government on this issue. Understandably, the trade associations were anxious not to jeopardize their relations with the government by appearing to criticize ministers or by openly expressing a loss of confidence in the government. Their errant members would have been the first to criticize them if they had!

The main circumstance in which a company's dissatisfaction with the UK Government's position can undermine the capacity of its trade association to mitigate the potential impact of the proposals is when the issue in question is subject to qualified majority approval by the Council of Ministers. In these circumstances the scope for a British trade body to influence the final policy agreement is diminished and a UK company with operations in other EC states can have greater effect by asking its EC subsidiaries to press its case through the appropriate national trade associations, and in some instances by lobbying other Member States' governments. This tactic is being deployed by a number of pan-European companies on various Social Charter proposals. Whilst this strategy may be effective for the companies concerned, it can reduce the credibility of the trade association in the eyes of the UK Government.

3.3 Improve/Safeguard the Trading Environment

Representative associations have also seen their role undermined in assisting their members to improve their general trading environment. This objective is, of course, a collective benefit which cannot be restricted to those members or companies which had actively campaigned for it. It would seem to make commercial sense in such circumstances to put a collective front forward. But, here too, the pressure group's role is not always as straightforward as one might expect.

In some cases, the national trade association is required to provide a front for an individual company, rather than simply a collective voice. Let us take the case of a UK-based company with operations in a number of EC countries. What does such a company do when faced with the Commission's latest proposals on informing and consulting employees? It cannot afford simply to dismiss the proposals out of hand and back the UK Government's opposition to formalized procedures and European works councils, for fear of upsetting its Continental employees. In at least one case, for instance, the company has decided to try to appease all parties. In those Member States where the principle of works councils already applies, the company is not opposing the proposals. But in the UK it is relying upon the CBI to oppose the measures, taking no part in the proceedings itself. In this way the pressure group can cover for a company wishing to avoid embarrassment.

The size and scope of a trade association's membership can be a limiting factor: the introduction of new minimum standards by the Community can be costly, but there is often the consolation that the standards will affect a company and its competitors equally and may even reduce the competition by pricing 'cowboys' out of the market. Unfortunately, a trade association representing all sizes and types of company within a sector is likely to face considerable opposition from its smaller members to any efforts to impose more stringent requirements upon them. Is it surprising, therefore, that an increasing number of larger companies seek representation on relevant British Standards Institution committees, albeit through their trade bodies, to assist them in negotiating EC-wide standards which can protect and even enhance their own market share?

The Community's growing appeal to British businesses as a source of uniform legislative minimum standards is also explained by companies' perceptions that such standards can sometimes limit their responsibilities in certain fields. This is particularly true in relation to environmental protection. For example, the UK Conservative Government's free-market policy has meant that it has been unwilling to legislate to require companies to undertake environmental audits and to publish the results. Though companies initially welcomed this policy, they are now beginning to wonder whether the absence of legal requirements in this field means that there is no limit to what they might be required to do. The scale and range of demands which the public, customers, shareholders, environmental pressure groups, and the government are now putting upon companies was not anticipated by them. The White Paper 'This Common Inheritance' and the Department of the

Environment leaflet made available to the public through leading supermarkets entitled 'Wake Up to What You Can Do for the Environment', are proving to have far more onerous implications for some companies than they would have expected from legal minimum standards.

Indeed, there is no limit to the 'voluntary' initiatives large companies might be pressed to introduce; in practice the 'voluntary' approach means that the level of public expectation rises continually. Competition between companies in the same sector to prove their environmental credentials is now so frantic, that as soon as a company decides on a particular initiative, it is outsmarted by its competitors. An entirely free market has lost its appeal and the prospect of the Community spelling out a minimum requirement, thereby levelling the playing field (a situation which companies always find reassuring!), is being looked at in a new light.

EC measures designed to open up new markets present further opportunities to improve a company's general trading environment. EC competition policy can be particularly helpful in this regard via the removal of restrictive trade barriers presented by specific national laws. British road hauliers, for example, have been arguing for some time, both individually and through the appropriate trade associations, that other countries' subsidies for road and rail freight transport distort competition within the EC. As a result, the European Commission in 1991 decided to investigate the Italian Government's incentives for road hauliers. A more widely publicized case involved the attempts by British, French, and Belgian interests to persuade the European Court of Justice that certain national laws on shop opening hours were against the principle of the Single European Market and contravened specific Articles of the Rome Treaty. To date (July 1991) none of these cases has been successful. As court cases are involved, the responsibility of championing the cause fell to an individual defendant in the UK case, but in those countries where mass appeals are more commonplace, a trade body can have a leading role even when the matter is referred to the European Court. The ruling by the European Court on the Belgian laws relating to Sunday trading involved a case taken by a regional trade union, albeit against an individual employer.

eg shopping on sundays in UK [handwritten margin note]

3.4 *New Business Opportunities*

Occasionally, EC policy which opens up new markets can present specific business opportunities to an individual company, as in the case of the draft directive designed to open up public procurement in all services, from advertising to waste disposal. Industrial service companies which provide a wide range of services have been anxious to persuade Commission officials that the full range of their particular services should be treated equally by the proposals— either in category A (which imposes the full procurement rules) or in category B (which requires only minimum disclosure), but not spread across both combinations groupings. (In this way, the same rules would apply to any multi-service contract.) Inevitably, such action has involved direct representations to the appropriate officials, leaving the relevant European trade association somewhat marginalized. In this case, however, corporate lobbying activities have been outpaced by commercial action, namely by a flurry of cross-border takeovers. It is interesting that takeovers have been given priority over preparations for cross-border tendering—reflecting a belief that despite the Commission's initiatives, a local (albeit foreign-owned) company is still more likely to win contracts than EC contenders from other Member States.

In other cases, company-specific business opportunities arise when a new EC directive awaits implementation by the national governments. The recently adopted draft directive on batteries and accumulators containing mercury, cadmium, and lead is a case in point. The proposal requires Member States to introduce measures to encourage recycling and reuse of spent batteries by 1993. By mid-1991, the DTI and the Department of the Environment had not given a great deal of consideration to exactly how this should be achieved in the UK. However, at least one leading battery retailer had already introduced initiatives of its own to encourage battery recycling, ostensibly on a voluntary basis. It hoped to gain competitive advantage by doing so, and ensure that future requirements were based on the arrangements it had introduced. Thus, some companies look upon EC policy as a useful market indicator. By relying on the lag effect between the formulation of an EC proposal and its implementation in the UK, they can mitigate the cost of compliance by introducing an initiative similar to that likely to be required, before it becomes law.

Pressure groups, however, have a limited role to play in relation to individual new business opportunities which a specific company might be seeking from its EC involvement. By definition, companies rarely want to share their gains with competitors, so they will not often be looking for help from their trade association in this respect—not, that is, in a positive sense. However, a group can be useful in these circumstances, in a negative capacity. Some companies have been known to use an interest group to try to delay EC and UK policy-making and stir up concern among their competitors on particular issues. In this way a company can buy time for itself to introduce a new product or service and put its competitors off the scent. This tactic is a favourite one among the leading food retailers in the UK and was deployed successfully by various companies in relation to their own-brand products in the run up to the introduction of fat content labelling and child-resistant closures on certain household chemicals.

Such initiatives are rarely discouraged, if not welcomed by the UK officials who are charged with implementing EC laws, many of whom lack any commercial experience. This is particularly true where the EC measure sets out the broad principles, leaving it up to each Member State to decide for itself how best to implement the principles in practice. In the face of staunch opposition from the relevant trade associations, who may argue that the EC proposals are unworkable, the emergence of a company which is prepared 'voluntarily' to give effect to the EC commitment can provide officials with a welcome break to a political deadlock. In an extreme case, the company may itself assume the characteristics of a pressure group if it is to its competitive advantage to do so. The classic example of this approach is the Body Shop which campaigns on environmental issues in relation to cosmetic products and, thereby aims to increase the appeal of its own products.

The introduction of qualified majority decision-making has meant that a number of pan-European companies are now in a position to usurp the traditional role of European trade associations. Whereas the latter have to reach agreements which satisfy the requirements of members representing not only different national interests but also different commercial interests within each national context, the pan-European company simply has to find a formula which is suitable to its own trading requirements. Not surprisingly, given a choice between listening to a pan-European company that has developed a workable solution, say to consulting and informing its employees on a European scale, and waiting for a negotiated solution from a European trade association, Commission officials will be more interested in the former. From the company's point of view, if Commission officials can possibly be persuaded to base their proposals on the company's procedures, a direct dialogue must be an attractive option.

This is not to suggest that pressure groups do not have a role to play in assisting individual members to identify company-specific opportunities presented by EC policy proposals. A pressure group can still play a key role in assisting a company to identify such opportunities, simply through the information it provides about pending EC policy. The subscription costs can be easily justified if the monitoring system throws up (albeit unwittingly) just one new business lead a year to a member company.

3.5 Insurance Policy

Business pressure groups have a more direct involvement in assisting their member companies to develop a favourable reputation among decision-makers, as an insurance policy to draw upon in times of crisis, for instance in a takeover situation or an environmental/public health incident. One of the most popular means for individual companies to introduce themselves to the Commission is as a member of a trade delegation to the relevant Commissioner or Director-General as such involvement emphasizes the company's status within a particular industry.

There is a growing trend, however, for established UK trade associations to face competition from groupings of both sides of industry. For example, the Industrial Participation Association (IPA), which organized a study tour of the European Commission for its members in 1991, boasts a membership of company directors and union leaders. It is looked upon particularly favourably by companies wishing to project a 'good employer' image and by the Commission, which is anxious to promote closer links between the social partners.

The attraction to corporate members of this grouping is the scope of its membership—beyond either specific sectoral or specific business interests. Such groupings recall the 'tripartite' arrangements of the 1970s. More commonplace, however, in the UK in the past few years have been issue-specific, *ad hoc* groupings of leading businesses, groupings of the 'great and the good'. Such groupings have been encouraged by the Conservative Government as a means of improving its links with industry. Only recently, the government announced the formation of another grouping of this kind—the Advisory Committee on Business and the Environment, comprised of senior managers from individual companies across a range of industries. Ten years ago such a committee would have consisted of trade association nominees. Increasingly, however, the government has preferred to by-pass the traditional representative associations and set up issue-specific groupings of individuals selected by ministers rather than nominated by trade bodies. This is particularly true where the government has decided to guide and encourage rather than to legislate, such as in the environmental field, and where it has looked to the private sector to fund its initiatives, as in the case of City Technology Colleges, new roads etc. Membership of these groupings is attractive to those companies wishing to project a particular image as leaders in their field, whether on environmental issues or training or whatever. But they are not simply image enhancers. Groups such as that on 'Business and the Environment' play a leading role in the development and negotiation of policy initiatives, such as the development of an EC-wide eco-labelling scheme.

4. CONCLUSION: MULTIPLE CHANNELS OF REPRESENTATION

In the UK at least, companies appear to use established trade associations more for information about EC developments than for influence over these developments. In practice, firms can select from a range of possible actions and different channels of influence according to the particular objectives which they are trying to achieve. In some circumstances, as suggested, lobbying initiatives undertaken by companies can actually undermine the effectiveness of representative groups. Only in tightly defined circumstances do companies appear to use existing trade associations to influence EC policy on their behalf—namely on issues of relatively low priority to the company which are usually technical in nature and offer no

THE CORPORATE BENEFITS OF LOBBYING

opportunities for individual commercial advantage. Where such opportunities exist, a company is more likely to take action independently. In connection with issues to which a company attaches high priority, direct action and/or the creation of a special one-issue campaigning group is often preferred to the established trade association, as a means of achieving the desired objective.

Trade associations can of course provide useful access to EC policy-makers but they are also valued for the access they provide to a company's competitors, and the opportunity to foster discord and delay. In short, we are not talking about the politics of pressure so much as about the politics of paralysis when we consider companies' use of traditional trade associations in relation to EC policy-making. Euro-groups which include British associations having to operate under these subtle constraints, can do little to obviate the adverse effects in terms of their own effectiveness. The phenomenon simply spreads into the Euro-group and renders it even more impotent than its national members. Meanwhile, pan-European companies are emerging as more effective providers of workable solutions to Community problems than are national or European pressure groups.

What of the future? Are there any signs that matters are likely to improve for the traditional forms of representative trade associations? This seems unlikely under the present government, because as suggested above, trade associations are being eclipsed by special campaign groups, and groupings of the great and the good. Indeed, government ministers are doing little to discourage the trend. Over the past twelve years the Conservative Government has actively tried to remove the intermediary role of trade associations from the policy-making process and has fostered closer links between departments and individual companies. This is not surprising as it is companies and not trade associations who are equipped to provide funding for government projects and who are directly involved in policy implementation. A Labour Government would herald a return to a more formalized basis for dialogue with 'the two sides of industry', but may not entirely rule out direct links with individual companies.

In the mean time, Conservative ministers have increasingly openly encouraged companies to make their individual views on EC proposals known in Brussels and Strasbourg. The latest case that comes to mind is the Secretary of State for Employment's plea to companies concerning a number of the Social Charter proposals. Significantly, in this case, British companies are also being urged to make their views known to other Member States' governments—a recognition of the UK Government's own weakness in the face of qualified majority decision-making.

The recent extension of qualified majority voting agreed in principle at the Maastricht summit will further undermine the ability of national trade associations to influence EC policy. Moreover, it is unlikely that European trade associations will be able to extend their remits beyond lobbying the Community institutions to lobbying individual Member States' governments. In consequence, Commission officials are likely to continue to look to pan-European companies to provide workable suggestions to EC policy stalemates, irrespective of their stated preference for dealing with representative Euro-groups.

A number of observers, especially trade association officials and policy-makers, have criticized companies for consistently preventing pressure groups from developing policies on EC issues which reflect more than agreement on the lowest common denominator; for liaising directly with EC and national institutions on EC issues, thereby sometimes undermining the voice of their pressure group and overloading the political system; and on other occasions for their reluctance to back up the pressure group's EC activities with sufficient financial or management resources.

However, cost-effective lobbying from a corporate point of view is not necessarily conducive to effective lobbying by a representative pressure group. There is an important difference between the two to a company interested in the impact of the EC on its bottom line. The former means that sometimes it pays for the pressure group (and even the company) to lose! Few issues are worth winning at any price, and in a recessionary climate, immediate commercial concerns often take precedence over longer term 'political' worries, despite the potential cost of 'short-termism' at the end of the day. Essentially, companies are ultimately answerable to their shareholders and as a result are more interested in competitive commercial considerations than in consensus politics. Whether established trade associations will ever be able to overcome the constraints which this situation places upon them is doubtful. This is not to suggest that they do not have an important part to play in the policy-making process on behalf of companies. But that part is circumscribed and the parameters are defined by their members. Perhaps, all along, we have simply asked too much of these representative organizations.

Looking to the future, unless the EC Commission and/or a future UK Government refuses to deal directly with individual companies and makes membership of a representative trade body 'compulsory' in some way, the growth of alternative forms of dialogue with individual companies will continue and the potential influence of UK trade associations and their respective Euro-groups in relation to EC policy will continue to be undermined.

14

Conclusion: A European Policy Style?

SONIA MAZEY AND JEREMY RICHARDSON

1. NATIONAL VS. EUROPEAN LOBBYING

Wyn Grant's chapter advocated the need to avoid being mesmerized by the growing importance of Europe as a centre of decision-making to the exclusion of analysing the continued importance of national lobbying as a means of influencing policy. In fact most national groups (and firms and quangos) are still heavily dependent on their 'sponsoring' ministries, for at least three reasons. First, despite the undoubted shift in power to Brussels and Strasbourg, much policy-making power still rests at the level of the nation-state. Many, if not most, key areas of social and economic life are still largely influenced by national governments as well as by the EC. Even with the further moves towards monetary union (and the existence of the Exchange Rate Mechanism, ERM), the management and development of national economies remains of central concern to national governments. Their room for manoeuvre is increasingly restricted in such areas as exchange rates, interest rates, schemes to attract inward investment, etc., yet many of the key national political issues can still be resolved without too much interference from the EC. Britain is perhaps the classic example of the 'semi-sovereignty' of national governments, notwithstanding its membership of the EC. In such key areas as privatization, reform of the professions, restructuring of the health and education services, prison reform, trade union reforms, it is difficult to see a dominant EC influence. All of these policy areas can be caught up in EC controls, of course, but the main thrust of these policy changes has been, nevertheless, determined in Whitehall and Westminster. Thus, any group which had abandoned national lobbying because it believed that power had shifted completely to Brussels would feel itself at a major disadvantage.

Secondly, even in those areas where key decisions are made in

Brussels (as we and others have argued, the trend is quite clearly for more and more decisions to be taken at the EC level), it is absolutely vital for national interests to maintain very close links with their national political/administrative systems. Both David Spence and Wyn Grant have argued that national ministries are a central conduit for lobbying the EC. In a sense there is a dependence which exists between groups and 'their' ministries, with the latter effectively being 'intermediaries' between the groups and the EC, particularly in the final stages of the policy-making process. Most groups are conscious that they must be careful not to alienate their own ministries by pursuing a contrary line to Brussels or Strasbourg. A typical comment to us was 'I would be nervous if we were clearly saying something at major odds with the DTI . . . we would need to take a policy decision on that . . . we wouldn't do it unless it was vital and we had exhausted all other lines of bargaining with the DTI.' This reflects the reality for groups, knowing as they do that the DTI (in this case) could easily ditch the group's case in the ministerial bargaining at the EC level— either because the DTI was in disagreement with the group's position, or because, despite being in agreement, it felt that the group's position could be sacrificed in a bigger trade-off in Europe, or because the DTI was simply lacking in sufficient expertise to grasp the precise nature of the issues involved.

More often, however, there is a recognition of mutual interests and interdependency in dealing with Europe, and a recognition that a common and co-ordinated strategy between group and national administrations is desirable. Intelligence is usually shared because both national officials and group leaders face the same problem— the need to obtain good advance warning of policy change emanating from the EC. Quite often, it seems, groups have better advance intelligence than do their own governments. In part this is due to the greater intensity of interest in European matters on the part of groups—they know where the shoe pinches and are therefore likely to make the greatest efforts to influence EC policies. The relevant national ministries are, of course, affected too, but often not to the same degree as their clients. Also, groups in any one sector almost certainly place more resources in the field whereas COREPER officers are usually covering a rather broad waterfront and often cannot develop the specialist knowledge which is so necessary if the significance of early signals from Brussels is to be fully appreciated.

An added advantage which many groups have is that they are also beneficiaries of the sharing of information (as suggested by Andrew McLaughlin and Grant Jordan) via Euro-groups, even though these groups may not always be effective in actual lobbying. Multinational firms are especially advantaged because of their capacity to monitor several different national agendas and because most EC decision-makers are conscious of the need for Europe to retain and attract multinationals. An added advantage for multinationals is that they also possess enormous technical expertise, which EC officials need, and this too enables them to gain early warning of policy change.

More empirical evidence is needed, but it seems likely that those Member States having a long tradition of close liaison between groups and government departments have some advantage in the lobbying process. As David Spence illustrates, Britain has a particularly well co-ordinated approach to Europe with its central administration. Equally, it has a long tradition of almost symbiotic relationships between governmental departments and interest groups (Richardson and Jordan 1979; Jordan and Richardson 1987; Richardson 1993), and this gives British groups some advantages over some of its EC partners. However, all states now recognize the need to develop a more co-ordinated approach between their interest groups and their national political administrative systems. There are of course difficulties in achieving this, as it involves interest groups in rather conflicting objectives because of the need both to maintain existing national links and to develop an equally symbiotic relationship with Brussels officials and Euro-MPs. Increasingly, we may expect tensions to develop as lobbying in these two different arenas of decision-making diverges, the more 'European' the groups become.

National lobbying will continue to be important, almost whatever happens in the process of greater European integration. Even if all major policy decisions in economic and social life are made at the EC level, the question of how policies are implemented will remain. It is almost inconceivable that the European Commission will be able to (or would be allowed to) develop a significant policy delivery capacity of its own. We are, therefore, likely to see a continuation (and possible extension) of the concept of subsidiarity, i.e. 'the Community should exercise those responsibilities—and *only* those responsibilities—that can be carried out more effectively by common policies at Community level than by the States acting separately' (Jacobs and Corbett 1990: 249). This means that there is, and will continue to be, plenty of scope for a degree of discretion in the implementation process and it will always be important for groups to lobby national, regional, and local governments—as well as agencies of various kinds—with regard to detailed implementation of Community policies. Whatever the true meaning of subsidiarity—even if it is agreed that it is about devolved administration, not devolved decision-making, leaving national and local governments little more than agents of Brussels (Adonis and Jones 1991: 19)—much can be gained by lobbying at the sub-EC level. Even where the concept of subsidiarity is not invoked, we still see an increasing implementation gap within the EC. This leaves the Commission with the problem of how best to ensure effective implementation of EC policies—whether via the Court, via the creation of new EC agencies (e.g. a new environmental agency is to be set up once a location can be agreed) or via national, regional, and local governments.

2. GROUPS AND THE PROCESS OF EUROPEAN INTEGRATION

The Europeanization of interests within (and beyond) the twelve Member States, can be, as we suggested in our study of the Federation of Stock Exchanges in Europe, a potential force in the process of European integration. The suggestion by the neo-functional theorists that groups would play a key role in the integration process may not have yet been proved correct. However, there is increasing evidence that economic interests (again, the multinational companies are probably the best example) are increasingly active in pressing for standardization, harmonization, and for a level playing field within Europe. They also recognize that, in terms of world competition, there is little alternative to cross-national collaboration if European industries are to be able to compete with those of the Pacific rim in the next century. Their desire to reduce uncertainty might also be expected to lead them to press for greater political as well as economic union within Europe. Essentially, the sooner the big questions of political union can be settled, the sooner a large uncertainty in the business environment will be removed. For example, Wyn Grant has drawn attention to the role of the European Round Table of Industrialists in the origins and development of the Single European Market. More recently the Round Table has argued, in its report, *Reshaping Europe*, that 'the unification of Europe is the only practical way to realise its potential and harness its resources . . . Deepening and widening are both needed, with the Community strengthening its policies and institutions as well as opening up to the needs of its neighbours' (ERT 1991*a*: 13).

In practical terms, the European Round Table has been pressing for a number of integrative measures such as a single European export control system ('differences in national regulations hamper efficiency, frustrate international co-operation between industries, and influence . . . in global competition', ERT 1991*b*); the future of indirect taxes in Europe ('ever since the original abolition of customs duties within the Community, the existence of wide disparities in indirect tax rates, and the means necessary to sustain them has constituted a glaring barrier to the free movement of people and goods across Europe', ERT 1988: 4); the need for new infrastructure networks ('infrastructure must be conceived and planned as a single European network. This means going beyond mere national aggregation of needs and overcoming a narrow uni-modal perspective. There is an urgent need to develop corresponding European institutional levels of competence to deal with infrastructure network decision-making', ERT 1991*c*: 8). Groups not directly involved in economic affairs have been equally vociferous in pressing for European integration. The World Wildlife Fund for nature has argued that 'too often, responsibility for nature conservation and environmental protection is spread among local and regional governments answering to different national ministries with no proper co-ordination, inadequate budgets and a lack of commitment to what are seen as second-order priorities' (WWF 1991: 6).

It would be wrong, of course, to see this type of pressure as necessarily leading to more European integration. However in discussing the concept of 'community settlement', Ernst Haas suggests that two of the six conditions for this sentiment to flourish are that

Interest groups and political parties at the national level endorse supranational action and in preference to action by their national government . . . [and] Interest groups and political parties organize beyond the national level in order to function more effectively as decision-makers *vis à vis* the separate national governments or the central authority and if they define their interests in terms of longer than those of the separate nation state from which they originate. (Haas 1958: 9–10).

His formal definition of political integration is as follows: 'Political integration is the process whereby political actors in several distinct national settings are persuaded to shift their loyalties, expectations and political activities towards a new center, whose institutions possess or demand jurisdiction over the pre-existing national states' (Haas 1958: 16). Much of the evidence in this volume indicates that we are witnessing that process at work and that the interest groups are often active in pressing for wider EC jurisdiction over the pre-existing nation-states. In essence, many of the groups within Europe—both at the national and supranational level—are actively pressing for a more federal Europe and for the EC to be more statelike in its actions. As organizations, interest groups have, therefore, developed very considerably in their integrative role from the rather limited role described by Lindberg in 1963. At that time, he saw 'most EEC-level interest groups as merely liaison groups with essentially secretarial functions and no role to play in co-ordinating national group views' (Lindberg 1963: 287–8). He suggested that interest groups,

would be of limited significance for political integration, unless participation in them comes to represent a fundamental restructuring of expectations and tactics. To what extent have collective needs at the regional level taken priority over national differences? Do the necessities of 'international lobbying' force compromise of initial positions? Do interest officials become more 'Europe-minded'? (Ibid.: 99).

His answer to these and other questions was very guarded, reflecting the relatively early stages of the development of European lobbying in the early 1960s. His caution was in part based on the fact that, at that time, 'the vital interests of relatively few are as yet directly affected by decisions of the Community institutions' (Ibid.). Crucially, however, he argued that

one can expect that over time the necessity for lobbying will force groups to emphasise collective needs rather than national differences. Such a development can be expected as the central institutions of the EEC become more active, as the types of actions taken involve the harmonization of legislation and the formulations of common policies (rather than the negative process of . . . barriers to trade), and as . . . groups become aware that their interests can no longer be adequately served at the national level alone. (Ibid.: 101).

Most of the available evidence suggests that groups in many if not most policy sectors have certainly recognized that supranational decisions are now inevitable for many policy problems and that it is often in their interests to engage in anticipatory activity in order to influence the shape and direction of European-level policy solutions. Thus, increasingly, groups themselves have recognized the logic and momentum of greater Europeanization of solutions. They are, therefore, beginning to play a very significant role in the process of European integration, as predicted by the neo-functionalists.

3. A EUROPEAN POLICY STYLE?

Gerhard Lehmbruch has suggested that more complex conceptualizations of the structure and process of interest intermediation beyond corporatism are attracting increasing attention. He argues that the metaphor of policy networks and typologies of economic governance may contribute to a better understanding of the role of the state or of administrative strategies in the emergence and dynamics of national and sector configurations in interest intermediation (Lehmbruch 1991: 122). He notes that empirical regularities in the interactions of organizations and public bureaucracies are sometimes 'discussed as contributing to a specific "administrative culture" (Jann 1983) or "policy style" (Richardson 1982), but that all too often these concepts . . . look like residual categories, the theoretical relevance of which for the comparative analysis of political structures is not quite clear (Lehmbruch 1991: 126). His proposal is that we should begin to analyse what he calls the 'configurative' aspect of interest intermediation: 'It is a structure made up of complex linkages between organizations, agencies, and other institutions the dynamic of which is not always sufficiently understood by isolating specific elements or relationships.' These linkages should be seen as hanging together in complex 'configurations'. Furthermore, he argues, to delineate a 'policy network' approach in combination with an emphasis on institutionalization might be a further step in trying to understand these configurative dynamics. Understanding the variability of policy networks is suggested as particularly important for the analysis of attempts to remodel patterns of state intervention, as cross-national research has shown that specific configurations of networks have either supported or constrained attempts at reform in such areas as telecommunications and health policy.

Our own research suggests that at the EC level there are indeed quite significant variations in the nature of policy networks (and that in some specific policy areas no networks may exist) but that there is at least a case to be made that the network concept is quite useful. More and more policy areas are now showing a high degree of 'group density' in the sense that many if not most of the interests have become organized and are active at the European level. They are also pressing their national administrations as part of this Europeanization of the policy process. As a result, it may be possible to argue that at least the cross-national differences in interest intermediation will be lessened as all national policy actors realize that one essential element of a European lobbying strategy is, as we suggested earlier, close co-ordination between national groups and national administrations. The French case is especially interesting for, as Suleiman has shown, the French bureaucratic élite has a tradition of autonomy from lobbies and a supposed tradition of resisting pressure (quoted by Lehmbruch 1991: 123).

Whether or not this is the case, there is absolutely no doubt that European-level policy-makers will face increased organization of interests and therefore increased pressure to somehow develop a more regularized and effective system of interest intermediation. Thus the European Parliament, in January 1992, held a public hearing on the need to have some system of registering lobbyists at the Parliament, essentially because the Parliament is now besieged by special interests from across Europe and beyond. Equally, Commission officials have found that increased interest mobilization demands some form of 'management'. Consequently, we see the Commission itself playing a role in the evolution of the system. As Lehmbruch notes, 'in critical junctures state bureaucracies have often played an important formative part of their own' (ibid.: 135). Thus, 'interactions of governmental bureaucracies with associations or other corporate economic actors seem to be of crucial importance in linking the macro- and meso-levels and result in the emergence of network configurations which will eventually become institutionalized' (ibid.: 136).

We do not yet know quite what form this institutionalization will take, but it is a reasonable prediction that some form of institutionalization will take place in order to render the system of European-level intermediation manageable. Wolfgang Streeck and Philippe Schmitter, however, see limits to the degree of institutionalization of concertation because of the absence of anything resembling a balance of class or sectoral interests, as neo-corporatism assumes an underlying social structure that could be plausibly conceived of as polarized in two large classes—'capital' and 'labour' (Streeck and Schmitter 1991: 146). As they argue, attempts to create Euro-corporatism failed and a centralized pattern of interest politics did not emerge at the European level, despite their belief that it was so common at the national level (ibid.: 139). We would agree with their analysis that there is no Euro-corporatism as such, but we doubt whether they are correct in arguing that 'the main concession governments seem to have made in return for business giving up previous claims for national protection was that the future European political economy was to be significantly less subject to institutional regulation—national or supranational' (ibid.: 149). In the lead-up to the Single European Act of 1992, they note that 'the project of European integration became finally and formally bound up with a deregulation project' (ibid.). In practice, much of what can be termed European integration is in fact about regulation, in part because regulation is a major resource to institutions when their financial budgets are severely constrained, as that of the EC is (so long as the Common Agricultural Policy (CAP) is in place). A small Commission with relatively few financial resources to hand out is, almost inevitably, going to turn increasingly to regulation as a cost-effective means of securing Europe-wide change in a number of policy areas. It seems unlikely, from the evidence so far, that Streeck and Schmitter are correct to suggest that supranational sovereignty will be used exclusively for the external reassertion of, as opposed to internal intervention in, the European economy. As Majone notes in his exploration of the growth of EC regulation,

One essential characteristic is the limited influence of budgetary limitations on the activities of regulators. The size of non-regulatory, direct-expenditure programmes is constrained by budgetary appropriations and, ultimately, by the size of government tax revenues. In contrast, the real costs of most regulatory programmes are borne directly by the firms and individuals who have to comply with them. (1989: 166)

Streeck and Schmitter see the future development of the European Community as clearly *not* neo-corporatist. Thus they see no mechanism in sight that could 'rationalize its political system, help crystallize its *mélange* of actors and processes, and establish corporatist monopolies of representation, interassociational hierarchies or for that matter a predominant position for the Commission's bureaucracy and technocracy' (Streeck and Schmitter 1991: 159). Their analysis poses the central question regarding the form of interest intermediation—namely, is the system so complex that it will prove impossible to introduce and institutionalize a stable set of standard operating procedures for managing interest intermediation? Our preliminary view is that there are tendencies in the system which suggest that both the Commission and the European Parliament wish to see a more regularized and effective system of intermediation and that the interests themselves are now coming to the view that effective lobbying requires a European-wide approach to policy-makers. Basically, the interests have recognized the reality of a federal Europe. Whatever terms we may use to describe the EC—whether it be federal, neo-federal, would-be-state, neo-state, or whatever, the reality for interests in Europe is that much of the regulatory framework under which their own policy areas are governed is now affected by EC intervention. While theorists may debate the precise labels to be used, if one is running an environmental pressure group in France, a chemical company in Germany, or hoping to build a motorway in Spain, the EC will play a very important role in what one is allowed to do. This is why there has been such an explosion of lobbying activity within the EC, such that the number and range of groups now seeking influence is likely to cause 'overcrowding' of some policy sectors (Gustafsson and Richardson 1980). One response to 'overcrowding' would be to return to the neo-corporatist ambitions of the Commission in its early years. However, it seems unlikely that anything like a corporatist system could be made to operate, at least until and unless the Euro-groups become much more effective organizations—both in terms of their technical expertise and their internal decision-making process. Thus, with a multiplicity of interests and a multiplicity of access points, it is difficult to envisage the Commission setting up a system which could be described in Schmitter's core definition of corporatism as 'monopoly of representation; hierarchic co-ordination across associations; functional differentiation into non-overlapping categories; official recognition or semi-public status; involuntary or quasi-compulsory membership; and some degree of heteronomy with regard to the selection of leaders and the articulation of demands' (Schmitter 1989: 64). Indeed he comments that 'I have become less and less convinced that corporatism—with or without one of its multiple prefixes or adjectives—will survive, much less be as much an imperative for the future of capitalism as Shonfield thought'. Of particular relevance to our interest in lobbying systems, he has argued that 'the notion of setting up a new neo-corporatist dynasty of the global or meta-level is positively frightening, given the transaction costs involved and the potential decisional perversities' (ibid.: 72).

What, then, might emerge? It seems unlikely that decision-making in the Commission will shift significantly from the sectorized and segmented approach which has developed so far. EC policy is, therefore, likely to continue to emerge from sectoral networks of some kind. The evolution of these networks is still under way and we might expect, therefore, a multiple model of EC policy-making to continue, in which interests play an increasingly important role but in which policy-makers make increased efforts to 'manage' the system. Andersen and Eliassen go so far as suggesting, in contrast to Schmitter's view of the possibilities of transnational neo-corporatism, that corporate structures are likely to be more important in the future, at the expense of the lobbying patterns of the late 1980s and early 1990s, although they appear to see this as dependent upon the emergence of a more parliamentary-based system (1991: 186). Despite the Maastricht Treaty, this possibility still seems problematic. The core of the process is likely to remain Commission-based, sectorally structured, and linked to a complex network of groups or organizations across Europe and beyond. Linking this decision-making structure to interests may not, however, be as difficult as one might think, bearing in mind that there is a relatively common political culture of decision-making within the majority of Member States. Writing nearly twenty years ago, Martin Heisler and Robert Kvavik captured the nature of the 'European Polity' model, as they called it, as follows, 'A decision-making structure characterized by continuous, regularized access for economically, politically, ethnically and/or sub-culturally based groups to the highest levels of the political system, i.e. the decision making sub-system' (1974: 48). They see this access as regularized and as taking a structured form—a pattern of co-optation noticed in Europe as early as the mid-1800s in Norway, for example. Our own evidence suggests that there are indeed strong tendencies for co-optation of some kind. By a process of trial and error, decision-makers will learn which groups are capable of co-optation and which are not. Equally groups will learn the basic rules of co-optation (e.g. see Ch. 5 particularly). As a result more stable and manageable networks of policy-makers and groups are likely to emerge.

References

Adonis, Andrew, and Jones, Stuart (1991), *Subsidiarity and the Community's Constitutional Future* (Discussion Paper No. 2; Centre for European Studies, Nuffield College, Oxford).

Andersen, Svein, and Eliassen, Kjell A. (1991), 'European Community Lobbying', *European Journal of Political Research*, 20: 173–87.

ERT (European Round Table) (1988), *Opening Up the Tax Frontiers* (Brussels: ERT).

——(1991a), *Reshaping Europe* (Brussels: ERT).

——(1991b), *Towards a Single European Export Control System* (Brussels: ERT).

——(1991c), *Missing Networks* (Brussels: ERT).

Gustafsson, Gunnel, and Richardson, J. J. (1980), 'Post-Industrial Changes in Policy Style', *Scandinavian Political Studies*, 3/1: 21–37.

Haas, Ernst B. (1958), *The Uniting of Europe: Political, Social, and Economic Forces 1950–57* (Stanford, Calif.: Stanford University Press).

Heisler, Martin, and Kvavik, Robert (1974), 'Patterns of European Politics: The "European Polity" Model', in Martin Heisler (ed.), *Politics in Europe: Structures and Processes in Some Postindustrial Democracies* (New York: David McKay), 27–89.

Jacobs, Francis, and Corbett, Richard (1990), *The European Parliament* (Harlow: Longman).

Jann, Werner (1983), *Staatliche Programme und Verwaltungskultur-Bekampfung des Drogenmissbruchs der Bundesrepublik Deutschland im Vergleich* (Opladen: Westdeutscher Verlag).

Jordan, A. G. and Richardson, J. J. (1987), *British Politics and the Policy Process* (London: Unwin Hyman).

Lehmbruch., Gerhard (1991), 'The Organization of Society, Administrative Strategies & Policy Networks: Elements of a Theory of Interest Systems', in Roland M. Czada and Adrienne Windhoff-Heritier (eds.),

Political Choice: Institutions, Rules, and the Limits of Rationality (Frankfurt am Main: Campus Verlag), 121–60.

Lindberg, Leon N. (1963), *The Political Dynamics of European Economic Integration* (Stanford, Calif.: Stanford University Press).

Majone, Giandomenico (1989), *Regulating Europe: Problems and Prospects* (Baden-Baden: Nomos Verlagsgesellschaft).

Richardson, J. J. (ed.) (1982), *Policy Styles in Western Europe* (London: Allen & Unwin).

——(1993), *Pressure Groups* (Oxford Readings in Government and Politics; Oxford: Oxford University Press).

——and Jordan A. G. (1979), *Governing Under Pressure: The Policy Process in a Post-Parliamentary Democracy* (Oxford: Martin Robertson, repr. Blackwells).

Schmitter, Philippe C. (1989), 'Corporatism is Dead! Long Live Corporatism!', *Government and Opposition*, 24/1: 54–73.

Streeck, Wolfgang, and Schmitter, Philippe C. (1991), 'From National Corporatism to Transnational Pluralism: Organized Interests in the Single European Market', *Politics & Society*, 19/2: 133–64.

WWF (World Wildlife Fund for Nature) (1991), *Nature Conservation in Europe: Agenda 2000* (Brussels: WWF).

Subject and Name Index

Italic numbers denote reference to illustrations.